Shamrocks and Pluff M[ud]
Southern City of Charleston, South Carolina

Shamrocks and Pluff Mud: A Glimpse of the Irish in the Southern City of Charleston, South Carolina

Donald M. Williams

Copyright © 2005 Donald M. Williams
All rights reserved.

ISBN : 1-4196-1317-0

To order additional copies, please contact us.
BookSurge, LLC
www.booksurge.com
1-866-308-6235
orders@booksurge.com

Shamrocks and Pluff Mud: A Glimpse of the Irish in the Southern City of Charleston, South Carolina

CHAPTERS

Chapter One: A Snapshot of the Irish in Charleston, South Carolina From 1670 To 1861 — 1

Chapter Two: The Celebration of St. Patrick's Day and the St. Patrick's Day Parade in Charleston — 23

Chapter Three: Irish Charitable and Benevolent Societies, Rifle Clubs, Social Clubs and Other Organizations — 43

Chapter Four: The Irish Volunteers and Other Irish Military Organizations — 85

Chapter Five: Charleston's Connection with the Fight for Irish Freedom — 121

Foreward

The first time I remember hearing anything about the Irish or St. Patrick's Day was when I was in the third grade of Sacred Heart Catholic School in Charleston, South Carolina. One day during school, I observed my friend Billy pinching our fellow classmate Joe, who was wearing a blue shirt and khaki pants. I asked Billy why he had pinched Joe, and I was informed that it was St. Patrick's Day and if you didn't wear green on St. Patrick's Day you would be pinched. I quickly surveyed my own wardrobe and, to my great relief, discovered that my mother had laid out a green shirt for me to wear that morning. I then asked Billy, "Why do people wear green on St. Patrick's Day?" He responded, "So you don't get pinched."

After my third grade experience, I always made sure that I wore something green on St. Patrick's Day, but didn't think much more about the Irish or St. Patrick's Day until about three years later. By that time I was in the sixth grade, and on March 17th my class, along with several others, gathered in the school auditorium for a St. Patrick's Day program. Each student was provided with a green hat made of construction paper and a shamrock covered song sheet containing the words to the most popular Irish songs. After singing for thirty minutes and witnessing two older students attempting to do an Irish jig, I thought to myself, Why do we celebrate St. Patrick's Day in Charleston? After all, there aren't any Irish people here, are there?

That evening, I posed my question to my mother who explained to me that we celebrate St. Patrick's Day in Charleston because the city has a long Irish heritage. She further explained that a large number of Charlestonians are descended from Irishmen, and as proof of this, pointed out the common Irish surnames of the people that we knew in Charleston: Condon, Duffy, McMahon, Molony and Regan. Then, to my surprise, she told me that I, too, was of Irish descent because her maiden name was Kennedy, and that my great-grandfather, Michael Kennedy, had come to Charleston in the early 1850s. She also told me that Michael Kennedy had left Ireland as a result of the "Potato

Famine." Of course, I had no idea what that meant at the time. Satisfied with my mother's explanation, I continued to celebrate St. Patrick's Day during my high school and college days. However, to be honest, the green beer was more of an incentive to celebrate each year than was my Irish heritage. This would soon change.

I enrolled in the University of South Carolina Law School in 1971, and during my time in Columbia, my friend George J. Morris sponsored me for membership in the Hibernian Society of Charleston, South Carolina. I became a member of this historic organization shortly before graduating from law school and quickly found that I enjoyed the camaraderie of the members of the society. I also discovered, somewhat to my surprise, that each time I entered the Hibernian Hall and gazed upon the portraits of the great men from Ireland and of Irish descent which adorn its walls that I felt a greater pride in being of Irish descent myself. I was hooked on the Irish for life, and even agreed enthusiastically when my wife Martie suggested that we name our daughter Michael after her Irish great-great-grandfather.

As my pride in my personal Irish heritage increased, so did my desire to learn more about the Irish heritage of the city of Charleston. In 1980 I became a member of the South Carolina Irish Historical Society and joined with P. Michael Duffy, Jerry McMahon, William B. Regan and others in their efforts to learn more about the Irish history of the city and state. We soon discovered that after the treaty establishing the Irish Free State was signed in the early 1920s, the Irish in Charleston almost completely assimilated into the general population. Most of Charleston's Irish organizations disappeared shortly thereafter and, except for the Hibernian Society and the Irish Volunteers, little was known about them.

My inability to easily discover Charleston's Irish past was frustrating to me at first, but it was not long before my frustration turned into enthusiasm. Sometime in the mid-1980s I decided to take it upon myself to gather as much information as I could about Charleston's Irish history in general, and in particular about the city's Irish organizations and the names of their members. My initial thought was to accumulate this information for my use and to share it with my friends. However, I eventually decided to make this information available to the public for genealogical and historical purposes. Now I offer it to all of you, to the Irish in all of us.

Donald Michael Williams
March 17, 2005

This book is dedicated to my loving wife Martie and daughter Michael who encouraged me and allowed me the time to write it, and to my mother Julia Kennedy Williams who gave me my Irish blood and sense of humor.

CHAPTER ONE

A SNAPSHOT OF THE IRISH IN CHARLESTON, SOUTH CAROLINA FROM 1670 TO 1861

It is not known when the first Irishman arrived in America, and this is a matter on which opinions differ. There are those who believe it was Saint Brendan the Navigator who, according to legend, sailed to the New World in the sixth century. Others believe it was an Irishman in the crew of Christopher Columbus. Still others believe that it was neither of them but some other Irishman.[1]

There are no specific claims that either Saint Brendan or Christopher Columbus reached the vicinity of Charleston. It is widely accepted that Captain Florence O'Sullivan, an Irish soldier of fortune, was if not the first, at least one of the first Irishmen to arrive in Charleston. O'Sullivan's name is listed among those on board the ship Carolina when it dropped anchor in April 1670 near the site of the original settlement.[2]

There may have been more Irishmen among the settlers, but the evidence is conflicting. On the way to Carolina, the expedition stopped at Kinsale, on the southern coast of Ireland, in hopes of obtaining twenty to twenty-five Irish servants for the venture. O'Sullivan assisted in this effort, but the Irish were reluctant to join the expedition because of the well-known English practice of sending Irishmen to the West Indies to be sold as slaves. Accounts differ as to whether or not any Irish servants were obtained there.[3]

After his arrival, Florence O'Sullivan became a well-known and prominent figure in the new settlement which was named Charles Towne. O'Sullivan was a deputy to one of the Lords Proprietors, served in the Colonial Assembly, and was appointed Surveyor General of the colony. In 1674, O'Sullivan was placed in charge of a signal cannon on an island at the entrance to Charleston Harbor. It was this assignment which immortalized his name. The island on which the signal cannon was located was later called Sullivan's Island and still bears that name.[4]

Another early Irish settler, Brian FitzPatrick, also became well known in the new settlement. FitzPatrick committed what has been referred to as "Charleston's first noteworthy slaying" in 1671 when he killed an Indian. It was rumored that FitzPatrick was acting as part of a conspiracy that involved Sir John Yeamans, an aspirant to the Governorship of the province. Interestingly enough, FitzPatrick escaped to Florida before the details could be sorted out.[5]

As Charles Towne grew, new Irish settlers joined their countrymen there. Although it is not known exactly how many Irishmen came to Charles Towne during the early years of its existence, one source states that a considerable number arrived in 1684.[6] The great majority of these Irishmen who came to Charles Towne during the early years of its existence were Protestant, but by 1685, it was noted that the population included a few Irish Catholics.[7]

Some of the new Irish arrivals were persons of means who gained prominence in the town and province as had O'Sullivan. James Moore, a descendent of Rory Moore, a leading figure in the Irish Rebellion of 1641, was one such man. He was appointed Governor of the province in 1700 and later served as Attorney General and Chief Justice of the court system. Moore's son, of the same name, also became Governor in 1719.[8] It is said that "both father and son seem to have inherited their share of the divine unrest of the Irish."[9]

Unlike the Moores, most of the Irish who came to Charles Towne during this time were poor and never attained any prominence. Many of these poor Irish came as indentured servants or redemptioners, who, upon their arrival, had to work off the expenses of their passage through a term of servitude. This term could be from two to seven years, but was usually four. The indentured servants usually signed their indenture contracts before beginning the voyage. The redemptioners, on the other hand, made the voyage free of indenture and were given a period of time after their arrival to locate someone who was willing to pay the costs of their passage. If they were unsuccessful, they too were sold into bonded servitude. After entering into their period of servitude, the status of these indentured servants was little better than that of the Carolina slaves. They could be sold at the whim of their master, just as any other property, and had very little control over their lives. However, unlike the slaves, the indentured servants knew that they would have their freedom one day.[10]

Although few in number, the Irish Catholic servants who

came to Charles Towne during the early years must have been quite troublesome, or else deeply hated for their religion, because in 1716 the General Assembly attempted to discourage their future immigration to the province. In that year, the General Assembly passed an act for the purpose of encouraging the immigration of white servants to the province to counterbalance the hostile Indians and the ever-increasing number of Negro slaves.[11] The act provided for the payment of a bounty for each white servant imported into the province, but also contained the following additional provisions:

> V. And whereas there hath been imported into this Province, several native Irish servants that are Papist, and persons taken from Newgate and other prisons, convicted of capital crimes, to the great prejudice and detriment to this Province, Be it therefore enacted by the authority aforesaid, That no person by this Act, required to purchase white servants, shall be obliged to purchase Irish servants, or persons convicted in England, or elsewhere, of capital crimes, nor is the Receiver obliged to take same.
>
> VII. And in order to prevent the imposing upon this Province persons of lewd and profligate lives, Be it further enacted, That all merchants or masters of vessels or others, shall upon their oaths, declare that to the best of their knowledge, none of the servants by them imported be either what is commonly called native Irish or persons of known scandalous characters or Roman Catholics, and if any merchant or other person, either in England or any other place abroad, shall ship any servant to this Province, he shall be obliged to send a certificate under the hand of the proper Magistrate, that such persons or servants, are Protestants, and be not reputed to be, or have not been legally convicted of any notorious crime; and with such a certificate, Irish servants, being Protestant, may be lawfully imported here, and receive the benefit of this Act, any thing therein contained to the contrary notwithstanding.[12]

Edward McCrady, a historian who studied South Carolina's Proprietary government, explained: "Such were the religious animosities of the time and the blindness of prejudice that the colonists appear to have been more afraid of the Irish papists than the Yamassee Indians, and regarded them no better than 'persons of lewd and profligate lives.'"[13]

Even if their immigration had not been discouraged, it is doubtful that many Irish Catholics would have settled in South Carolina prior to the American Revolution. The Irish who immigrated to America from 1700 to 1776 were mostly Protestants from Ulster, and there were not many Irish Catholics among them. Further, pre-Revolutionary South Carolina had little to offer the Catholic Irishman who wanted to continue to practice his religion. Papists had been excluded from those granted religious freedom by act of the General Assembly in 1697 and this exclusion continued until after the Revolutionary War. There was no Catholic Church in South Carolina, nor even a priest to administer the sacraments.[14] There is evidence that some Irish Catholics did immigrate during this period, however. In 1775, two Catholic Irishmen were tarred and feathered in Charlestown.[15]

Although Irish Catholics were not welcome in pre-Revolutionary South Carolina, the same cannot be said of Irish Protestants. After South Carolina became a royal colony, the number of Negro slaves continued to increase much more rapidly than the white population. There was a constant threat of slave insurrection, and new efforts were made to attract white Protestant settlers from Ireland and other parts of Europe to diminish this threat. In addition, the early settlers had resisted leaving the coast, and new settlers were needed to tame the previously unsettled inland areas.[16]

In 1731 South Carolina officials offered free land to white Protestants who would settle in the province. A number of Irish Protestants responded to this offer in 1732 and established a settlement on the Black River. The site of their settlement was named Williamsburg. Many of these settlers died as a result of the unfamiliar climate and the back-breaking labor required to clear the wilderness.[17]

After the establishment of Williamsburg, Protestant immigration from Ireland to South Carolina virtually dried up during the remainder of the 1730s and most of the 1740s. A number of reasons have been advanced to explain the lack of Irish Protestant immigration during this period, but the most compelling reason was probably Britain's involvement in various wars. It was simply too dangerous to travel by sea from Britain or Ireland to South Carolina during this time.[18]

Peace returned in the late 1740s, and South Carolina authorities increased their efforts to attract white Protestant settlers. An act was passed in 1752 under which poor Protestant immigrants from Europe would be provided with tools, corn, and other provisions. Another act was passed in 1754 providing for the payment of the costs of land surveys for Protestant settlers. A small number of Irish Protestants took advantage of these bounty schemes during the 1750s and settled in South Carolina.[19]

The South Carolina General Assembly was disappointed with the number of white Protestants who had immigrated to the colony following the enactment of the bounty schemes of the 1750s and decided to make one more effort to attract European Protestant settlers. In July of 1761, an act was passed under which monies would be paid to assist European Protestants with the expenses of their passage to South Carolina. Under this act, Protestants over the age of twelve received a payment of four pounds sterling while Protestants between the ages of two and twelve received a lesser sum. The act further provided that the money to be paid for the passage of these Protestants would be paid directly to the owner or master of the vessel in which they were brought into the province unless the cost of the passage had been previously paid.[20]

Irish Protestant immigration to South Carolina increased rapidly after the passage of the Act of 1761 and remained steady until the beginning of the American Revolution. During this period large numbers of Irish Protestants took advantage of the bounty schemes and immigrated to South Carolina through the port of Charles Towne.[21] Historian Alexander Hewatt, in describing immigration to South Carolina during this period, wrote:

> But of all other countries, none has furnished the Province with so many inhabitants as Ireland. In the northern counties of that Kingdom the spirit of emigration seized the people to such a degree, that it threatened almost a total depopulation. Such multitudes of husbandmen, labourers and manufacturers flocked over the Atlantic, that the landlords began to be alarmed, and to concert ways and means for preventing the growing evil. Scarce a ship sailed for any of the plantations that was not crowded with men, women and children. But the bounty allowed new settlers in Carolina proved a great encouragement, and induced numbers of these people, not withstanding the severity of the climate, to resort to that province. The merchants, finding this bounty equivalent to the expences of the passage, from avaricious motives persuaded the people to embark for Carolina...Many causes may be assigned for this spirit of emigration that prevailed so much in Ireland...But of all other causes of emigration oppression at home was the most powerful and prevalent.[22]

The crowded conditions on these immigrant ships sometimes led to disaster. In 1767, a ship bound for Charles Towne was loaded in Belfast with 450 passengers, which was over twice the number the ship was designed to carry. To make matters worse, the greedy captain reduced the provisions for the voyage, and many of the passengers became ill. Over one hundred passengers died during the voyage, and upon the ship's arrival in Charles Towne the wardens of St. Philip's Church had to be called upon to assist the survivors.[23]

Large numbers of these Irish immigrants who arrived at the port of Charles Towne during the 1760s and early 1770s moved on to settle other parts of the province. In fact, in describing Irish immigration to South Carolina during this time, historian David Duncan Wallace reported that the Irish "fairly swarmed into the upcountry."[24]

Those Irishmen who did remain in Charles Towne, however, seemed to be especially suited to perform labor in the lowcountry of South Carolina. This is evidenced by the following excerpt from a letter written from Charles Towne in 1773:

> The Irish are considered as welcome guests as they are generally industrious, and in this low and marshy country have a value in being what others deride them for—Bog Trotters.[25]

As in earlier years, a number of these "Bog Trotters" who came to Charles Towne between mid-eighteenth century and the Revolutionary War were brought over from Ireland as indentured servants.[26] Apparently, not all of these Irish indentured servants felt that they were treated as welcome guests in the city, and some decided to run away in search of a better life. The indentured servants who chose to run away were pursued by their masters just like runaway slaves. Advertisements offering rewards for their return were common in local newspapers. One such advertisement was placed by Peter Timothy, a printer, in the *South Carolina Gazette* in 1751:

> ROBERT WHITAKER, Born in Ireland, of a very short stature, with thick, short legs, small, black Beard and a likely Visage, aged about 25 Years; a Printer by Trade, an indented Servant to the Printer hereof, having ran away from his Master on Thursday Night, the 27th of June: Whoever brings him to the Subscriber, or secures him so that he may be had again, shall have Five Pounds reward and such Charges as are allowed by law. PETER TIMOTHY[27]

Another advertisement placed in the same newspaper in 1767 reveals that dissatisfaction among Irish indentured servants was not limited to those of the male gender:

> RAN AWAY, the 8th of December last, from the Brick Barracks, an Indented Servant Girl, named Elizabeth Ash, aged about 17 years, short, lusty, ruddy-faced and remarkably sluttish; born in Ireland, and lately brought from thence, in the ship Belfast Packet; wore when she went away a new black quilted serge petticoat, a new printed linen gown, a long ear'd cap and straw hat; and is supposed to be gone towards the Irish Settlements in the back country. Whoever delivers her at the said Barracks, shall have £ 10 reward and reasonable charges; and whoever harbours or entertains her, will be prosecuted with the utmost rigor by RALPH PHILLIPS.[28]

For some of Charles Towne's Irish indentured servants who chose not to run away, their period of servitude turned out to be a blessing in disguise. These were the fortunate ones who learned a valuable skill or trade from their masters during their period of indenture. After obtaining their freedom, they were often able to use that skill or trade to aid them in achieving the financial security that eluded so many of their fellow countrymen. One example was John Hennessey, who arrived in Charles Towne in 1764 and was indentured to a carter. After serving the four-year period of his indenture, he purchased horses and wagons and went into business for himself. By 1778 he had acquired property worth £ 460 including a brick house.[29]

At about the same time the pre-Revolutionary Irish immigration to South Carolina was reaching its peak, the split between the American colonies and the British mother country was beginning to widen. After suffering years of British oppression at home, it would have been very difficult for these Irishmen to contain the joy they must have felt each time the colonists successfully challenged British authority. The following excerpt from the *South Carolina Gazette*, which appeared on March 21, 1771, is evidence that the Irish in Charlestown did not try very hard:

> Monday last being the Anniversary of the Repeal of the Stamp-Act,...the same was celebrated here in a suitable manner particularly by...the sons of St. Patrick, at Mr. Dillon's.[30]

At the time the final break with Britain occurred, two of South Carolina's most outstanding leaders, Edward and John Rutledge, were both of Irish descent. Their father, Dr. John Rutledge, had arrived in Charles Towne from Ireland around 1735. Doctor Rutledge's family had been residents of County Cavan, Ireland, for many years.[31]

Edward Rutledge was one of four South Carolinians to sign the Declaration of Independence. His older brother John became President and Commander-in-Chief of South Carolina in 1776.[32] In that capacity, John was responsible for preparing the defense of South Carolina against the expected invasion by the British. Just prior to the Battle of Fort Moultrie, General Charles Lee, who commanded the Continental troops in Charlestown, was considering giving orders to evacuate Sullivan's Island. John Rutledge, who disagreed with General Lee's assessment of the situation, responded in typical Irish fashion. He sent the following note to General Moultrie, the Commander of the Island:

> General Lee wishes you to evacuate the Fort. You will not without an order from me. I would sooner cut off my right hand than write one.[33]

Irish immigration to America, which had been interrupted by the Revolutionary War, began anew shortly thereafter. At least five thousand Irishmen left their country to seek a new life in America during 1783. Thereafter it is estimated that a similar number, or more, departed from Ireland to America each year during the remainder of the eighteenth century.[34]

Those Irishmen who chose to come to Charleston immediately after the American Revolution discovered upon their arrival that the city had fallen on economic hard times. Many of Charleston's post-Revolutionary War Irish immigrants were unable to find employment upon their arrival and found themselves in desperate economic straits. There was no formal Irish organization in the city to relieve the distress of these immigrants and they were forced to rely upon public and private charity. Finally, in 1787, the Friendly Brothers of Ireland was organized to render assistance to these immigrants.[35]

In addition to the economic hardships, the Irish Catholics who chose to immigrate to Charleston immediately after the Revolution had to deal with the same restrictions on the practice of their religion which had existed prior thereto, but things were beginning to improve. The first mass was celebrated in Charleston in 1786 at the request of a few Irishmen by a priest who had been on board a ship which had taken shelter in the harbor from a storm. The service was held in a private residence on Tradd Street rather than in a public place due to the religious prejudices that still existed in that year. In attendance was Margaret Ryan, a native of County Cork. Her participation in the city's first mass was such a momentous event in Margaret's life that it was noted in her obituary in the *United States Catholic Miscellany* over fifty years after the occurrence of the event.[36]

Two years after the celebration of the first mass, the tolerance of Catholics in Charleston had increased considerably. In 1788, a French priest took up residency in Charleston. This priest celebrated mass in public and was even bold enough to use newspaper advertisements to encourage the Irish Catholics in the city to attend.[37] On August 8, 1788, the following notice appeared in the *City Gazette*:

> The Assembly of the Roman Catholics, convened on Sunday last, have elected two church wardens:
> Mr. Hubert, for the Dutch nation;
> Mr. Chupin, for the French nation.
> There will be two elected for the Irish nation; the election will take place next Sunday after mass. All gentlemen of that nation are requested to attend.[38]

The French priest was replaced by an Irish priest, Reverend Matthew Ryan, who also arrived in Charleston in 1788. Father Ryan, who was described as "very pious," became the first resident Irish priest in Charleston. A long line of Irish priests would follow.[39]

On August 24, 1789, a Methodist meeting house on Hasell Street was conveyed by the Sheriff of the Charleston District to the Trustees of the Roman Catholic congregation, who were mostly Irish. St. Mary's Roman Catholic Church was established on this property as the first Catholic church in Charleston as well as in the Carolinas and Georgia.[40]

In 1790, South Carolina finally adopted a new constitution based on the Federal Constitution, which removed all restrictions on the practice of religion. At last, the Irish Catholics who chose to immigrate to Charleston could continue to practice their religion. Many of the old prejudices against Catholics and Irishmen would continue, but at least now there was a Catholic church and a priest.[41]

In 1798, the people of Ireland again attempted to throw off the yoke of British oppression by revolution. This revolt was crushed with great cruelty, sending off a new wave of Irish political refugees to America. A large number of Irishmen arrived in Charleston, and it quickly became apparent that a formal organization was needed to render assistance. The Hibernian Society of Charleston, South Carolina was founded in 1799 to meet that need.[42]

The Irish have always been able to find humor in the most dire circumstances, and at least one of the political refugees who settled in Charleston after the Irish Revolution of 1798 was able to do so. Mr. Timothy Kennedy, who took part in the revolt, had been sentenced by the British to be hanged, but was later pardoned. In reflecting on his sentence, Mr. Kennedy is reported to have said "that he did not object to a drop or two for friendship sake, but that the drop to have been given him by order of the government would have been the death of him."[43]

The religious animosities which some residents of Charleston felt towards Irish Catholics who came to Charleston following the American Revolution do not appear to have been shared by most of their Protestant countrymen. In fact, the relationship between the Irish Catholics and Irish Protestants who came to Charleston appears to have been very good. The Hibernian Society of Charleston, the city's most prestigious Irish organization, never had any religious qualification for membership and included both Catholic and Protestant members. This organization also elected a Catholic priest, Reverend Simon Felix Gallagher, as its first president under its completed organization in 1801.[44]

Not all of the Irish Catholics and Irish Protestants who came to Charleston could, however, put aside the ancient religious animosities which had existed in Ireland for hundreds of years. John Blair, who traveled from Larne, Ireland, to Charleston on the Sally of Savanna in 1796, made the following entry in his diary on June 19 of that year:

> At 6:00 A.M., we had a Pretty General Scuffle between two Parties we have on Board, Namely, Defenders, or Roman Catholics; and Break of Day Boys, or Protestants. It was occasioned by the former accusing the latter, of a murder that was committed in Ireland; they intend going to the law as soon as we arrive in America.[45]

Just as they had done during the American Revolution, the Irish who came to Charleston rose to positions of leadership in the state of South Carolina and the new American nation thereafter. One such

Irishman was Aedanus Burke, who was born in County Galway, Ireland, on June 16, 1743. Burke arrived in South Carolina around 1775 and served in the American Army during the Revolutionary War. After the war, Burke was elected Associate Judge of the Court of Common Pleas and the Court of General Sessions and also served in the South Carolina House of Representatives from 1783 to 1788. In 1789 Burke was elected to the First United States Congress. While in Congress, Burke became friends with Aaron Burr and acted as his second in a duel. Burke did not seek re-election to Congress after the end of his term and returned to his judgeship. In 1799, Burke was appointed Chancellor of the Court of Equity, a position in which he served until his death in Charleston on March 30, 1802.[46]

Another post-war Irish American leader was O'Brien Smith, who had immigrated to South Carolina shortly after the American Revolution. Smith began his political career in 1788 when he served as a delegate to the State Convention, which was considering the ratification of the Federal Constitution. Smith voted against the ratification, but this action did not hinder his career in politics. In 1789, he was elected to the South Carolina House of Representatives and in 1800 to the South Carolina Senate. In 1805, Smith was elected to the United States House of Representatives where he served until 1807. Like Burke, Smith did not seek a second term in Congress. Instead he returned to South Carolina, and, in 1808, was elected to the South Carolina House of Representatives from St. Michael's and St. Philip's Parishes. Thereafter, Smith continued to serve in that body until his death in Charleston on April 28, 1811.[47]

Many of the Irish immigrants who arrived in Charleston during the eighteenth century, both before and after the Revolutionary War, came directly to Charleston from Ireland. The square-rigged sailing ships of this period had difficulty sailing into the wind and lacked modern navigational aids. Accordingly, these vessels depended to a great extent upon a clockwise pattern of prevailing winds and currents to take them from Europe to America and back again. Charleston, which was located on the western edge of this clockwise pattern, became a major colonial port in terms of direct transatlantic commerce in both goods and people, including the Irish.[48]

Direct Irish immigration to Charleston was beginning to decline by the end of the second decade of the nineteenth century, and indirect Irish immigration from other American ports, particularly New York, was taking its place. After the war of 1812, chronometers and thermal navigation came into widespread use, enabling mariners to more accurately determine their position. In addition, new ship designs were introduced which enabled vessels to tack when sailing against the wind. These navigational aids and design innovations freed sailing ships from their dependence on the winds and currents that had brought European goods and immigrants to Charleston. Vessels were now able to cross the ocean from Europe to ports located in the northern part of the United States at much higher latitudes in a fraction of the time that it had previously taken them to get to Charleston.[49]

New York quickly moved ahead of Charleston in transatlantic commerce and also became a major landing point for Irish immigrants coming to the United States. According to one source, during the years 1815-1819, two hundred and two ships from Irish ports arrived in New York. During this same period, only thirty-two ships from Irish ports arrived in Charleston.[50]

In the subsequent years leading up to the Civil War, New York became the major landing point for Irishmen coming to the United States, aided in part by the emergence of Liverpool, England as the major port of embarkation for the Irish going to America. Liverpool began competing with Irish ports for the Ireland-to-America immigration trade shortly after steamship service was introduced between the two countries in 1823.[51] The Irish quickly came to prefer ships leaving from Liverpool to those leaving from Irish ports because the ships from Liverpool sailed on schedule, and because the "emigrant ships in Irish ports were the worst on the seas—rickety, overcrowded, dirty vessels, alive with vermin."[52] By the 1840s, Liverpool had very few competitors in the immigration trade between Ireland and the United States. Most of the ships that sailed to the United States from Liverpool were bound for New York.[53]

Charleston remained an important port in the South, but played only a minor role in the immigration trade with Ireland and the other countries of Europe during the nineteenth century. The most immigrants to arrive in Charleston from Europe in any one year between 1819 and 1861 were fewer than two thousand. Unfortunately, it is impossible to determine how many of these European immigrants were Irish, since the immigration officials in Charleston insisted on listing Irish immigrants as British. However, it is probably safe to say that most of Charleston's Irish immigrants during the nineteenth century first landed in the United States at one of the major immigration ports in the North, such as New York, and then later came to Charleston.[54]

Apparently, even some of those Irishmen who intended to come directly from Ireland to Charleston ended up in another port as a result of fraud and deceit by unscrupulous ship owners and agents. In 1819, for example, the owner of ship sailing from Dublin advised potential passengers that, "Such as intend to visit New York, Philadelphia, Baltimore, or Charleston will find this vessel by far the cheapest conveyance, she being the only vessel for Upper Canada, which is so convenient to the above places."[55] Another group of Charleston-bound Irishmen were told by agents "that Boston was the nearest port-only a 'short walk away.'"[56]

At about the same time that Charleston's role as an immigration port was beginning to decline, there were economic forces at work which greatly increased Charleston's need for Irish labor. In 1808 the United States Congress placed a ban on further importation of slaves into the country. Thereafter, the only source for slave labor were areas such as Charleston which had imported slaves for many years prior to the ban. This limited supply of slaves was subjected to an ever-increasing demand for laborers on the cotton plantations of Georgia, Alabama, and Mississippi. Slave prices skyrocketed, and slaves were used only for the safest tasks. There was a need in Charleston for cheap white labor to work on construction jobs which were too risky for the use of expensive slaves. The people of Charleston turned to the Irish to meet that need. Contractors from Charleston were sent to New York to obtain Irish laborers for construction projects in the city and throughout the state of South Carolina.[57]

In 1821, a group of Irishmen was brought to Columbia to dig a canal five miles in length from the bridge at Granby. The climate was harsh, and the work was hard and dangerous. Many of these Irishmen died within a year or two of their arrival and were buried in the walls of the canal.[58]

Laborers were also needed to build the South Carolina Railroad, which was being constructed between Charleston and Hamburg, on the Savannah River, in the 1830s.[59] In order to attract these laborers advertisements such as the following were run in Charleston newspapers:

> Laborers are wanted to work on the Railroad; wages at the rate of $8 per month will be paid promptly and provisions found. Apply to the agent of the Company on the road.[60]

Irish laborers responded to the advertisements and became a part of the labor force employed to construct the railroad. Unfortunately, white laborers proved to be very susceptible to the diseases which plagued the swampy regions along the railroad's route. Many of these laborers, fearing for their lives, left the railroad's workforce. Those who remained were able to demand great increases in their wages.[61]

The Charleston fire of 1838 also created a need for Irish labor. This fire destroyed a substantial portion of the city, and laborers were needed to work on numerous rebuilding projects. A significant number of white laborers came to Charleston for this purpose. These workers were packed into overcrowded boarding houses, creating a most unhealthy condition. An epidemic of yellow fever broke out, and 125 Catholic victims died between August 11 and October 26, 1838. Eighty-three of these were Irish.[62]

After the city was rebuilt, the Irish continued to come to Charleston to work on the construction projects which were considered too dangerous for slaves. In 1842, Irish laborers were working on several such projects in the city. One of these was the opening of drains and the transfer of earth to various parts of the city.[63]

Plantation owners near the city of Charleston also used Irish labor prior to the Potato Famine. Although these plantation owners would not allow Irishmen to work in the fields with slaves, they used Irish labor for construction projects on the plantations. In 1843, Edmund Ruffin, conducting an agricultural survey of South Carolina, observed forty-three Irishmen building a dike for a rice field on one of the plantations along the Cooper River.[64]

The Irish who came to Charleston from northern immigration ports in search of work faced many difficulties, not the least of which was the hot, humid climate that was so radically different from that of Ireland. Every new Irishman who arrived in the city had to undergo an unpleasant acclimation process, as described by one who went through it:

> The surface of the skin becomes raw and irritable, frequently wearing the appearance of broiled flesh; heat blisters cover the entire surface of the skin, and the victim tortured with a smarting sensation, banishing sleep and rest. The choral melody of millions of mosquitoes stinging or rather biting the exposed part of the body, both night and day, increases pain and induces a nervous irritability of long duration; the bite of a mosquito and ant are equally poignant; the former possesses more virus, and after the pain ceases, leaves a white blister behind. The beds are protected at night by a gauze netting called mosquito-bars, without which it is impossible

to sleep or rest. I have frequently worn gloves and knotted a handkerchief over the face at night when otherwise unprotected, which the excessive heat of 90 degrees rendered intolerable, and breaking them loose I preferred insomnolence and a promenade, after a day's hard labor.

Barely to exist, and make no effort of mind or body, is sufficient labor for many constitutions during the summer months in our seaports...[65]

Another difficulty faced by many of the Irish who came to Charleston was unemployment. Those who did not arrive in Charleston with a job, or who lost a job after arriving, found their employment opportunities limited. They were forced to compete for the lowest-paying city jobs against free blacks, who were generally better skilled. In addition, they found that some occupations were not open to them at all because they were white.[66]

Those Irishmen unable to find employment returned to the North or were forced to rely upon private or public charity for support. In 1825, the Charleston poor house had 448 inmates of whom 122 were Irish. In subsequent years, things got worse. In the period between 1830 and 1849, the poor house in Charleston admitted 4,047 foreigners, with forty-eight percent coming from Ireland.[67] The Hibernian Society rendered what assistance it could to as many of these immigrants as possible. This aid took many forms, ranging from financial assistance for food or shelter to providing the cost of passage back up North.[68]

Bishop John England, Charleston's Irish-born Roman Catholic Bishop, in 1840 warned the Irish against coming to the South:

> Our southern states are the worst places to which an Irishman can emigrate, except he is a merchant with good capital, a mechanic in the way of building or tailoring (with as much as spare means as would support him for a couple of months), steady habits and untiring industry.[69]

In spite of such warnings, a steady stream of Irishmen came to Charleston and to other parts of the South in the years prior to the Civil War. In fact, at the time of the Civil War "the Irish were the largest foreign-born group in the South".[70]

Along with the Irish workers, Irish Catholic clergymen came to Charleston to minister to the spiritual needs of the growing number of Catholic residents. The most prominent of these was the above-mentioned Bishop John England. Born in Cork, Ireland, on September 23, 1786, he received his ecclesiastical training at the College of Carlow and was ordained to the priesthood in 1808. After his ordination, he served in various positions in the Diocese of Cork, including president of the Diocesan Seminary, Chaplain of Prisons and Parish priest in Bandon.[71]

In 1820, the Catholic Church established the Diocese of Charleston, which included the states of South Carolina, North Carolina, and Georgia, and appointed John England its first Bishop. Bishop England aptly served his Diocese for a period of twenty-two years. During his tenure, he increased the number of Catholic Churches in the Diocese from about half a dozen to fourteen. He also established a seminary, a girls' school and the first distinctly Catholic newspaper in America, the *United States Catholic Miscellany*.[72]

In addition to tending to the spiritual needs of the Catholics of his Diocese, Bishop England also assisted his fellow Irishmen with their worldly needs by supporting the activities of the Hibernian Society of Charleston. The Bishop joined the Society on June 4, 1821, shortly after he arrived in the city, and remained an active member for the rest of his life. He was the main speaker at the laying of the cornerstone of Hibernian Hall in 1839 and again at the Hall's opening in 1841. At the time of the Bishop's death in 1842, the members of the Society resolved to wear black crepe on their left arms for a period of thirty days in testimony of their respect for him.[73]

By the beginning of the 1840s, many of the people of rural Ireland survived on a daily diet which consisted almost exclusively of potatoes. In 1845, a great blight literally destroyed the potato crop. This occurred again in each of the following three years, causing a terrible famine in Ireland. It is estimated that over one million Irishmen died of starvation and disease as a result of the famine. Another one million immigrated to North America. Large numbers of these Irishmen immigrated to the United States, through northern immigration ports of which New York was the most prominent.[74]

The Irish who landed in New York and the other northern immigration ports between 1845 and the Civil War tended to linger in the port of landing rather than travel further west in search of homesteads.[75] These Irishmen, "carried, with certain exceptions, a prejudice against farming," which to them symbolized all the problems which they had left Ireland to escape.[76] In addition, "the Irish were a gregarious, novelty-loving people, and the bright lights and crowds in New York and Boston were more attractive than the monotony and loneliness of life along the Frontier."[77] This tendency to linger in the port of landing, along with the large number of Irishmen arriving, led to widespread poverty and unemployment among the Irish in New York and other northern immigration ports. To some of these poor unemployed Irishmen, Charleston appeared to be a city which would offer them a chance for employment and a better life.[78]

Fortunately, for those Famine Irish who landed in New York and desired to travel to Charleston, the means of transportation between the two cities had greatly improved by the time of the Famine. At the beginning of the nineteenth century, the quickest way to travel from New York to Charleston was by sailing ship, a voyage of about ten days. By the 1840s, however, steam-powered passenger vessels had reduced the time of the voyage to three days. It was relatively easy for the Irish in New York to take advantage of these steamers to come to Charleston even for a few months in search of employment. Consequently, a large supply of Irish labor was available for the numerous construction projects in Charleston during the latter part of the 1840s and throughout the 1850s.[79]

Irish labor was used extensively in the construction of the facilities utilized by the Charleston Light and Gas Company to supply gaslight to the City of Charleston. The Charleston Light and Gas Company was incorporated in December 1846 and in May 1847 began the construction of Charleston's first gas plant on the west side of Church Street between Cumberland and Market Streets. This facility, completed in December 1848, consisted of several brick buildings, tool sheds and a workshop. During this project, 125,000 cubic feet of earth and other materials were removed from the site and disbursed to various parts of the city. At least one hundred Irishmen were employed in this operation.[80] These Irishmen, unaccustomed to Charleston's climate, labored in the August and September sun in "a pit ten to twenty six feet deep with not a current of air to fan their burning bodies."[81]

After Charleston was lit with gas in April 1848, the demand for this modern convenience increased rapidly, creating more employment opportunities for the Irish. A second gas facility was constructed on King Street near Vanderhorst Street, between May and November 1849. A third gas facility was constructed on Cannon Street during the summer of 1853.[82]

Another project which employed a large number of Irish laborers was the construction of the United States Custom House at the corner of East Bay and Market Streets. Congress had appropriated money for this project in 1848, and in 1849 Fitzsimons' Wharf was purchased for the site. The building, as designed, was to be constructed in the Roman Corinthian style in the shape of a cross surmounted by a dome, the highest point of which was to be 160 feet above the pavement.[83]

In January 1852, excavation began on a pit seventy feet long, thirty feet wide, and ten feet deep, in preparation for the erection of the construction of the north wing of the Custom House. Twenty-one thousand cubic feet of earth, mud and other materials were removed from this pit by laborers who were mostly Irish. In August of that year, 196 of the 211 laborers working on the project were Irish. The work on the Custom House continued in 1853, and an additional 143,000 cubic feet of earth were excavated that year. At least 202 Irishmen were employed in this endeavor.[84]

Charleston's waterfront and its related activities provided another source of employment for the Irish. By the mid-1850s, they were well established as a part of the work force. John W. DeForrest, an author who visited Charleston in 1855, wrote:

> The crowd of porters & coachmen that met us on the dock presented not above half a dozen black faces. Instead, I saw the familiar Irish & German visages whom I could have met on a dock at Boston or New York.[85]

It seems that there was no job too dirty or too dangerous for the Irish if the price was right, as will appear from an incident which occurred on the Charleston waterfront in 1854. In July of that year, a group of Irish laborers were unloading the ship *Aquatic* at Union Wharf. During this operation, the men noticed that the customs officer had not boarded the ship as was customary. They questioned the officer about this and were told that there was yellow fever on the ship, to which they replied "And, by jabbers, is it yellow fever that's aboard this vessel, and divil a turn more will we give the windlass." An immediate renegotiation of wages took place, and the Irishmen continued to unload the vessel. Of the seventeen Irishmen who unloaded the *Aquatic*, three died of yellow fever. It was reported that the rest were "ready to unload another yellow fever vessel at the same wages."[86]

In the early 1850s, Irish labor was also used to construct the Northeastern Railway, which was being built to link Charleston's port with the interior. It has been said that the Irish introduced rioting to America as a means of settling industrial disputes, and it was during the construction of the Northeastern Railway that a number of Irishmen attempted to introduce these methods to Charleston. In March 1855, some of the Irishmen who were working as laborers in the construction of the railroad went on strike for a raise in wages from $1.00 a day to $1.25 a day. When their demands were not met, the men rioted and had to be subdued by several companies of militia.[87] At their subsequent trial, Judge Withers made the following comments about the Irish:

> I know your native Ireland has contributed a rich contingent to the best blood of mankind—it has heightened the charms of song—it has furnished the electric power of eloquence—it has glorified the battle field—its bone and muscle have subdued the wilderness and made it to "blossom as the rose." But truth demands admission that the Emerald Isle has likewise afforded us the most troublesome specimens of humankind—it may not be peculiar in that respect.
>
> It is but too true, that a great proportion of those we receive in Charleston from Ireland, manifest a proclivity to turbulence...[88]

Notwithstanding Judge Withers' remarks, it is doubtful that the Irish who came to Charleston were any more turbulent or troublesome than their fellow countrymen in the North. The Irish who came to America during the nineteenth century, whether to the North or the South, had to compete fiercely with each other and with others for menial, low-paying, dangerous jobs just to exist. It was inevitable that this fierce competition would sometimes lead to violence. It must be admitted, however, that the Irish contributed more than their share to the problems of those charged with enforcing the laws in Charleston. Of the 617 males committed to the House of Corrections in the period from November 1856 through October 1857, 401 were Irish. During the same period, 128 of the 171 females committed to the House of Corrections were Irish.[89]

On the other hand, the Irish also contributed more than their share to the ranks of those charged with enforcing the laws in Charleston, the City Guard. The members of the Guard, which eventually evolved into the Charleston City Police Department, were paid sixty cents per day, and no particular skills were required. Many Irish laborers looked upon the Guard as a second job, and the records for 1849 and 1850 show that over half of the Guard members were Irish. Apparently, the "Irish cop" was a familiar sight in antebellum Charleston.[90]

The living conditions of many of the poor famine-era Irish who came to Charleston were as bad as those in the northern seaports.

Large numbers of these Irishmen were forced to live in tenements and boarding houses located in crowded, disease-ridden neighborhoods.[91] In an 1855 Medical journal, a Charleston physician described the conditions under which these immigrants lived:

> ...their abodes abound with filth, which gives rise to emanations which are in the highest degree offensive. Each family of those people usually occupied a single room; a house with four or six rooms, being occupied by four or six families, will thus contain from 20 to 30 human beings. The occupancy of many houses in one vicinity in this manner gives rise to an accumulation of filth enough to generate an atmosphere, which if not capable of originating an epidemic disease, readily receives and propagates the germs which are introduced from abroad.[92]

The same conditions were observed by Frederick Law Olmstead when he visited Charleston in 1856: "I saw as much close packing filth, and squalor, in certain blocks, inhabited by laboring whites in Charleston, as I have witnessed in any Northern town of its size..."[93]

One Charleston neighborhood associated with the Irish who came during the Potato Famine was the area around Market Street and Lingard Street. This neighborhood was described in 1849 as being inhabited by the Irish and Dutch of the lower classes.[94] Another famine-era Irish neighborhood was situated on land westward of Franklin Street, opposite the Marine Hospital, which had been filled with garbage and gave off an unpleasant odor. This neighborhood, which was later described as "embodying nearly everything bad about this City", was reached by way of an alley which was later named "Cromwell Alley."[95]

A third famine-era Irish neighborhood was located east of Meeting Street on both sides of Calhoun Street. By the 1850s, this area was thickly settled with Irish Catholics. Many of the lots in this neighborhood were low and boggy and had no drainage because they were located below the level of the street. These lots constantly had stagnant water standing on them, creating deplorable and unhealthy conditions.[96]

The conditions under which the famine-era Irish were obliged to live, coupled with their lack of natural immunity to American diseases, made them very susceptible to the fevers and other epidemics which periodically visited Charleston. This was particularly true of yellow fever, which was referred to as "stranger's fever" because it struck foreigners much more frequently than it did natives.[97] An editorial in one of Charleston's leading medical journals discussed yellow fever in Charleston:

> The Irish Celts, and the lower classes from Southern Europe, are most susceptible to the disease, and succumb most readily to its deleterious influence. The Teuton, whether German, English, or American, are less liable to be attacked, and are more apt to recover when affected by the disease.[98]

During the first few years after the beginning of the Irish Potato Famine, the city of Charleston was relatively free of yellow fever. Then in 1849, a year in which numerous white laborers were engaged in the extensive excavations of drains on Hasell and Market Streets, the fever struck. One hundred and twenty-three people died of the fever. Of these, sixty-six were Irish.[99]

Three years later, in 1852, yellow fever returned to Charleston at a time when the city was holding its elections for Mayor and Aldermen. The Irish and Germans, as usual, were actively engaged in these elections and, the fever spread quickly through these two groups. This epidemic of yellow fever killed 302 people including 150 Irishmen. At least one-third of the Irish who died in the epidemic were fresh off the boat. They had arrived in the city while the fever raged and had little or no natural immunity.[100]

In 1854, two-fifths of the population of Charleston were struck with yellow fever, which caused 627 deaths. Two hundred and fifty-six of those who died were Irish.[101] There were so many Irishmen dying that one Charleston lady "blamed the 'besotted Irish' for continuing the epidemic because they continued to immigrate to Charleston and keep the fever up by giving it constant fuel."[102] The Irish kept on coming, and so did the fever. Epidemics of yellow fever occurred in Charleston again in 1856 and 1858.[103]

The beginning of the Civil War marked the end of large-scale Irish immigration to Charleston. After the war, the Irish did not come to America in the large numbers that they had during and immediately following the Potato Famine, and war-torn Charleston offered very little opportunity for those who did come. Although attempts were made to entice the Irish to come to Charleston both from Ireland and from New York, these efforts met with very little success.[104]

CHAPTER TWO

THE CELEBRATION OF ST. PATRICK'S DAY AND THE ST. PATRICK'S DAY PARADE IN CHARLESTON

The celebration of the Feast Day of St. Patrick, the Patron Saint of Ireland, has been observed in Charleston, South Carolina since at least 1749. In March of that year "an Ode to St. Patrick's Day" was printed in the *South Carolina Gazette* on behalf of the Irish Society.[105]

In the early years, St. Patrick's Day was celebrated with a dinner where the natives of the Emerald Isle joined together to partake of a sumptuous meal and spend the evening "with that Mirth and Jollity, ever conspicuous to the Natives of that Country."[106] These dinners often featured excellent entertainment along with the fellowship and food. One such St. Patrick's Day dinner was attended by Josiah Quincy, Junior, of Massachusetts, who visited Charleston in 1773 while on a tour of the Carolinas. Quincy made the following entry in his diary concerning the occasion:

> March 17…Dined with the sons of St. Patrick. While at dinner, six violins, two hautboys, &c. After dinner six French horns in concert,—most surpassing music. Two solos on the French horn, by one who is said to blow the finest horn in the world. He has fifty guineas for the season from the St. Cecilia Society.[107]

As the number of Irishmen in Charleston increased at the beginning of the nineteenth century, the way in which St. Patrick's Day was celebrated began to change. The traditional dinner in the evening was still hell, but other activities were added. The celebration of St. Patrick's Day gradually became an all-day affair.

The Irish who came to America liked nothing better than to march on St. Patrick's' Day in full regalia with the other members of the social or military organizations to which they belonged, and as early as 1779 a St. Patrick's Day parade was held in New York City.[108] The Irish who came to Charleston were no exception, and a parade was added to the morning activities in the early 1800s.[109]

The St. Patrick's Day parade in Charleston originated with the Irish Volunteers, who began the day with a procession to a Catholic church where a Mass was celebrated. Although it is not known when the Irish Volunteers held their first procession, the custom dates back to at least 1823. On March 17 of that year, this organization marched to St. Finbar's Cathedral on Broad Street where they were treated to an oration by Charleston's Irish Catholic Bishop, John England.[110] Not long thereafter, the St. Patrick's Benevolent Society joined the Irish Volunteers in the procession, and these two organizations remained the mainstays of the parade throughout its history.[111] It is interesting to note that Charleston's Hibernian Society did not usually take part in the parade. For reasons unknown, its members marched only occasionally in St. Patrick's Day parades during the nineteenth century.[112]

Charleston's St. Patrick's Day parade was actually two separate processions. The first was a march from the point of rendezvous to a Catholic church where a Mass and oration were held. Prior to the Civil War, this church was usually the Catholic Cathedral on Broad Street or St. Patrick's Church on St. Philip Street. After Mass, the line was reformed for the march from the church to the point of dismissal.[113]

The Irish population of Charleston greatly increased during the late 1840s and early 1850s with the influx of immigrants fleeing the Irish Potato Famine. New Irish organizations sprang up, each with the desire to march on St. Patrick's Day. The Irish Mutual Benevolent Society was formed in 1849.[114] It was followed in quick succession by the Meagher Guard, the Montgomery Guard, and the Emmett Volunteers, all of which were in existence by 1854.[115]

On St. Patrick's Day in 1854, most of these new organizations elected to join in the parade to the Cathedral along with the Irish Volunteers and the St. Patrick's Benevolent Society. However, the Meagher Guard decided to hold its own parade, and marched to St. Patrick's Church in the upper wards.[116] Thereafter, for the remainder of the 1850s, there were two separate St. Patrick's Day parades in Charleston. One marched to the Cathedral on Broad Street and the other to St. Patrick's

Church.[117] In 1860, these two processions were combined, and most of Charleston's Irish organizations marched together to the Hibernian Hall to hear an oration by Michael Patrick O'Connor.[118]

In 1861 there were again two St. Patrick's Day parades in Charleston. One was held by the St. Patrick's Benevolent Society, which marched to the Cathedral where an address was given by the Rev. Dr. Moore. The other procession was held by the Irish Volunteers and the Montgomery Guard, both of which were in State service preparing for the confrontation between South Carolina and the United States Government over Fort Sumter. These two military units, after assembling at Hibernian Hall, marched through the principal streets of the city to Magnolia Parade Ground where they engaged in target practice.[119]

The St. Patrick's Day parade was apparently discontinued during 1862, 1863, and 1864 because no mention of it was made in the Charleston newspapers during those years.[120] The Irish Volunteers, Montgomery Guard, and Meagher Guard, which usually marched in the parade, were engaged in the war effort, and it probably would have been viewed as unpatriotic for others to parade in their absence.[121] In addition, the city of Charleston was put under martial law in 1862 and was under the fire of Union guns after August of 1863. It would have been both difficult and dangerous to stage a parade during those years.[122]

On March 17, 1865, less than one month after the Union Army occupied Charleston, a St. Patrick's Day parade was held in the city by the St. Patrick's Benevolent Society. The members of the Society assembled at Masonic Hall at the corner of King and Wentworth Streets at half past eight and marched in a body to St. Mary's Church on Hasell Street. At the church the usual services were held, and an eloquent discourse was given by the Rev. Dr. Baker. Thereafter, the parade was reformed and marched back to Masonic Hall.[123]

The following year, the St. Patrick's Day parade was expanded to include new participants. Marching in the 1866 procession were the St. Patrick's Benevolent Society, the local Circle of the Fenian Brotherhood, and the band of the Sixth United States Army Infantry, which had been supplied for the occasion by General Sickles, the occupation commander of Charleston. This parade, like the one the previous year, formed at Masonic Hall, but this time the destination was St. Joseph's Church on Anson Street. St. Joseph's would remain the destination of the parade for the rest of the 1860s.[124]

In 1870 the destination of the parade was shifted to St. Patrick's Church in the upper wards, where it remained until 1872. Thereafter, the Cathedral Chapel on Queen Street became the parade's destination for the rest of the 1870s. This decade brought new participants to the parade: the Irish Rifle Club, the Irish Volunteer Rifle Club, and St. Joseph's Total Abstinence and Beneficial Society all marched for the first time. The newly reorganized Irish Volunteers and Montgomery Guards rejoined the parade during this same period.[125]

A convention made up of representatives of the various Irish civic and military organizations was organized in the 1870s to plan the parade and elect a marshal.[126] Each organization considered it a great honor to have one of their members chosen as marshal of the parade. There was a lot of jealousy between organizations, and this was ever increased when the person elected marshal was a member of more than one group. In the 1870s, Colonel James Cosgrove, a member of the St. Patrick's Benevolent Society and officer of the Irish Volunteer Rifle Club, was chosen as one of the marshals. Another member of the Benevolent Society asked Colonel Cosgrove whether he would wear the green scarf of the Society or the uniform of the Rifle Club. Colonel Cosgrove called on his Irish wit and responded "that he had sent to Ireland to get the 'collar of gold which King Malachi won from the proud invader.'"[127]

Charleston's St. Patrick's Day parade varied from year to year, both in size and pageantry. Newspaper accounts show that the parade on occasion included over four hundred participants.[128] The parade of 1876, as reported in the local paper, was probably typical:

THE RENDEZVOUS

The Irish Rifle Club, Irish Volunteer Rifle Club, St. Patrick's Benevolent Society and St. Joseph's Total Abstinence and Beneficial Society, formed into line soon afterwards in King Street, the right resting on Wentworth Street. Headed by the Eutaw Band and commanded by Lieut. J. F. Walsh, of the Irish Rifle Club, this division marched down King Street to the rendezvous at Hibernian Hall, where they were joined by the Irish Volunteers, Lieut. James Cosgrove commanding.
The line was then formed in the following order:
1. Irish Rifle Club, 45 men; Lieut. J. F. Walsh commanding. Second Lieut. N. A. Quin. Third Lieut. M. Hogan. The uniform consisting of a cadet gray frock coat trimmed with green, black pants and gray capies, surmounted with white and green plumes.
2. Irish Volunteer Rifle Club, 30 men; Capt. Phil Fogarty commanding, Second Lieut. P. O'Neil; Third Lieut. W.

H. O'Brien. The company was divided into two sections, one of which appeared in the old uniform and the other in the handsome uniform recently adopted by the corps, a description of which was published in The News and Courier of Wednesday last.

3. Irish Volunteers, 35 men; First Lieut. James Cosgrove commanding, Second Lieut. William Moran, Third Lieut. P. Brady. The uniform of the Company is of dark blue cloth, trimmed with green, black felt hats and green plumes. The rank and file are almost entirely composed of old veterans.

4. Montgomery Guard, 34 men; Capt. A. G. Magrath commanding, First Lieut. P. E. Gleason, Junior, Second Lieut. T. J. Kennedy.

The civic division of the parade was headed by the Eutaw Band, and was composed of the St. Patrick's Benevolent Society, 30 strong, and the St. Joseph's Total Abstinence and Beneficial Society, 60 strong. The members of both organizations were clothed in the regalia of their respective orders, that of the first named consisting of a broad green ribbon worn around the neck, and of the latter, a four inch scarf of green satin, bordered with gold and adorned with the insignia of the society, worn across the shoulder.

TO THE CHURCH

The line was formed about half-past 9 o'clock, and was then turned over to Captain John Burke, Chief Marshal, and President James F. Redding, Assistant Marshal of the day, Lieut. J. P. Walsh, of the Irish Rifle Club, commanded the military division, which carried the old colors of the Irish Volunteers and the American colors. A squad of mounted policemen, under the command of Lieut. Fordham, preceded the column, which countermarched in Meeting to Queen, and proceeded thence to the Cathedral Chapel. Here the military presented arms while the societies filed into the church, the band playing "St. Patrick's Day in the Morning."[129]

A rare glimpse inside the church at one of the St. Patrick's Day Masses is provided by the following account from the March 18, 1884 *News and Courier*:

During the celebration of the Mass, the battalion stood in single rank formation in the central aisle, facing the altar, and at the reading of the gospel presented arms. At the elevation of the Host, the battalion knelt and at the Pontifical benediction again presented arms. During these ceremonies two sentinels were stationed at the entrance to the sanctuary and two at the main entrance, facing inward. The commanding officer stood near the main entrance, facing the altar and the other officers near the altar rails. The collection was taken up by the officers of the two companies and a representative of the St. Patrick's Benevolent Society.

Bishop Northrop, who occupied the Episcopal throne in the sanctuary during the services, and who was announced to deliver the annual address on the occasion, announced at the onset of his remarks that he had no idea of taking advantage of his position to preach a sermon. If he once began on the subject of Ireland, he said, it would be difficult to set a limit to any address that he might deliver. Though there had never been any formal union of Church and State in the Green Isle there had always been the closest, strictest and most endurable union of love and faith in the hearts of Irishmen. Piety and patriotism had always gone hand in hand in the hearts of the sons of Ireland from time immemorial. In conclusion he could not refrain from congratulating his hearers upon the celebration of St. Patrick's Day. It was a matter of congratulation that in Charleston the Irish Catholic soldiers and Irish Catholic citizens always commenced the celebration by first kneeling at the altar and offering prayers to Almighty God...[130]

A parade which was definitely not typical was the St. Patrick's Day parade of 1877. Reconstruction was coming to an end, and the people of Charleston were in a mood to celebrate. This was reflected in the large number of organizations that chose to take part in the parade. These included: the Washington Artillery, the Fifth Artillery Band, the Palmetto Guards, the Washington Light Infantry, the German Fusiliers, the Sumter Guards, the St. Patrick's Coronet Band, the Irish Rifle Club, the Irish Volunteers, the Montgomery Guards, the Montgomery Guards Coronet Band, the St. Patrick's Benevolent Society, and the St. Joseph's Total Abstinence and Beneficial Society.[131]

After attending the traditional Mass at the Cathedral Chapel, the parade participants reassembled and proceeded down Meeting Street to South Battery, then to East Battery. At the corner of South Battery and

East Battery the parade was halted while a salute of thirty-two cannons was fired by the Washington Artillery in honor of the thirty-two counties of Ireland and of South Carolina. The procession then continued along East Battery, East Bay Street, Market Street, Meeting Street, Columbus Street and King Street to the Academy of Music, where the parade was dismissed and a collation was served to the participants.[132]

The point of commencement of Charleston's St. Patrick's Day parade varied from year to year throughout its history, and it was not until the 1880s that a regular point of commencement was established. In 1883 the Irish Volunteers, who had originated the parade and participated in it almost every year, moved their headquarters to a site on Vanderhorst Street around the corner from Marion Square.[133] Shortly thereafter, the starting point of the parade was shifted to Marion Square. From then, until World War One, the parade began at Marion Square or at the nearby Irish Volunteers Hall.[134]

The rifle clubs went out of existence in the late 1870s and early 1880s, and were replaced in the parade in the 1890s by Charleston's newly formed Divisions of the Ancient Order of Hibernians. Division No. 1 of the Ancient Order of Hibernians first marched in the parade of 1890. Divisions No. 2 and No. 3 were formed shortly thereafter, and by 1895 all three of Charleston's divisions were participating in the parade.[135]

After the turn of the century, the Hibernian Society apparently reversed its position on marching on St. Patrick's Day and became a regular participant in the parade. It is not known what caused this change of heart, but the Society took part in the parades of 1911, 1912, 1915, 1916 and 1921. The P. N. Lynch Council No. 704 of the Knights of Columbus also began marching in the parade of 1911 and participated every year thereafter.[136]

The St. Patrick's Day parade was not held in 1917 because the Irish Volunteers, the chief organizers of the parade, were absent from the city, serving on the Mexican border. The next year the United States entered into World War One, and the parade was omitted from the St. Patrick's Day celebrations of 1918, 1919 and 1920 due to the war and conditions that existed thereafter.[137]

In 1921, after an absence of five years, the citizens of Charleston were ready for the return of the St. Patrick's Day parade. At a meeting of the Knights of Columbus held during the winter of that year, it was decided to revive the time-honored tradition of parading on St. Patrick's Day. A parade committee consisting of J. W. Wallace, Sr., M. J. Hanley and J. J. Regan was appointed to attend to the details and invite the other participants.[138]

The revived parade of 1921 was one of Charleston's largest St. Patrick's Day parades. The cause of Irish freedom had been rapidly gaining momentum since the end of the First World War, both in Charleston and throughout the United States. The city's residents of Irish descent decided to go all out to show their support. The parade formed at the Customs House under the direction of the marshals of the day, Messrs. Martin J. Hanley, John J. Regan, William M. Rowland, W. J. Leonard, James B. Lannon and J. P. Kiley. Almost five hundred people participated, including representatives from the Hibernian Society, the Friends of Irish Freedom, the Ancient Order of Hibernians, the Saint Patrick Benevolent Society, the P. N. Lynch Council No. 704 of the Knights of Columbus, and the Holy Name Societies of various parishes. The line of march was from East Bay to Broad Street, to Meeting, to King, to Vanderhorst, to St. Philip Street, and on to St. Patrick's Church where the Mass was celebrated.[139]

On occasion, after the parade was dismissed, a collation was held for the participants.[140] The more customary practice, however, was for the various Irish organizations to go their separate ways so that they could conduct individual meetings or other activities with their own members. At noon on St. Patrick's Day, the Hibernian Society traditionally held its annual business meeting. At this meeting, the Society elected the officers for the ensuing year.[141] The St. Patrick's Benevolent Society also usually held a midday meeting to elect new officers.[142]

In the afternoon of St. Patrick's Day in the 1850s, it was traditional for the city's Irish militia companies to hold target practice. These exercises, which often included invited guests, took part at various locations in Charleston and in Mount Pleasant, but were most often held at the Magnolia Parade Ground.[143] The companies sometimes conducted individual target exercises, and sometimes joint ones. The March 18, 1859 edition of the *Charleston Daily Courier* reported the results of a joint target exercise by the Irish Volunteers, the Montgomery Guards, and the Meagher Guard:

> The target firing of the Irish Volunteers, Captain E. Magrath, resulted as follows:
> First Prize—Magrath Medal—Private John Noonan.
> Second Prize—Silver Medal—Private James Powers.
> Third Prize—O'Connell Medal—Private Michael Hennessy.
> Fourth Prize—Plume—Private Wm. O'Connor...

The target contest of the Montgomery Guards was reported as follows:
Corporal Gorman, 1st Prize—Silver Medal
Private Sullivan, 2d Prize—Silver Cup
Private Murry, 3d Prize—2d Silver Cup
Private Walsh, 4th Prize—Company Plume...
The target firing of the Meagher Guard was reported as follows:
First Prize—Silver Cup—John O'Rourke
Second Prize—Silver Tankard—Private John McCaffer
Third Prize—Silver Watch—Private Hy. McConell.[144]

After the Civil War, these target exercises did not occur on a regular basis. However, when they were held, the site was usually the Hibernian Park on Meeting Street Road. The Irish Volunteers also on occasion held a formal military lunch after the parade.[145]

In the evening of St. Patrick's Day, a number of Charleston's Irish organizations held traditional anniversary dinners which were the highlight of the day's activities. These dinners, which started out as simple meals, eventually evolved into grand banquets. The banquet of the Hibernian Society was the most prestigious.[146]

In the early years, the Hibernian Society did not have a permanent meeting place and its anniversary dinners on St. Patrick's Day, like those of most of Charleston's other Irish organizations, were held at rented facilities. These included, among others, Burger's Tavern, the Carolina Coffee House, St. Andrew's Hall and the Carolina Hotel.[147] Then, on March 17, 1841 the Hibernian Society held its anniversary dinner in the newly completed Hibernian Hall. Since that date, the Society's anniversary dinners have been held at the Hibernian Hall.[148]

The Hibernian Hall was, of course, appropriately decorated each year in preparation for the anniversary dinner. The following description of the decorations for the anniversary dinner of 1897 was printed in the Charleston *News and Courier*:

> The Hall was handsomely decorated for the gala occasion and the design was formulated and carried out by Capt. Gannon an enthusiastic member assisted by several members of the committee. At the south end, where stands the president's chair, three enormous flags, "Old Glory," the "Harp of Erin" and the brave "Palmetto" joined folds to guard the honored guests. Above their heads in letters of red, white and blue

tissue were the words "Cead mille failthe." (Ten thousand welcomes.) Each pillar supporting the ceiling was wound with tri-colored ropes of tissue and the chandeliers were hung with the same bright colors...
The tables were placed north and south, with cross tables at either end, and were tastefully arranged. [149]

The first order of business for the members of the Hibernian Society and their invited guests was to partake of a sumptuous meal. The menu, of course, varied from year to year, but one particular "gastronomical extravaganza" was the meal served at the banquet of 1868.[150] The menu for this feast was reprinted in the *Charleston Daily Courier*:

BILL OF FARE
Oysters on half shell.
SOUP.
Cooter. Green Turtle.
FISH.
Broiled Fresh Kennebec Salmon, cream sauce.
Boiled Rock, shrimp sauce. Baked Shad.
BOILED.
Irish Mutton, caper sauce.
New York Turkey, oyster sauce.
Ham. Tongue.
Buck County Capons, mushroom sauce.
COLD DISHES
Dinde d'esosses aux Boudins Blanc aux truffles.
Chicken Salad. Shrimp Salad.
Pate de Foie Gras, aux truffles.
ENTREES.
Brazed Quails. Larded sweet Bread on spinach.
Oyster patties. Mutton Chops on mashed potatoes.
Pigs Feet, tomato sauce. Deviled Crabs.
Maccaroon Pies.
RELISHES.
Celery, Currant and Blackberry Jellies.
French Mustard. Worcestershire Sauce.
Chow Chow. Picaclilly.
ROAST.
New York Turkey, gravy sauce. A la mode Beef.
Saddle of New York Mutton, mint sauce.

Buck County Capons, truffle sauce
Ducks, with olives. Baked Ham, champagne sauce.
GAME.
Wild Turkey, brown gravy.
Haunch Venison, currant jelly
Prairie Hens, wine sauce.
Mallard Ducks. Pheasants. Quails on toast. Snipes
VEGETABLES.
Boiled and Baked Irish Potatoes.
Parsnips. Onions. Turnips. Asparagus. Green Peas.
Baked Sweet Potatoes. Rice. Bread.
ORNAMENTS.
Fancy Pyramids. Baskets of Candied Fruit.
PASTRX.
Plum Puddings, Madeira wine sauce
Baked Almond Puddings.
Apple, Cranberry, and Peach Pies.
Assorted Small Tarts.
Charlotte Russe. Calves' Feet Jelly. Bisquet Giace.
Vanilla and Pine Apple Ice Creams.
Cheese. Fruit Cakes. Ladies' Fingers.
DESSERT.
Oranges. Apples. Bananas. Figs. Raisins. Almonds.
English Walnuts. Hazel and Pecannuts.
COFFEE.[151]

The Irish have always paid due attention to drink as well as to food, and the Hibernian banquet of 1868 was no exception. In its account of the event the *Charleston Daily Courier* goes on to state: "Of course there was no lack of those good liquids which are essential to the proper enjoyment of such a repast, and so the table gratefully bore numerous testimonials to the productive industry of the Widow Cliquot, to say nothing of the Sauterne, St. Julien, &c."[152] It was further reported by the newspaper that thirteen bottles of champagne were consumed at this banquet in eleven minutes.[153]

After dinner was finished, it was customary for the president of the Hibernian Society to rise and propose the first "regular" toast. This was followed by a series of regular toasts which were appropriate to the occasion and responded to by designated persons.[154] The regular toasts varied slightly over the years, but those given at the Hibernian banquet of 1857 were typical. These included: "The Day," "Ireland,"

"The State of South Carolina," "The President of the United States," "Our Benefactors," "Our Sister Societies," "The City of Charleston" and "Woman."[155]

In the 1850s, the Hibernian Society began inviting prominent public figures to address the banquet in response to one or more of the regular toasts, thus adding to the prestige of the Society. Prior to the Civil War, these speakers included Irish patriots Thomas Francis Meagher, William Smith O'Brien and Archbishop John Hughes of New York. The tradition was continued in the 1900s, and the Vice President of the United States, James S. Sherman addressed the Society in 1911.[156]

In the nineteenth century it was the custom, after the regular toasts were completed, to open the floor for "volunteer" toasts. These were sometimes quite numerous and could last until the early hours of the morning.[157] Volunteer toasts over the years included the following:

> The Emerald Isle—The land of my forefathers; may its fields continue to flourish when the tyranny that now oppresses it is only known in story.
> The true heart and pure hand with which an Irishman greets both his friend and his enemy.
> The Land we live in—The asylum of the oppressed of all nations.[158]
> The Shamrock—The pride of Irishmen and a plant that modestly, but perseveringly makes its way in every clime.[159]
> The Harp of Erin—May its cords be ever strung in the cause of liberty.[160]

The only risk assumed by most of the makers of these volunteer toasts was that they might be pelted by a roll or heckled if their toast was unpopular. In 1866, one brave man risked much more. When the floor was opened to volunteer toasts at the Hibernian banquet that year, Dr J. Dickson Bruns arose from his seat and toasted "The health of Jefferson Davis." In a state occupied by the Union Army and controlled by a reconstruction government, this toast could have subjected him to immediate arrest. The *Charleston Daily Courier* reported that Dr. Bruns made his toast: "Carefully avoiding the utterance of ANY SENTIMENT which could excite ill feeling towards the Government."[161]

The St. Patrick's Benevolent Society held an anniversary dinner each St. Patrick's Day evening similar to that of the Hibernian Society. The Irish Volunteers, Irish Mutual Benevolent Society and Irish Volunteer Rifle Club also occasionally held such dinners. Unlike the parade, anniversary dinners continued throughout the Civil War. However, these dinners were a far cry from the grand banquets held before and after the war. [162]

The Hibernian Society gave its annual banquet in Hibernian Hall in 1861, but in 1862 cancelled the banquet and instead held a simple collation. [163] In reporting on the St. Patrick's Day activities of the Hibernian Society that year the *Charleston Daily Courier* stated:

> The attendance at the business meeting, or collation in the evening at their Hall, was not large and it was a creditable proof of the devotion which the members have exhibited and are now exhibiting in defence of their city, state and country, that few of those were of military age or liability. Of these few, some if not all were on short furloughs for this purpose. [164]

In 1863, the Hibernian Society again held a collation in its hall in the evening of St. Patrick's Day. [165] Then in 1864, after it was forced out of the hall by Union shellfire, a defiant Hibernian Society held its anniversary dinner in the street at the southeast corner of Thomas and Radcliffe Streets. [166] The following account of this dinner was printed in the *Charleston Daily Courier*:

> The 62nd anniversary of the Hibernian society of this city was celebrated on Thursday, 17th inst.—St. Patrick's Day—with features of excellent cheer and encouragement that would have agreeably surprised some of our distant friends who estimate the condition and prospects of Charleston by the reports of frightened fugitives from duty...
>
> The Society with some guests—the few out of many invited who could seize this always acceptable opportunity—sat down to a repast, which the Stewards modestly called a collation. If it was not a good dinner, we would be obliged to any caterer for a dinner. The Stewards had fortunately engaged the services of Vanderhorst & Tully, who full sustained their reputation as caterers, purveyors and cooks, in spreading a feast which would have been acceptable at any time. In deference to the duties which detained from the festival many members who usually keep the feast, there was no formal program, or scheduled ettiquette. The President, at proper interval announced the following sentiments, which were well received:

The Day we Celebrate—The Anniversary of a Patron Saint of a People who, in their struggles for liberty, may be often crushed but never subdued.

The President of the Confederate States—The patriotism, the ability, and the efficiency with which he has discharged the duties of his high office, entitle him to the admiration, the gratitude, and confidence of the Confederacy.

Charleston, "the Cradle of the Rebellion"—Unconquered and unconquerable. Cease, viperse ye gnaw a file.

The Defenders of Charleston—By their gallantry they have won an imperishable name in history, and entitled themselves to eternal gratitude of those whose homes and hearthstones they have protected from the ruthless invader.

Col. Stephen Elliott of Fort Sumter—the gallant son of a worthy sire: in the language of President Davis, "he has added new lustre to a name already illustrious." [167]

The Hibernian Society finally cancelled its St. Patrick's Day dinner in 1865.[168]

The St. Patrick's Benevolent Society held anniversary dinners during all of the war years, but it was the dinner of 1865 that is the most noteworthy. The Union Army had occupied Charleston in February of 1865, but the St. Patrick's Benevolent Society did not let that interfere with their plans to hold the annual St. Patrick's Day dinner the following month. On March 17, 1865, the Society adorned its meeting place at Masonic Hall with both the banner of the Society and the flag of the United States of America. It then extended an invitation to General Stewart L. Woodford, the Commander of the United States occupation forces in the city, to address its St. Patrick's Day dinner. General Woodford graciously accepted and addressed the gathering which included about one hundred and fifty members of the Society and their invited guests. It was stated in the accounts of this dinner that the speaker "prided himself in his remarks on his Irish ancestry, and at the time gave a permit for the supply of liquid refreshments required."[169]

Since very few Irish organizations in Charleston require that a person be Irish to be a member, and given the fact that everyone loves being Irish on St. Patrick's Day, it was not unusual to find participants of many ethnic origins at Charleston's St. Patrick's Day banquets. This sometimes led to confusion on the part of visitors from places such as New York or Boston, where there were large Irish populations. Such a visitor was a priest from New York who attended the banquet of the

Hibernian Society in the early 1900s. During the banquet, this priest remarked to someone that "some of these young men do not look like Irishmen."[170] The priest "was told that there were different nationalities in the Society and that one of the golden rules embodied in the constitution was that neither politics or religion should be discussed, but that when the delegation from the St. Patrick's Benevolent Society came to exchange greetings, he would see men distinctively Irish." The Benevolent Society's delegation entered the hall shortly thereafter. It was made up of a German, an Italian, and a Jew.[171]

While the Hibernian Society and St. Patrick's Benevolent Society were holding their banquets, which were all-male affairs, other Irish organizations hosted balls and other activities in the evening of Saint Patrick's Day in which the ladies could also participate. One of the first Irish organizations to do this was the Emmett Volunteers which held a military ball in 1855 where the members of the company could show off their uniforms and fancy footwork to the members of the fairer sex. In describing this ball, the *Charleston Courier* stated: "The members of the company and many friends rallied in the evening at their convenient and spacious hall, at 90 Meeting St., where many daughters of the Emerald Isle were found joining in the dance, which was kept up with much harmony and enthusiasm until a late hour."[172] Another organization to include women in its evening activities on St. Patrick's Day prior to the Civil War was the Montgomery Guard which held a ball in 1859.[173]

The Irish Rifle Club held a Saint Patrick's Day ball at the Academy of Music in 1875.[174] The *News and Courier* of March 18, 1875 made the following reference to this event:

> Ball of the Irish Rifle Club
> The ball of the Irish Rifle club, at the Academy of Music in the evening, was a charming finale to the day's festivities. The scene was beautiful, made up as it was of the fair daughters of Erin, their courtly gallants, and members of the various kindred organizations. Music and merriment prevailed until a late hour, every attendant being delighted, and profuse in expressions of the gallantry of the club and Irishmen generally.[175]

This ball was apparently successful, and the following year a similar event, which was described as the "Second Annual Calico Ball," was held. The committee in charge of arrangements for the ball consisted of: J. J. Grace, J. F. Walsh, N. A. Quinn, P. F. May, D. Spellman, M. F. Twohill,

Wm. Maguire, D. F. Gleason, D. O'Neill, M. Hogan, E. E. Kenny, Jas. Walsh, T. O'Gorman, M. J. Harlow, John Hynes, J. Armstrong and James Foley.[176]

The Irish Rifle Club went out of existence in the early 1880s, creating the need for an organization to carry on the tradition of holding a ball on the evening of St. Patrick's Day. The Emerald Social Club, described as "an organization composed of young and festive representatives of the Emerald Isle in this city," met this need. The initial St. Patrick's Day ball of this club was held in 1885.[177]

The Montgomery Guards, which had reorganized after the Civil War, also held balls on an annual basis after Reconstruction.[178] One such ball was mentioned in the *News and Courier's* coverage of Charleston's St. Patrick's Day activities in 1890:

> The Montgomery Guards celebrated St. Patrick's Day with a grand and successful ball. The event was in keeping with this famous command. Everyone who was fortunate enough to attend will long have pleasant recollections of last night's pleasures.
> The ball was given in the spacious hall of the Carolina Rifles. The music was furnished by the Borning Band. The grand march, in which there were about forty couples, was lead by Lieut., Wm. Comar and Mrs. George Simonin.
> The committee who deserve the success of the Montgomery Guards' annual ball consisted of the following members: J. A. Goutevenier, Chairman; Sergt. T. J. Delany, Sergt. M. P. McLaughlin, Sergt. J. M. Hayes, Treasurer Isaac Dixon, Private Daniel Maher, Private Thomas Duffy, Private James Maher, Secretary J. S. Carey.[179]

In 1892, the first annual Saint Patrick's Day ball of the Ancient Order of Hibernians was held. This ball, which took place initially at the Irish Volunteers Hall on Vanderhorst Street, inaugurated a tradition of St. Patrick's Day evening entertainment by the Ancient Order of Hibernians which would last almost thirty years. The committee on arrangements for this initial ball consisted of: W. J. Comar, Chairman; M. A. Walsh, J. A. Noland, M. F. White, F. F. Buero, J. F. Dean, E. G. Enright, J. P. McCaffrey and John J. Furlong. The admission price was one dollar.[180]

In 1908, the Ancient Order of Hibernians moved the ball to the Knights of Columbus Hall on Calhoun Street and expanded it into a grand entertainment. Over the years, this entertainment included, besides music and dancing, meals, plays and lectures.[181] In 1912 it was estimated that over twelve hundred people stood in line to get into the affair.[182] The grand entertainment of 1916 featured, along with Irish songs and dances, an address on "Why We Celebrate St. Patrick's Day" and a one act comedy entitled "A Day at Ballyhoo Fair."[183]

An examination of contemporary Charleston newspapers reveals that the celebration of St. Patrick's Day in Charleston rapidly declined, both in size and enthusiasm, after the treaty establishing the Irish Free State was signed at the end of 1921. The celebrants by this time were mostly sons and grandsons of Irish immigrants who had never even seen Ireland, and who considered themselves Americans and Charlestonians, not Irishmen. When the Irish Free State was established, they probably felt that Ireland had finally won its freedom, and they were ready to completely assimilate into American life. The St. Patrick's Benevolent Society, Division No. 2 of the Ancient Order of Hibernians, and the Ladies Auxiliary of the Ancient Order of Hibernians all remained in existence until after 1925 but apparently either curtailed or eliminated their St. Patrick's Day celebrations after 1921. The *News and Courier* does not report any St. Patrick's Day activities by any of these organizations in 1922 or for any other year through 1929.[184]

The P. N. Lynch Council No. 704 of the Knights of Columbus, although not an Irish organization, included many members of Irish descent and continued to hold St. Patrick's Day celebrations after 1921. This council sponsored Charleston's St. Patrick's Day parade in 1922 which commenced at the United States Customs House and marched to St. Patrick's Church where a solemn High Mass was celebrated.[185] In 1923 and 1924 the Knights continued their sponsorship of the St. Patrick's Day parades which marched from the Knights of Columbus Hall on Calhoun Street to St. Patrick's Church.[186] Apparently, the parade was not held on a regular basis after 1924 because it is not mentioned in the newspaper accounts of Charleston's St. Patrick's Day activities during the remainder of the 1920s.[187]

In the 1920s and 1930s, the Hibernian Society continued to celebrate St. Patrick's Day in pretty much the same way they had always done. At noon on St. Patrick's Day, the Society held a members-only business meeting and luncheon at which the officers for the ensuing year were elected. In the evening of St. Patrick's Day, the Society held a grand banquet attended by members and their guests and addressed by a prominent speaker.[188]

During World War Two, the Hibernian Society modified its

St. Patrick's Day celebration. The Society considered canceling the banquet in 1942, but decided to proceed. The speaker at this banquet was Senator Harry S. Truman, who would later become President of the United States. The following year the banquet was cancelled, and the Society held a buffet supper for the remaining war years.[189]

After the war the Hibernian Society resumed its normal celebration of St. Patrick's Day. The guest speakers at banquets during the 1950s, 1960s and 1970s included, among others: John J. Hearne, Irish Ambassador to the United States; Sam J. Ervin, Jr., U.S. Senator; Robert C. Byrd, U.S. Senator; M. Scott Carpenter, Astronaut; John N. Mitchell, Attorney General of the United States; General William C. Westmoreland, Chief of Staff of the United States Army; and Gerald R. Ford, Vice President of the United States.[190]

In the 1970s Saint Patrick's Day began to be celebrated in Charleston with renewed enthusiasm. This is evidenced by the revival during this period of one of Charleston's most venerated St. Patrick's Day traditions, the St. Patrick's Day parade. The parade was revived by the Hibernian Society which added it to the Society's morning activities on St. Patrick's Day. The Hibernian Society's St. Patrick's Day parade, which is made up of the members of the Society and their invited guests, usually begins on East Bay Street at around 11:00. It then proceeds down either Broad or Market Street to Meeting Street and then to Hibernian Hall.[191]

The South Carolina Irish Historical Society joined in the city's St. Patrick's Day celebration in 1979 and in that year instituted a new Charleston St. Patrick's Day tradition. It raised the Irish flag over the old Irish Volunteers Hall on Vanderhorst Street on St. Patrick's Day in 1979. The following year the Society raised the Irish flag over the Charleston County office building at the Old Citadel, thus symbolically over the county. The flag-raising ceremony was moved to the Charleston City Hall in 1981. Since then, the Irish flag has flown over the City of Charleston on every St. Patrick's Day.[192]

In the 1990s the Ancient Order of Hibernians, the Knights of Columbus, and the South Carolina Irish Historical Society began attending Mass together on the morning of St. Patrick's Day. After the Mass, held at St. Patrick's Church, the members of these organizations form their own St. Patrick's Day parade. This parade marches down King Street tracing the route of many of Charleston's previous St. Patrick's Day parades.[193]

Thus, after over two and a half centuries, the celebration of St. Patrick's Day in Charleston is alive and well. The city again has two

St. Patrick's Day parades, and the size and enthusiasm of the crowd participating in the celebration increases with each passing year. The city's celebration will never rival that of its neighbor Savannah in size, but the celebration of St. Patrick's Day in Charleston will always be a special tradition in a city known for its traditions.

CHAPTER THREE

IRISH CHARITABLE AND BENEVOLENT SOCIETIES, RIFLE CLUBS, SOCIAL CLUBS AND OTHER ORGANIZATIONS

As each new ethnic group arrived in Charleston, its members formed clubs and societies for the purposes of socialization and mutual assistance. The Irish who arrived in Charleston followed the same pattern beginning in the 1700s. The majority of these early Irish organizations did not last very long, but as each succeeding wave of Irish immigrants arrived in Charleston, new Irish clubs and societies sprang up.

THE IRISH SOCIETY

ORGANIZED CIRCA 1749

One of the earliest references to an Irish organization in Charleston is to a group known as the Irish Society. In an issue of the *South Carolina Gazette* covering the period from March 13 to March 20, 1749, there appeared an ode to Saint Patrick written by Joseph Dumbleton. It was dedicated to the president and members of the Irish Society.[194]

THE SONS OF ST. PATRICK

ORGANIZED CIRCA 1771

Another Irish club mentioned in early Charleston newspapers is the Sons of St. Patrick. A meeting of this organization, held at Dillon's Tavern in Charleston, is mentioned in the *South Carolina Gazette* on March 21, 1771. Unfortunately, nothing is known of its purpose or the composition of its membership.[195]

ST. PATRICK'S CLUB OR FRIENDLY BROTHERS OF ST. PATRICK

ORGANIZED CIRCA 1773

The next Irish club to appear in Charleston newspapers is the St. Patrick's Club or Friendly Brothers of St. Patrick, which was mentioned in 1773. On St. Patrick's Day of that year, the club elected the following officers: Thomas Knox Gordon, president; James Parsons, vice-president; and Thomas Phipps, treasurer and secretary. Edward Rutledge, one of South Carolina's signers of the Declaration of Independence, was named a club steward. This group apparently went out of existence around the time of the Revolutionary War.[196]

THE FRIENDLY BROTHERS OF IRELAND

ORGANIZED 1786

After the American Revolution, a society by the name of the Friendly Brothers of Ireland was formed in Charleston. This group first met at the City Tavern on November 18, 1786. The stated objects of the society were to "assist the distressed, to inculcate by precept and example obedience to the laws of the State and adherence to moral principles." At the initial meeting Pierce Butler, one of South Carolina's early United States Senators, was elected president of the society. The other officers were: James Lynah, vice-president; Daniel O'Hara, treasurer; and Samuel Corbett, secretary. Bartholomew Carroll and George Archibald were elected as stewards.[197]

In January of 1787 the members of the Friendly Brothers of Ireland filed the following petition for incorporation with the South Carolina State Senate:

> To the Honorable John Lloyd Esq. President and The Honorable the other Members of the Senate.
> The humble Petition of Us Whose Names are hereunto subscribed in behalf of ourselves and others associated with us, by the name of The Friendly Brothers of Ireland
> Witnesseth
> That Whereas many Emigrations have taken place from Ireland and others likely to follow, Whereby numbers for want of Immediate Employ Have suffered great Inconveniences on their Arrival in this Country, to prevent as much as in us lies

such distress in future, We have for this and other charitable purposes formed ourselves into a Society under the above name as by reference to our rules may fully appear
It is therefore the humble prayer of this Petition, That we be Incorporated and Vested with such powers as may be most conductive to promote the good Intentions of said Society.
And your Petitioners
As in duty bound Shall
Ever Pray
Petition 27th January 1787
P. Butler
J.A. Lynah V: P:[198]

Unfortunately, nothing more is known about this Society after the filing of the petition for incorporation.

THE HIBERNIAN SOCIETY OF CHARLESTON FOUNDED 1799

COMPLETED ITS ORGANIZATION 1801

Charleston's longest-lasting Irish organization is the Hibernian Society of Charleston, which was established on the 17th of March, 1799. The Society was formed for the dual purposes of "true enjoyment and useful beneficence." In other words, social enjoyment among its members and rendering aid to Irish immigrants.[199] In commenting on the Society's beginnings, Thomas Stephens, its president from 1846 to 1847, wrote:

> It was originated by eight generous Irishmen, not long arrived, viz: THOMAS MALCOM, EDWARD COURTNAY, WILLIAM HUNTER, JAMES HUNTER, JOSEPH CROMBIE, ANDREW SMYLIE, JAMES QUINN, AND JOHN S. ADAMS, who, according to the poet Crafts, met heart in hand, at each other's residence, every second Thursday, to converse and to contribute towards a fund to relieve distressed emigrants; and every fourth Thursday, engaged themselves in sentiment and song and supper; and so continued until, from increased numbers, it became more convenient to assemble in some hotel...[200]

It took the Society two years to complete its organization, and by resolution it has dated its completed organization to March 17, 1801. During that period, the Hibernian Society adopted its constitution, rules, seal and motto. The seal chosen was, naturally, the harp. The motto was, Non ignara mail, miseris succurrore disco. This motto, when literally translated means, "Being familiar with misfortune, I learn to assist the unfortunate."[201]

The Society also adopted a badge to distinguish it from other organizations, described in the Society's rules as follows:

RULE XXI
Each member shall supply himself with a silver badge, exhibiting the Irish Harp, surrounded with the words, "Hibernian Society Charleston, South Carolina." To be suspended by a green ribbon, and worn on the left breast on St. Patrick's Day; which shall be the distinguishing badge of the members of the Society; and for which badge he shall pay TWO DOLLARS AND TWENTY-FIVE CENTS.[202]

The Hibernian Society never imposed any ethnic or religious qualifications for membership and was open to all who wanted to participate. This was later codified in the Society's constitution and rules, which provided that the Society was "open for the admission of respectable persons of any nation or religion provided that they have obtained the age of twenty-one years."[203]

The Society's members at the time of its completed organization on March 17, 1801 were: John S. Adams, Joseph Anthony, Edward Courtney, Joseph Crombie, John Crow, Thomas Denny, M.D., Rev. Simon F. Gallagher, Dominick A. Hall, James Hunter, William Hunter, Peter Kennedy, John Loggan, Thomas Malcom, Dennis M'Gowen, Humphrey Minchin, William M'Kelvey, Charles M'Kenna, Cornelius O'Driscoll, Henry O'Hara, Henry Peyton, Edmund M. Phelon, James Quin, Thomas Reilly, M.D., O'Brien Smith, William Smith, and Andrew Smylie.[204] The Hibernian Society remained an unincorporated association for several years, then, on December 19, 1805, it was incorporated by act of the South Carolina Legislature.[205]

The fee for admission to the Society was initially two dollars. This was raised to five dollars in 1801, ten dollars in 1807, fifteen dollars in 1812 and twenty dollars in 1818, where it remained until after the Civil War. In addition, each member had to pay a monthly subscription of one dollar. One-half of the subscription fee could be spent on meeting nights and the remainder was applied to the expenses of the Society.

Later, the monthly subscription for "country" members (those living outside the city) was reduced to fifty cents.[206]

Although the admission fees and monthly subscriptions as set out above may not appear large by today's standards, they were not insignificant in the days when an Irish railroad worker was paid eight dollars a month. Consequently, many of the early members of the Hibernian Society were persons of means. This was reflected in the men who served as the group's early presidents. Simon Felix Gallagher was a Catholic priest, but was also a professor at the College of Charleston. O'Brien Smith was a politician who served in the South Carolina Legislature and the United States Congress. Simon Magwood was a successful businessman, and James Adger was reported to be the fourth-richest man in the United States.[207]

Members who could not meet their financial obligations to the Society were expelled. The rules provided that any resident of Charleston who did not pay his arrears for six months, and any country member who did not pay his arrears for twelve months, would be read off and no longer considered a member. There were no exceptions, and one of the eight founders of the Society, was read off for non-payment of arrears.[208]

In 1818, the members received some assistance with their financial burden thanks to the Society's first major bequest which occurred when it took charge of the estate of Judge Aedanus Burke. Burke, who was born in Ireland, came to South Carolina prior to the Revolutionary War. After his arrival he became quite successful, serving as a state judge and a member of the U. S. House of Representatives. In his will he directed that his estate be used "for the sole purpose of giving a little aid to such poor Irish emigrants and their successors as shall arrive in this Country." This initial bequest was followed by others from Simon Magwood, Walter Goodman, and John Blair.[209]

In order to carry out the charitable purposes of the Society, a committee on relief was established. This committee was given the power to assist emigrants from Ireland and their descendants. The payments made by the committee started out modestly at twenty-five to thirty dollars per month, and increased to over two hundred dollars per month. The committee was also given the power to provide funds for the burial of a member if necessary.[210]

The Hibernian Society, like most other Irish societies in Charleston, held monthly meetings for the social enjoyment of its members. Early meetings were held at various places around the city, including Burger's

Tavern on Queen Street, Corbett's Thatched Cabin on Meeting Street, and the Carolina Coffee House.[211]

In the 1820s the Society began considering constructing its own meeting house, but nothing concrete was done until 1831 when a site on Meeting Street across from Chalmers Street was acquired for the hall. After purchasing the site, members embarked on the tedious process of selecting the right design for the hall. They even considered building a combination hall and hotel, but that idea was eventually discarded. Several prominent architects of the time submitted proposals, among them Robert Mills. Finally, the group settled on the design of Thomas U. Walter of Philadelphia, who would later become known for his work on the United States Capitol in Washington, D.C.[212]

A budget for construction of the hall was approved by the Society in 1838, but work was delayed due to a fire that swept the city that same year. The cornerstone of the Hibernian Hall was finally laid on March 18, 1839 at a ceremony attended by representatives of fourteen of Charleston's other fraternal societies. Over the next twenty-two months a handsome edifice was constructed according to Walter's plans in the Classic Greek Revival Style of architecture.[213]

The Hibernian Hall was officially opened on January 20, 1841. A crowd of over two thousand attended the ceremony, including Bishop John England who gave the oration. Thereafter, the Hibernian Society has held its monthly meetings, and grand Saint Patrick's Day banquets at the Hibernian Hall.[214]

During the time the Society was planning and constructing its hall, it continued its charitable activities. The group rendered assistance in 1836 to the families of the Irish Volunteers who went to Florida to fight the Seminole Indians. In 1838 it contributed funds to the Saint Patrick's Benevolent Society which was assisting the victims of a yellow fever epidemic in the city. Thereafter, during the 1840s and 1850s, the Society was kept busy rendering assistance to the ever-increasing number of Irish workers who flocked to Charleston to build the new United States Custom House, the Northeastern Railway, and numerous other construction projects in and around the city. Besides feeding the hungry, aiding the sick and burying the dead, the Society's records reflect that a considerable amount of funds were used to return Irishmen and their families to the northern U.S. cities from which they had come.[215]

The Hibernian Society, as the oldest and best established Irish society in South Carolina, took the lead in 1847 in organizing relief efforts to assist the victims of the Irish Potato Famine. On February 2, 1847, a committee was formed consisting of James Adger, Alex.

Robinson, Thos. Reiley, H. W. Conner, John Robinson, Alex. Black, R. Martin, O. L. Dobson and W. Patton to coordinated these efforts. This committee in turn set up subcommittees in each of the wards of the City of Charleston and coordinated with those in other parts of the state willing to contribute to the relief effort. In addition to money, the committee solicited staples such as rice, corn, flour, and meal which were carried by the South Carolina Railroad free of charge if marked with the word "Ireland." Approximately twenty thousand dollars was raised in South Carolina for the needy Irish people.[216]

In 1861, with the outbreak of the Civil War, the Hibernian Society whole-heartedly embraced the Southern Cause. During the conflict the Society contributed funds to both of the city's Irish companies and to the families they left behind. The group also allowed the use of its hall for balls given for the city's military units and for fundraisers such as the Ladies' Fair to benefit the Confederate gunboat *Palmetto State*. In addition, numerous members of the Hibernian Society volunteered for service in the Confederate Army, including the secretary and treasurer, both of whom died in the war.[217]

At the end of the Civil War in 1865, the Hibernian Society, like much of the South, was in financial ruin. During the war, the Society had invested most of its funds in Confederate stocks and bonds, which became worthless with the South's defeat. In addition, the Hibernian Hall was in great need of repair due to Union shelling and four years of neglect. To make matters worse, state and city taxes were reimposed on the hall. Consequently, the Society was only able to contribute a nominal amount to assist Irish immigrants during the latter part of the 1860s and early 1870s. Fortunately, the great influx of the Irish to Charleston had ended with the Civil War.[218]

The membership of the Hibernian Society remained small during the 1880s and 1890s, and its financial position did not improve significantly during those decades. In fact, it got worse. Hibernian Hall was seized by the State in 1882 for non-payment of taxes and was almost sold at foreclosure in 1893. It took all of the Society's financial resources just to survive during this period.[219]

In 1893, in sad recognition of the Society's financial inability to carry on one of its original purposes of useful beneficence, the provision providing for aid to emigrants from Ireland was removed from its rules. Although it was later reinstated, the Society never again expended any appreciable sums on assistance to Irish emigrants. It has been the Society's other original purpose, "true enjoyment among its members," which has accounted for its survival to the present day.[220]

The Hibernian Society celebrated its one-hundredth anniversary in 1901. As Saint Patrick's Day fell on a Sunday that year, the Society was presented with the opportunity of stretching its celebration over a two-day period. On Sunday, the Society celebrated by marching in procession with the Irish Volunteers, the Saint Patrick's Benevolent Society, and Divisions No. 1 and No. 2 of the Ancient Order of Hibernians to the Pro-Cathedral where a solemn High Mass was celebrated. The following day, the members of the Society and invited guests heard an address by former President Augustine T. Smythe in Hibernian Hall. Smythe recounted the history of the Society during its first hundred years, which account was published in the *News and Courier*.[221]

As the Hibernian Society began its second century, it experienced an increase in membership. With one hundred thirty-four members in 1900, the Society grew to one hundred eighty-nine by 1904, and reached two hundred forty-two members by 1912. This expansion was accompanied by a strengthening of the Society's financial position, and by 1915 the organization was finally on sound financial ground.[222]

The Society's return to financial stability enabled its members to turn their attention to the final struggle for Irish freedom between 1919 and 1922. The cause of Irish independence had always been dear to the members of the Hibernian Society, and during the nineteenth century several prominent Irish patriots had visited the Society and others had received its financial aid. During this final struggle, such prominent members as Colonel James Armstrong advocated the Irish cause at meetings of the Society, and the Hibernian Hall was used for meetings in support thereof. Some members also actively participated in national Irish American organizations, which kept political pressure on the governments of the United States and Britain. Foremost among them was Mayor John P. Grace, who rose to the office of vice president of the Friends of Irish Freedom, the most powerful Irish organization in America.[223]

After the treaty was signed establishing the Irish Free State in December 1921, the Hibernian Society, like most Irish organizations in America, lost much of its Irish identity. Unlike many other Irish organizations, however, it did not go out of existence. The Hibernian Society was unique among Irish organizations in that it had a grand hall with a fine back bar which its members could enjoy. This, along with the fact that the Society was one of Charleston's oldest and most revered societies, with a membership open to persons of all ethnic and religious backgrounds, helped it to attract members throughout the roaring twenties, the Great Depression and World War Two.[224]

At the end of World War Two, the membership of the Hibernian Society stood at two hundred and fifty, and the club was in excellent financial condition.[225] In the post-war years, its membership and financial strength continued to grow. Thus, the Society was able to return to its original charitable purposes. In 1976 the Hibernian Society of Charleston Foundation was established, its purpose to "provide funds for education and other worthy purposes." In keeping with this goal, the foundation has provided scholarships to students at local colleges.[226]

In the post-World War Two years, the Hibernian Society has hosted several high-ranking officials from the Republic of Ireland. John J. Hearne, the Irish Ambassador to the United States, was the Society's St. Patrick's Day speaker in 1954. A subsequent Irish Ambassador to the United States, John G. Molloy, visited Hibernian Hall on March 21, 1975. John Bruton, the first sitting Prime Minister of Ireland to tour the southern United States, visited Charleston on March 20, 1997. A reception was given in his honor at Hibernian Hall by the Hibernian Society and the South Carolina Irish Historical Society.[227]

On March 17, 2001 the Hibernian Society celebrated its two-hundredth anniversary with a grand banquet. The guest speaker was Albert Reynolds, the former Prime Minister of the Republic of Ireland. Mr. Reynolds was instrumental in the peace process for Northern Ireland and signed the Joint Declaration of Peace along with British Prime Minister John Major. The Hibernian Society has now embarked on its third century of "true enjoyment and useful beneficence" in Charleston.[228]

THE ST. PATRICK'S BENEVOLENT SOCIETY OF CHARLESTON

ORGANIZED 1817

Another organization which served Charleston's Irish citizens in both the nineteenth and twentieth centuries was the St. Patrick's Benevolent Society of Charleston, organized in 1817.[229] This organization remained active for over one hundred years. The purposes and objects of the Society were set out in its original petition for incorporation:

> That your Petitioners have associated together for the purposes of aiding and assisting all such Emigrants and other persons who may from time to time come to this State with the View to Settle within the Same, and whose Situation may

claim and require the assistance arising from the funds of your Petitioners.

That the object of your Petitioners is to extend relief to the unfortunate and distressed whose Government and poverty have driven them from their native Country to Seek Shelter and Protection in the land of freedom and Independence.[230]

These purposes and objects were expanded somewhat by the time they were codified in the Society's 1835 constitution. The Preamble of this constitution stated:

> PREAMBLE—The primary object of the St. Patrick's Benevolent Society of Charleston, South Carolina, is to administer relief to such Irish immigrants as might arrive in the City in distress; It is next desirable to promote kind feeling and affectionate intercourse between Irishmen of every denomination of every station in society and every political party and their friends; and also to uphold the character and dignity of the land of their birth and of their forefathers; and as far as in their power, to console and to aid the widows and orphans of members whom an inscrutable providence might cast upon their protection.[231]

In keeping with the objects of the Society, Article I of the same constitution provided that membership was "open to Irishmen and their descendents or friends of whatever religion or political denomination or place of nativity who might be disposed to take on the obligations of the society and further its objects."[232] In later years, it was required that candidates for membership be between 18 and 50 years of age and in sound bodily health, but no religious or ethnic qualification was specified. Although there was no ethnic qualification for membership in the Society, the same was not true for those seeking the offices of president or vice-president. The constitution and by-laws provided that none but Irishmen or their descendents could fill these positions.[233]

Like the Hibernian Society, the St. Patrick's Benevolent Society adopted its own seal:

> The Seal of the Society shall be a circular plate, two inches in Diameter, with a figure of St. Patrick, with full flowing beard and full canonical robes and crosier resting on the ground near his right foot; his right hand holding the same on a line with

the elbow and left hand extended on a line with the elbow; the three last fingers closed, and the thumb resting on them, the index finger pointing from him; his right foot resting on a serpent, and a cluster of shamrock growing from beneath his feet; the plate to have inscribed upon its face, the motto "God Save Ireland" and St. Patrick's Benevolent Society, 1817, encircling the border.[234]

John Magrath became president of the Society in 1817 and continued in that office until 1849 when he resigned due to ill health. The Society owed its existence during its first thirty-two years in great measure to the able leadership and efforts of President Magrath. Under his lead, the organization embarked on a course of charitable and benevolent activities that would last into the twentieth century.[235]

In 1836, the Benevolent Society rallied to the assistance of the families of the combatants when the Irish Volunteers were sent to Florida to fight in the Seminole Indian War. In 1838, the Society rendered relief to the sick and indigent during the yellow fever epidemic which ravaged Charleston. The yellow fever returned to Charleston in 1852, killing 310 people, of whom 220 were Irish or German. The epidemic became so severe that there was a need for a special hospital. On September 2, 1852, the Sisters of Our Lady of Mercy opened St. Mary's Relief Hospital in an uncompleted wing of Roper Hospital. The St. Patrick's Benevolent Society paid the expenses of this hospital.[236]

During the Civil War, the Society again rallied behind Charleston's Irish combatants. A new company known as the Irish Volunteers for the War was formed for service with the Confederate Army in Virginia. The St. Patrick's Benevolent Society and the Hibernian Society encouraged the Irishmen of the city to join this company by assuring them that these societies would assist their families while they were away. The company's rolls were quickly filled.[237]

In addition to its other charitable activities, the Benevolent Society, both before and after the Civil War, contributed to the support of the orphans in the care of the Sisters of Mercy. These children seemed to have held a special place in the hearts of the members of the Society as members never missed an opportunity to take up a collection for their benefit. This was especially true on St. Patrick's Day, when all Irishmen were feeling generous.[238]

The Sisters of Mercy showed their appreciation for the Society's generosity by presenting them a banner on St. Patrick's Day 1873. This banner was described in the *Charleston Daily News*:

The St. Patrick's Benevolent Society carried a beautiful banner about three feet square, green on one side, displaying a harp and the name of the society embroidered in gold. The opposite side is white upon which is embroidered the figure of St. Patrick attired in parti-colored vestments. It is bordered all round with deep gold fringe, and is ornamented with gold cords and tassels.[239]

After the Civil War, when the great flow of Irish immigrants to Charleston came to an end, the focus of the Saint Patrick's Benevolent Society became the assistance of its members. In these dark days of reconstruction and financial hard times, when the Hibernian Society encountered grave financial difficulties, the St. Patrick's Benevolent Society grew in financial strength and membership.[240]

The treasury of the Benevolent Society, in the post-Civil War years, was zealously protected and used exclusively for the benefit of the Society's members to relieve their needs and to aid them in their hours of illness. In the 1880s, a member who became sick or was injured in an accident was entitled to $5.00 per week for a period of four weeks; thereafter, the allowance was reduced to $2.50 per week for six weeks. After that, it was reduced to $.50 per week.[241]

A burial plot at St. Lawrence Cemetery was also maintained by the Society for the benefit of its members. The Benevolent Society seems to be unique among Irish organizations in Charleston in this regard. Its constitution provided for a payment of $75.00 upon the death of a member, but in the event the member was interred in the Society's plot, the benefit would be reduced to $65.00. The plot at St. Lawrence can still be located, but unfortunately it does not contain any gravestones.[242]

Besides being a charitable organization, the St. Patrick's Benevolent Society was also very much a social organization, holding monthly meetings and other gatherings where the members could enjoy each other's fellowship. Since the Benevolent Society, unlike the Hibernian Society, never purchased its own meeting hall, these get-togethers were held in different locations over the years. In the 1850s and 1860s, the monthly meetings were held at the Masonic Hall on King Street. During the 1880s and early 1890s, meetings were held at various times at the Catholic School building on George Street, the German Fusiliers Armory on George Street or at Hibernian Hall. By the mid 1890s, the Society had settled upon the Irish Volunteers Hall on Vanderhorst Street, and its meetings were held there until the Society went out of existence.[243]

In addition to holding its own social functions, the Benevolent Society accepted almost every invitation to join in activities with other Irish organizations. The Society was a regular participant in Charleston's St. Patrick's Day parade. Members took part in the laying of the cornerstone of Hibernian Hall on March 17, 1839, the laying of the cornerstone of the new St. Patrick's Church on March 17, 1886 and in the centennial celebration of the Hibernian Society on March 17, 1901.[244]

The 100th anniversary of the St. Patrick's Benevolent Society was celebrated March 17, 1917 with a grand banquet at the Charleston Hotel. The speaker for the evening was Colonel James Armstrong, a Civil War veteran, past president of the Hibernian Society, and an entertaining orator. Colonel Armstrong presented a humorous account of the history of the Benevolent Society, which was published by the Society.[245]

The St. Patrick's Benevolent Society marched in Charleston's St. Patrick's Day parade in 1921, but was not very active thereafter. It did not participate in the parades of 1922, 1923 or 1924. The Society apparently went out of existence around 1926, as it was not listed in the Charleston City Directory of 1927.[246]

THE CHARITABLE SOCIETY OF IRISH VOLUNTEERS OF CHARLESTON

ORGANIZED CIRCA 1822

The Charitable Society of Irish Volunteers of Charleston was apparently an Irish charitable society formed by members of Charleston's Irish Volunteer Company. The organization was incorporated by act of the South Carolina Legislature in 1822, but little else is known about this group.[247]

ASSOCIATION OF THE FRIENDS OF THE IRISH IN CHARLESTON

ORGANIZED CIRCA 1829

In 1829 a group by the name of the Association of the Friends of the Irish in Charleston gave $100.00 to the relief fund of the Hibernian Society of Charleston. Nothing else is known about this organization.[248]

THE EMERALD ISLE BENEVOLENT SOCIETY OF CHARLESTON

ORGANIZED 1831

The Emerald Isle Benevolent Society of Charleston was a charitable organization formed in February or March of 1831. By November of that year the Society had about fifty members and petitioned the South Carolina House of Representatives to be incorporated.[249] The purpose of the Society was set out in its petition for incorporation:

> ...the relief of distressed emigrants from Ireland and of the widows and Orphans of members and to promote a good understanding and affectionate feelings between countrymen and their friends...[250]

The Emerald Isle Benevolent Society was incorporated on December 17, 1831.[251] Unfortunately, no membership lists of this organization have been located, but the following were some of its officers and committee members:

1831

OFFICERS: Demis Kane, President, Legrand Capers, Vice-President, Robert Lemall, Treasurer, and James Fox, Secretary.[252]

1832

OFFICERS: Captain D. Kane, President; John King Jr., Vice-president; Samuel Rowan, Treasurer and Charles L. White, Secretary.

COMMITTEE ON RELIEF: Messrs. M'Donald, Rooney, M'Clelland, Schnieder and Cantwell.[253]

1833

COMMITTEE ON ARRANGEMENTS FOR ST. PATRICK'S DAY: Capt. Alex. M'Donald, P. Cantwell, Wm. A. Murphy, Wm. Jno. Smith and Saml. Bowan.[254]

The Emerald Isle Benevolent Society of Charleston held Saint Patrick's Day banquets in 1832 and 1833, but did not participate in Charleston's Saint Patrick's Day parade. The Society's last Saint Patrick's Day banquet was held in 1833 at the Rame's Room which was located on

Meeting Street opposite Guignard Street. The *Charleston Courier* does not report any Saint Patrick's Day activities of the Society in 1834, and it is assumed that it went out of existence prior to March of that year.[255]

IRISH MUTUAL BENEVOLENT SOCIETY OF CHARLESTON

ORGANIZED CIRCA 1849

The Irish Mutual Benevolent Society of Charleston was formed in Charleston around 1849.[256] The Society was incorporated by the State Legislature in 1851, for the purpose of "promoting charity and alleviating suffering among their fellow members."[257] The officers and committee members of the Society for the years 1850 through 1853 were:

1850
OFFICERS: Thos. Ryan, President; Geo. W. Black, 1st Vice-President; Alexr. Owens, 2d Vice-President; Jno. F. O'Neill, Treasurer and Jno. Bresnan, Secretary.
COMMITTEE ON FINANCE: Jno. Dougherty, Henry F. Baker and Jno. J. Cagney.
COMMITTEE ON RELIEF: Richard Hogan, Jno. Burns, Jas. Kennedy, Jas. Early, Jno. Blake, Thos. M'Manus, Jno. Commins, Jas. Armstrong, Peter M'Cormick, Thos. Maguire and T. L. Quackenbush.[258]

1851
OFFICERS: Thomas Ryan, President; George W. Black, First Vice-President; Alexander Owens, Second Vice-President; Lawrence Burke, Treasurer, John Bresnan, Secretary, and O. A. White, Physician.
COMMITTEE ON FINANCE: John Burns, Chairman; C. E. Kanapaux, John J. Cagney and James Todd.
COMMITTEE ON RELIEF: Richard Hogan, Thomas Burke, James Kennedy, James Early, John Blake, T. F. McManus, James Armstrong, Peter McCormick, Thomas Maguire, T. L. Quackenbush and John Burke.[259]

1852
OFFICERS: Thomas Ryan, President; Geo. W. Black, 1st Vice-President; A. A. Allemong, 2d Vice-President; John

Burns, Treasurer, Jno. T. Bresnan, Secretary and O. A. White, Physician.
COMMITTEE ON RELIEF: Richard Hogan, Chairman, Thomas Burke, James Kennedy, Patrick Brady, John Blake, T. F. McManus, Peter McCormick, Geo. Sergeant, T. L. Quackenbush, John Burke and Thomas Kenny.
COMMITTEE ON FINANCE: Jno. T. O'Neill, Chairman, Jno. J. Cagney, John Burke, Dennis O'Callaghan.[260]

1853

OFFICERS: Thos. Ryan, President; G. W. Black, 1st Vice-President; A. A. Allemong, 2d Vice-President; Joseph Murray, Secretary and John Burns, Treasurer.
COMMITTEE ON FINANCE: W. B. Ryan, John Dougherty, George Sergeant, and John Rielly.
COMMITTEE ON RELIEF: John Burke, R. Hogan, Thos. Burke, James Kennedy, P. Brady, Jno. Blake, T. F. McManus, Peter McCormick, George Sergeant, T. L. Quackenbush, and James Carroll.[261]

The Irish Mutual Benevolent Society did not last long, but was active during its short tenure. The organization held monthly meetings on the first Thursday of each month at the Masonic Hall on the corner of King and Wentworth Streets. Its members were also regular participants in Charleston's St. Patrick's Day parade. The Society was not listed in reports of Charleston's St. Patrick's Day activities of 1855, apparently having gone out of existence prior to March 17th of that year.[262]

THE SOCIETY OF UNITED IRISHMEN

ORGANIZED CIRCA 1853

Another Irish society which existed in Charleston in the early 1850s was the Society of United Irishmen. This group met on Wednesdays and Saturdays at 90 Meeting Street. In 1853 E. McDonough served as president. During a visit of Thomas Francis Meagher to Charleston in March that year, Meagher was extended an invitation by the Society to visit its hall, and he requested to enroll as a member. After Meagher's departure from Charleston, the Society was instrumental in the formation of the Meagher Rifle Guard, a militia company which also met at 90 Meeting Street.[263]

RIFLE CLUBS

After the surrender of the southern armies in the spring of 1865, the Confederate soldiers who returned to South Carolina felt helpless to protect themselves, their families, and their property from potential abuses and retaliation by the newly-freed slaves. As a matter of self-defense they formed rifle clubs which, although organized for supposed social purposes, actually served as a volunteer police force. Before the Civil War, German rifle clubs had existed in several southern states and the federal government did not oppose the formation of similar clubs after the war. One of South Carolina's first rifle clubs was formed in Charleston in 1869, and many more would follow.[264]

The citizens of Charleston of Irish birth or descent formed two rifle clubs during the Reconstruction period: the Irish Rifle Club and the Irish Volunteer Rifle Club. The Irish Volunteers and Montgomery Guards were also reorganized, and the Emmett Guards organized during Reconstruction for the same purposes as the rifle clubs. However, these three organizations did not use the words "rifle club" as part of their names.[265]

THE IRISH RIFLE CLUB OF CHARLESTON, S.C.

ORGANIZED 1871

The Irish Rifle Club of Charleston, S.C. was formed in 1871.[266] Unlike many of Charleston's rifle clubs, this one adopted a military uniform, which was described in an article in the *Charleston Daily News* on March 18, 1872: "black pants, with a light gray coat trimmed with palmetto buttons, green collar and cuffs, and neatly corded across the breast. The hats were black, with gold cord and tassel, and were looped up on the left with a green rosette pinned in with a miniature gilt harp."[267] The same article described the colors of the club: "an old Fenian flag, green on one side, and on the other white, with 'Irish Rifle Club' handsomely embroidered upon it and surmounted by the immortal shamrock."[268]

The club was incorporated by act of the Legislature on January 16, 1873 as The Irish Rifle Club of Charleston, S.C. The incorporators of the club were James Armstrong, president; James J. Grace, first vice president; D. O'Neill, second vice president, and A. G. Magrath, Jr., third vice president. The secretary of the club was J. F. Walsh and A. E. Kenny was its treasurer. P. Cleary, P. J. May, J. F. Byrnes, William Fowley and John Burke Jr. served as the club's wardens. The defensive purpose of the club was revealed by the weapon it adopted, which was a rapid-fire Winchester.[269]

The Irish Rifle Club had its headquarters at Byrnes Hall on the east side of King Street opposite Liberty Street, where the club held meetings on the first Thursday of each month. Membership records have not survived, so it is impossible to know the maximum number of members the club had at any one time. However, we know there were at least seventy-eight members in 1874.[270]

In 1875, the Irish Rifle Club adopted a new uniform which was described in the March 18th *News and Courier*:

> The club donned their new and exceedingly neat uniforms, consisting of a cadet gray cloth coat, trimmed with green cloth and a regulation cap, surmounted by a white plume tipped with green. In front of the cap was the monogram "I.R.C." in silver letters encircled by shamrock. The pants were black, and the trappings of the officers stylish and in keeping with the uniform.[271]

THE IRISH VOLUNTEER RIFLE CLUB OF CHARLESTON, S. C.

ORGANIZED 1872

The Irish Volunteer Rifle Club was organized in 1872, and incorporated on January 28, 1873 as The Irish Volunteer Rifle Club of Charleston, S.C. The incorporators of the club were Francis L. O'Neill, Phillip Fogarty, Thos. E. Hogan, D. W. Erwin, and Robert F. Toughey. The clubs wardens that year were P. O'Neill, T. J. Lyons, E. O'Neill, J. J. McManus and M. J. Lynch. The directors were James Quinn, E. O'Day, James O'Brien, G. B. Sprague and M. Sullivan. John E. Burns was secretary, S. Fogarty was treasurer, and R. F. Touhey the club's solicitor. This club was a little larger than the Irish Rifle Club and had at least 107 members in 1874.[272]

The Irish Volunteer Rifle Club of Charleston also adopted a military uniform, which was described in the *News and Courier* in 1876:

> It consists of a cadet gray military dress coat, trimmed and faced with olive green, three rows of palmetto buttons down the breast; pants of cadet gray with one inch olive green stripes down the seams; white waist belts with brass breastplates containing the letters I.V.R.C. The cap is of the same cloth

surmounted by a green and white plume, and having a sunburst in the front encircling the monogram of the company. The uniform will at a later date be completed by handsome epaulettes of green and gold. [273]

The mere presence of the armed rifle clubs in the city of Charleston must have served as a powerful deterrent to trouble. There were no riots or other incidents requiring the exercise of their power between the time of their formation and the beginning of 1876. The rifle clubs would be much more active later that year.[274]

During the summer of 1876, the Democratic Party in South Carolina began preparing for a political campaign in which it would seize back control of the state from the Republicans. In August, Wade Hampton was nominated as the party's candidate for Governor and began waging a bitterly-fought political campaign across the state. The rifle clubs, which by this time had an estimated 14,350 members statewide, exerted a powerful influence for Hampton in this campaign. These clubs acted as local operational units for the Democrats' political mobilization. Their public displays of armed force also played a major role in Hampton's policy of "bloodless coercion," under which Republican candidates and their supporters were discouraged from participating in the political process.[275]

In April 1877 Wade Hampton became Governor of South Carolina and the federal occupation troops were withdrawn. The old state militia was reorganized, and there was no longer any need for the rifle clubs. The Irish Volunteer Rifle Club of Charleston apparently went out of existence prior to March 1878 because the club did not participate in the St. Patrick's Day activities that year, as was its usual custom. The Club may have merged into the Irish Volunteers, which again became a part of the state militia.[276]

The Irish Rifle Club of Charleston first became a part of the reorganized militia and elected the following officers: James Armstrong, captain; J. F. Walsh, first lieutenant; John Hines, second lieutenant; M. P. Clear, third lieutenant; James Walsh, first sergeant; W. H. Armstrong secretary and E. E. Kenny, treasurer. This organization later became a social club and remained in existence at least until 1882.[277]

UNITED IRISH ASSOCIATION

ORGANIZED CIRCA 1872

The United Irish Association is listed in the Charleston City

Directories of 1872 and 1873 with the following officers and committee members:

> OFFICERS: James Brennan, President; M. Caulfield, Vice-President; Garret Byrns, Treasurer; and Stephen Moloney, Secretary
> EXECUTIVE COMMITTEE: Nicholas A. Quinn, James Hogan, Patrick Slattery, Michael Kelly and Patrick Cleary.[278]

Nothing is known about the purpose of this organization, but its members apparently knew how to celebrate St. Patrick's Day. In reporting on Charleston's St. Patrick's Day activities in 1872, the *Charleston Daily Courier* stated that the members of the United Irish Association, "at their Hall in Hayne Street, were not unmindful of the obligation they owed the day, and celebrated its memories in flowing bowl and telling speech until they had exhausted the hours of the night."[279]

HIBERNIAN PARK ASSOCIATION

ORGANIZED 1874

In October 1874, a group of Irishmen banded together to form the Hibernian Park Association. The purpose of this group was "the promotion of good fellowship among its members, and the advancement of their interests by purchase of grounds suitable to provide amusement for themselves and their families."[280] The constitution of the Association provided that none but Irishmen and their descendants could become stockholders.[281]

The officers of the Hibernian Park Association at the time of its organization were: B. Callaghan, President; W. M. Moran, Vice-President; James F. Redding, Secretary; George Addison, Treasurer and R. F. Touhey, Solicitor. The members of the Board of Directors were: George Addison, P. Fogarty, T. Roddy, D. O'Neill, D. W. Erwin, M. Hogan, P. Gleason, M. H. Collins, James Cosgrove, Edward Daly, M. Storen, W. M. Borne, P. Brady, T. O'Brien, E. F. Sweeney, S. W. Egan and T. Coligan. The association held monthly meetings on the second Monday of each month and anniversary meetings on the first Monday in October each year.[282]

It took the members of the association over a year to find a suitable piece of property for their pleasure ground. Finally, on January 1, 1876, the Hibernian Park Association acquired two parcels of land approximately four miles from the city of Charleston on the main road, now Meeting Street Road. The purchase price was three thousand dollars. During the next five months, members of the Association constructed a park that would rival anything in Charleston at the time. The area included a dance hall, a restaurant, bar room, target shooting range, a bowling alley and various benches for pleasant conversation.[283]

Prior to opening the park, the decision was made by the members of the association to incorporate, and in March 1876 the Hibernian Park Association was incorporated by act of the South Carolina Legislature. The incorporators were B. Callaghan, Wm. Moran, D. W. Erwin, P. Fogarty, James Cosgrove, B. F. McCabe, A. G. Magrath, Jr., T. O'Brien, T. A. Beamish, S. Fogarty, M. Storen, J. D. Kennedy, M. Hogan, P. Brady, B. Boyd, Wm. Byrne, John Hynes, Thomas Roddy, J. F. Redding, Edward Daly and Robert F. Touhey.[284]

The Hibernian Park opened on June 21, 1876 with great pomp and circumstance. A grand military parade was formed in front of Hibernian Hall consisting of three companies of Cavalry, two of Artillery, nine of Infantry, and three military bands. These were accompanied by carriages containing the Honorable M. P. O'Connor, Orator of the Day; ex-Governor William Aiken; the Honorable George S. Bryan; B. Callaghan, President of the Hibernian Park Association; Captain F. W. Dawson of the *News and Courier*; the Honorable Thomas Y. Simons; Captain John Burke; and the Honorable Alex Melchers. At eight o'clock in the morning the parade was turned over to Captain Edward Daly, the Grand Marshal of the Day. The march was taken out by columns of fours and paraded through Broad Street, East Bay Street, Market Street, Meeting Street, Hasell and King Streets to the Ann Street Depot of the South Carolina Railroad where a special train for excursions to the park was waiting. The parade was then dismissed. The Cavalry proceeding up Meeting Street Road and the Infantry, together with a large number of ladies and civilians, embarked on a special train of ten cars which was filled to its utmost capacity.[285]

The scene upon arriving at the park was described by a reporter of the *News and Courier*:

> A ride of about five minutes brought the party to the park. There the most careful and elaborate preparations had been made for the occasion. The grand old oaks that shelter the park from the rays of the sun were decorated with swings, which afford amusement for the ladies and children. Convenient seats are arranged in various portions of the ground and

everything looked clean and neat. The large hall was neatly whitewashed and bore a sign with the inscription "Tara's Hall". Upon the building were displayed the Palmetto, the United States and Irish colors. A long table spread beneath the sheds of Oaks literally groaned with sandwiches and was flanked on either side by innumerable kegs of lager on ice. The disembarkation occupied but a few moments and the park was speedily crowded with gay throngs of pleasure seekers. The military was masked in front of a large platform erected in the center of the grounds and by half past ten the Inaugural Ceremonies began.[286]

As soon as the crowd had gathered around the platform at which the dignitaries were seated, Mr. Callaghan, the president of the Hibernian Park Association, thanked the people for coming and introduced the speaker of the day, Michael P. O'Connor, one of Charleston's finest orators. Mr. O'Connor then delivered a speech in which he outlined the contributions of the Irish to the United States and the progress they had made since their arrival. The opening ceremonies were then concluded, and the crowd spread out through the park for a pleasant afternoon of dancing, shooting and general merriment. [287]

During the decade after its opening, the Hibernian Park was used extensively by the members of the association and their friends. The park became the home of an annual "People's Festival" which was usually held in May or June of each year under the auspices of the Irish Volunteers and the Montgomery Guards or the Hibernian Park Association itself. This festival lasted for several days and included, among other activities, target shooting, music and dancing. The Hibernian Park was also a favorite spot for picnics held by the St. Patrick's Benevolent Society and various groups associated with Charleston's Catholic churches, and for target shooting by Charleston's Irish militia companies on St. Patrick's Day.[288]

By the 1890s the glory days of the Hibernian Park had come to an end. The Hibernian Park Association continued to hold title to the property, but around 1898 the name of the park was changed to Tuxedo Park. Finally, in 1907, M. F. Kennedy as president of the Hibernian Park Association and John J. Burke as its secretary executed a deed on behalf of the Association conveying the Hibernian Park property to Joseph Maybank for seven thousand dollars. Thereafter, the property was subdivided. The land which was formerly the Hibernian Park is today located at the southeast intersection of Meeting Street Road and Cherry Hill Lane. The area is known as Hibernian Heights.[289]

THE UNITED IRISHMEN OF AMERICA AND SOUTH CAROLINA

ORGANIZED 1876

Charleston's Irish organization of perhaps the shortest duration was the United Irishmen of America and South Carolina, which was formed in 1876. This organization arose out of a meeting of the Irish citizens of Charleston held at the Hibernian Hall on September 14, 1876. The object of the meeting was to consolidate Charleston's Irishmen behind Wade Hampton in his bid for the Governorship of the state. At this meeting the following were nominated as officers and committee members: For president, John H. Devereux; for vice-presidents, Thomas S. O'Brien, J. D. Aiken, R. S. Cathcart, A. McLoy, P. Brady, C. R. Cassidy; for recording secretary, J. F. Redding; for corresponding secretary, H. J. O'Neill; for treasurer, S. Fogarty. Executive Committee: James Cosgrove, D. A. J. Sullivan, D. W. Erwin, R. C. Barkley, J. E. Holmes, P. P. Toale, J. W. Reid and P. Moran.[290] The following resolution was also passed:

> Resolved, that we, Irishmen, and the descendants of Irishmen, citizens of the United States and of this State, do hereby organize ourselves as a body, to be called the United Irishmen of the State of South Carolina, for the purpose of effectually aiding our fellow citizens in securing the redemption of the State, and promoting and perpetuating honest government within its borders. [291]

On September 28, 1876 the group formalized its organization under the name the United Irishmen of America and South Carolina. The idea was to seek assistance for the people of South Carolina from people of Irish blood from all over the United States.[292]

The officers selected at that time were John H. Devereux, President, and James F. Redding, Secretary. The Managing Committee was made up of: Ellison A. Smyth, Edward McCrady, B. Callaghan, E. F. Sweegan, Charles R. Cassiday, John Hynes, and James Power, with James Cosgrove for Sullivans Island and Christ Church Parish. It was said that this was "a judicious mixture of Catholic and Protestant Irish."[293] After Hampton assumed the Governorship in April of 1877, this organization no longer had a purpose, and it is assumed it went out of existence at that time.

EMERALD SOCIAL CLUB

ORGANIZED CIRCA 1885

After the Civil War, many social clubs were established in Charleston. The Emerald Social Club first appeared in the Charleston city directory in 1885.[294] The *News and Courier* that year stated that "The Emerald Social Club is an organization composed of young and festive representatives of the Emerald Isle in this city."[295] The club last appears in the city directory of 1890. Its officers that year were E. Barry, President, and A. J. Noland, Secretary.[296]

THE ANCIENT ORDER OF HIBERNIANS

Most of the Irish organizations in Charleston never made it a requirement that one be Irish or of a particular religious affiliation to belong. One notable exception was the Ancient Order of Hibernians. Membership in this national organization was open only to persons who were Irish or of Irish descent and who were Roman Catholics.[297]

The purpose of the AOH was set out in the preamble to its Constitution and By-Laws adopted in 1871:

> The members of this Order do declare that the intent and purpose of the Order is to promote Friendship, Unity and True Christian Charity among its members, by raising or supporting a stock or fund of money for maintaining the aged, sick, blind and infirm members and for no other purposes whatsoever.[298]

The AOH, as it was often called, was first organized in this country in 1836. The basic unit or branch of the AOH is called a Division, and there is evidence that a Division was established in Charleston prior to the Civil War. Apparently, this Division did not survive the war, and it was not until 1889 that another Division was established in the city.[299]

On November 3, 1889 the members of Division No. 1 of the Ancient Order of Hibernians were initiated at the Irish Volunteers Hall in Charleston. National Delegate P. J. O'Connor of Savannah, along with other AOH officials from Atlanta and Augusta was on hand for the ceremony. The initial officers of the Division were: Dennis Kennedy, President; E. M. Barry, Vice President; W. J. Casey, Recording Secretary;

M. J. Danehey, Financial Secretary; B. P. Cunningham, Treasurer; and Jno. J. O'Herin, Sergeant-at-Arms. The meetings of this Division were held at the Irish Volunteers Hall.[300]

Division No. 2 of the Ancient Order of Hibernians was established in Charleston on July 24, 1892 with sixty-six charter members. This Division's first officers were: E. F. Sweegan, President; M. D. Maguire, Vice President; J. J. Corcoran, Financial Secretary and Treasurer; S. F. Dawson, Sergeant-at-Arms; M. P. Mclaughlin, Recording Secretary; P. Devereux, Sentinal; J. F. Condon, Chairman Standing Committee; W. J. Storen, Marshal and Rev. J. J. Monaghan, Chaplin. This Division also held its meetings at the Irish Volunteers Hall.[301]

A Division No. 3 of the Ancient Order of Hibernians was also established in Charleston, probably in late 1894 or early 1895 as it is first listed in the city directory in 1895. The officers of Division No. 3 that year were: Thos. Hogan, President; James Cosgrove, Vice President; James McGrath, Financial Secretary; and J. A. Barbot, Treasurer. This Division, unlike the other two, did not last very long. It does not appear in the Charleson city directory for 1900.[302]

A state AOH board was established shortly after Division No. 1 was organized, with F. J. Devereux as its president; a county board was also established. These boards were comprised of the officers of the divisions together with officers chosen by them.[303]

In keeping with its purposes, the By-Laws of the Order provided for a sick allowance and death benefit for its members. Section 15 of the 1871 By-Laws dealt with these matters:

> When any member of this Order falls sick, a visiting committee belonging to the Division of which he is a member shall visit him; and should they neglect to do so, each of them shall be fined a sum of one dollar. When said committee shall report the state of his health, and if it be so that he is not able to attend to his daily labor, the President shall give an order on the Treasurer, signed and countersigned by the Secretary, for the sum of five dollars for each week during his sickness; and should he die, the sum of fifty dollars shall be allowed to defray his funeral expenses.[304]

Besides its existence as an Irish organization, the Ancient Order of Hibernians was a Catholic organization in which religion played a major role. Upon the death of a member in good standing, the 1871 By-

Laws provided that a Division would have a High Mass said and any officer or member neglecting to attend the funeral would be fined.[305]

As one might suspect, St. Patrick's Day was an official holiday of the AOH. The national constitution in effect in 1871 provided:

> The seventeenth day of March shall be a national holiday of the Order, to be celebrated by a public procession of its members, and any member failing to parade shall be fined a sum of three dollars, unless excused by the Board of directors of the Division.[306]

The Charleston Divisions of the AOH followed the directive of the Constitution and participated in the St. Patrick's Day parade each year. In addition, a ball and grand entertainment was usually held in the evening at the Knights of Columbus Hall on Calhoun Street under the auspices of the Ancient Order of Hibernians.[307]

The Ancient Order of Hibernian was unique among Irish organizations in Charleston in that it was one of the few such groups to have a ladies' auxiliary. Division No. 1 of the Ladies Auxiliary to the Ancient Order of Hibernians was formed in Charleston at the Irish Volunteers Hall on March 28, 1901. The organizational meeting was presided over by County President B. P. Carey, assisted by Brothers T. F. Sughrue, J. L. Kiley, M. E. Powers and F. J. Quinlivan, of the County Board. Fifty-three charter members were inducted.[308] From among the charter members the following officers were selected:

> Division Officers: Mrs. C. O. Schott, President; Mrs. D. O'Brien, Vice-President; Mrs. Margaret Vaughan, Recording Secretary; Miss Delia Donelan, Financial Secretary; Mrs. T. F. Sughrue, Treasurer; Miss Annie Leonard, Sergeant-at-Arms; Miss Mary Hogan, Assistant Sergeant-at-Arms; Miss Marie Benedikt, Sentinel.[309]
> County Officers: Mrs. W. J. Condon, President; Miss Kate A. Lucas, Vice-President; Mrs. F. F. Buero, Secretary; Mrs. J. P. Corcoran, Treasurer.[310]
> State Officers: Miss M. Gravell, President; Mrs. Hattie Donelan, Vice-President; Miss Kate L. Sughrue, Secretary; Mrs. J. L. Kiley, Treasurer; Mrs. K. Mollenhauer, Chairman Standing Committee.[311]

Charleston's Division No. 1 of the Ladies Auxiliary did not march on St. Patrick's Day, but did participate in the Mass and helped to put on the annual ball and grand entertainment. In 1921 the Ladies Auxiliary was also instrumental in organizing a branch of the Celtic Cross Association for the purpose of raising funds for the aid of the people of Ireland.[312]

Division No. 1 of the Ancient Order of Hibernians apparently went out of existence around 1921, as it is not listed in the Charleston city directory for 1922. Division No. 2 is last listed in the directory of 1925-1926 and the Ladies Auxiliary is last listed in the directory of 1929.[313]

On October 27, 1997, Charleston Division 1 of the Ancient Order of Hibernians was re-chartered at the Knights of Columbus Hall on Calhoun Street. The initial officers of this re-chartered division were President Jimmy Finnigan, Vice President Billy Clarey, Secretary John Gilbert and Treasurer Michael Bolchoz. The initial membership numbered about sixty.[314]

IRISH FRIENDLY SOCIETY

ORGANIZED CIRCA 1890

The Germans had their Friendly Society in Charleston and so did the Irish. Unfortunately, the Irish Friendly Society did not last nearly as long as its German counterpart. The Irish Friendly Society existed in Charleston from 1890 to 1892. Its officers were Patrick Moran, President and J. W. Casey, Secretary.[315]

THE SOUTH CAROLINA IRISH HISTORICAL SOCIETY

FOUNDED 1979

The South Carolina Irish Historical Society was founded in 1979 by a small group of Charlestonians of Irish descent. The founders of the Society were a group of people who were not only interested in their own Irish heritage, but who were also interested in the Irish heritage of Charleston and South Carolina. They had discovered over the years that the general public was not aware of the contributions that the Irish had made to the City and State. Therefore, they decided to form an organization to raise this awareness. Although founded in Charleston, the decision was made to name the new organization the South Carolina Irish Historical Society to show the groups interest in the Irish heritage of the entire state. The purposes of the Society, as set out in its charter, are:

To promote and preserve the Irish heritage in South Carolina.

To provide a repository for information and items of significance to the South Carolina Irish community.[316]

Unlike some of the city's other Irish organizations, which hold monthly meetings, the South Carolina Irish Historical Society chose to hold its meetings four times a year. These meetings are held on St. Bridget's Day (February 1st), St. Patrick's Day (March 17th), St. Brendan's Day (May 16th), and September 17th, which is half-way to St. Patrick's Day. The place of these meetings is usually Tommy Condon's Irish Pub and Restaurant on Church Street in Charleston.[317]

Since its inception, the Society has grown to over two hundred members and has been very active. It has contributed books on Irish subjects to the local library and participated in numerous activities highlighting the state's Irish heritage. The Society has also been instrumental in the effort to construct an Irish memorial in the City of Charleston.[318]

The South Carolina Historical Society's St. Patrick's Day activities include the raising of the Irish flag over the Charleston City Hall and marching in Charleston's St. Patrick's Day Parade. In addition, during the month of March each year, the Society sponsors an Irish music show which features professional Irish entertainers from Ireland and other parts of the United States.[319]

The presidents of the South Carolina Irish Historical Society from its inception through 2004 are: P. Michael Duffy, 1979; Gerald F. McMahon, Jr., 1980; Robert H. McDowell, 1981; J. Barney Clarey, Jr., 1982; Thomas C. Condon, 1983; Francis X. McCann, 1984; Donald M. Williams, 1985; Judith M. McDowell, 1986; John McAlister, 1987; Stephen D. Regan, 1988; Michael C. Robinson, 1989; Frederick W. McMahon, 1990; Betty R. White, 1991; Richard C. Neapolitan, 1992; Edward W. Duffy, 1993; Frank E. Eaton, 1994; Rose Kavanagh, 1995; James J. Kerr 1996; David P. McCann, 1997; Peter F. O'Malley, 1998; Michael J. Power, 1999; James Dodds Moore, 2000; James J. Brady, 2001; Peggy T. Droze, 2002; Rosemary Bouvette, 2003; and Heather O'Malley Jenkins, 2004.[320]

Judge Aedanus Burke, a member of the First United States Congress
who left money to aid Irish emigrants
(Courtesy of the Hibernian Society)

O'Brien Smith, early Captain of the Irish Volunteers
(Courtesy of the Hibernian Society)

Rev. Simon Felix Gallagher, President of the Hibernian Society 1801-1803
(Courtesy of the Hibernian Society)

John F. O'Neill, President of the St. Patrick's Benevolent Society in 1858
(Courtesy of the Hibernian Society)

Hibernian Hall

Grave of Captain John Mitchel

HIBERNIAN SOCIETY.

THE fifty-fourth Anniversary of this Society will be celebrated on the 17th instant, (St. Patrick's Day.) The members will assemble at their Hall, at twelve o'clock M., to transact the usual business, and elect officers.

Dinner ordered at 4½ o'clock. Members intending to dine will please call on the Treasurer for their tickets.

W. P. O'HARA,
March 17 Secretary.

MONTGOMERY GUARDS.

THE COMPANY will assemble at their usual rendezvous, properly armed and accoutred, This Morning, at 8 o'clock precisely, for the purpose of celebrating the day by target shooting at Magnolia. By order. P. OLEARY,
March 17 1 O. S. M. G.

IRISH VOLUNTEERS.
70TH ANNIVERSARY, MARCH 17, 1855.

THE Company will assemble at their usual rendezvous at 9 o'clock precisely, for the purpose of celebrating the day by target exercise at Magnolia.

Previous to which a discourse will be delivered before them by the very Rev. Dr. RYDER, at the Cathedral, in Broad-street, at 10 o'clock. They will further unite in its celebration by a supper in the evening, at Military Hall, at 7½ o'clock.

Tickets may be had of any of the undersigned.

Lieut. B. O'NEILL,
WM. BARRAGAN,
JAS. BUCKLEY, } Committee of Arrangements.
M. BURKE,
M. QUINN,

March 17 1

ATTENTION, MEAGHER GUARD.

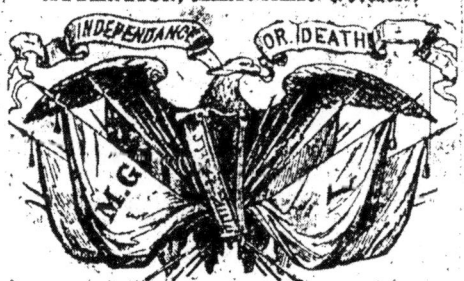

YOU are ordered to assemble at Military Hall, at 8 o'clock, A. M., on the 17th inst. At 9 o'clock, the Company will proceed to St. Patrick's Church, where an Oration will be delivered by the Very Rev. P. N. LYNCH, from thence to the Target Ground, to contend for the Company prizes.

The Company will re-assemble at Military Hall at 8 o'clock, P. M., in citizens dress, to partake of the festivities provided for the occasion.

By order of the Captain.
March 17 1 B. O. CONNER, O. S. M. G.

Armory of the Irish Volunteers

Meeting notice of Montgomery Guards

Michael Patrick O'Connor, main speaker at the dedication of
Hibernia Park
(Courtesy of the Hibernian Society)

James Redding, President of Charleston's Grattan Branch of the Irish
National League of America.
(Courtesy of the Hibernian Society)

Edward F. Sweegan, State President of Ancient Order of Hibernians in 1901
(Courtesy of the Hibernian Society)

Irish Volunteers on the Mexican Border in 1916

Delegates to the Irish Race convention of 1919 pose in front of the statute of Sergeant Jasper

SHAMROCKS AND PLUFF MUD

Terence MacSwiney, Lord Mayor of Cork,

Eamon de Valera, second gentleman from right, upon his arrival in Charleston

Left to right: Rev. J. A. G. Irwin, Eamon de Valera and Andrew Riley at Charleston's City Hall

W. Turner Logan, president of the Charleston chapter of the Friends of Irish Freedom
(Courtesy of the Hibernian Society)

Mayor John P. Grace, national vice president of the Friends of Irish Freedom
(Courtesy of the Hibernian Society)

CHAPTER FOUR

THE IRISH VOLUNTEERS
AND
OTHER IRISH MILITARY ORGANIZATIONS

Over the centuries, the Irish have acquired the reputation of being excellent soldiers. Unfortunately, more often than not, this reputation has been gained in the service of countries other than their own. British occupation prevented Irishmen from bearing arms in the service of their country. British oppression and famine forced hundreds of thousands of them to emigrate to other countries. After their arrival, the Irish became loyal citizens of the places in which they settled and were always in the forefront of those volunteering for military service.

The Irish who came to Charleston were no different, and the officials of the city and state could always rely upon them to respond to a call to arms. This was especially true during the struggle for Southern independence when many an Irishman made the ultimate sacrifice for his adopted city of Charleston and state of South Carolina. Confederate Captain John C. Mitchel, who was killed on July 20, 1864 while in command of Fort Sumter, epitomized the spirit of these Irish soldiers.[321] His last words were, "I willingly give my life for South Carolina; Oh! that I could have died for Ireland!"[322]

THE IRISH VOLUNTEERS

ORGANIZED CIRCA 1794

The first Irish militia unit to form in Charleston was The Irish Volunteers. At least one source dates the organization of this company to 1798, but it may have been earlier. A March 27, 1919 article in the *Charleston American* states that the unit was organized on June 20, 1794. According to this report, a group of citizens held a meeting on that date at the Globe Tavern for the purpose of forming a company to be called the Irish Volunteers of Charleston, S.C. At this meeting Charles Crowley was elected Captain of the company, and Michael Crowley was elected First Lieutenant.[323]

During the first few years of its existence, the Irish Volunteers acted almost exclusively as a social club, with its first opportunity for potential military action not coming until 1812. It was in June of that year that the United States declared war against Great Britain. The state was required to provide troops for the federal government, and the Volunteers, not having any love for the British, immediately signed up for service. Those looking for action were disappointed, however, since there was very little activity along the South Carolina coast during the war. The company's duties were limited to patrolling the coast and working on the city's defenses.[324]

In 1832, it again appeared that the company would soon be drawn into military action when the state of South Carolina passed the Nullification Ordinance. After passage of the ordinance, the members of the Irish Volunteers placed their loyalty to the state above their loyalty to the country. The company began preparing to aid the state in repelling an invasion by the federal government, and not even Charleston's Irish Catholic Bishop, John England, could persuade them to support the Union. Fortunately, cooler heads prevailed and a clash between state and federal authorities was avoided.[325]

Four years later, the Irish Volunteers were finally called upon to fight. The Seminole Indians rose up against the citizens of Florida in 1836, committing horrible atrocities. The situation became so bad that the people of Charleston felt compelled to render assistance. In January 1836, Governor McDuffie issued orders calling for a draft of men from the Fourth Brigade of militia to serve in Florida for three months. The Irish Volunteers immediately volunteered to go to Florida, and the draft was suspended.[326]

On February 10, 1836, the company, under the command of Captain George Henry, departed for Florida, arriving in St. Augustine several days later. The first fight in which the unit engaged the Indians occurred on March 10th about fifty miles from St. Augustine. In this action, the company sustained its first battle casualty, Michael Kennedy, who was killed.[327]

The company fought the Indians a second time on March 22, 1836 along the St. Johns River near Volusia. The Indians fired from across the river, and the Irish Volunteers crossed the river to engage them. After a short skirmish, the Indians were forced to retreat without inflicting any casualties on the Volunteers. This battle was the company's last of the campaign, and in May 1836 the Volunteers returned to Charleston.[328]

In December 1860, when South Carolina seceded from the Union, the Irish Volunteers immediately offered their services to the state. Their offer was accepted, and they were immediately put to work. State officials had just been embarrassed by the surprise move of Major Anderson and his troops from Fort Moultrie to Fort Sumter and they did not want to be embarrassed again. It was expected that the United States government would send a ship to relieve Fort Sumter, and great pains were taken to see that this did not happen. A battery, manned by cadets from the Citadel, was established on Morris Island adjacent to the main ship channel so that fire could be brought to bear on any relief ship. In addition, Captain William H. Ryan of the Irish Volunteers and a detachment of men from the Fourth Brigade were placed on board the guard ship *General Clinch* with orders to patrol the Charleston Bar at night and warn of any Union relief expedition. On the night of January 9, 1861, Captain Ryan's party sighted the *Star of the West* crossing the Charleston Bar. The *General Clinch* immediately turned towards the city and raced up the harbor, firing rockets to alert the gunners. The Citadel cadets on Morris Island saw the signal and fired on the ship, causing it to give up the relief effort.[329]

The Irish Volunteers remained in the service of the state until after the surrender of Fort Sumter. Thereafter, they resisted the temptation—succumbed to by many Charleston military units—to immediately rush off to Virginia to fight the Yankees. Instead, they chose to stay in Charleston as part of the state militia, ready to defend the South Carolina coast from any invasion.[330]

It was during these first months after the fall of Fort Sumter that the Sisters of Mercy in the city of Charleston made a flag for the Irish Volunteers. This flag was presented to the company on September 16, 1861 at Saint Finbar's Cathedral. The flag displayed the harp of Ireland, surrounded by a mingled wreath of shamrock, oak and palmetto on one side, and on the reverse side, the palmetto and crescent moon with the superscription, "Et Presidium, et Dulcecus Deus." It was borne into the church by Rev. L. Fillion, the company chaplain. Reverend Fillion then handed the banner to Bishop P. N. Lynch, who, assisted by three other priests, blessed it according to the pontifical forms of the Catholic Church for such occasions.[331] After the blessing, the Bishop made a short speech and then presented the flag to the company's Captain with the following words: "To you, then, I commit this banner. In your hands I know it will never be stained by cowardice, or by any act that will disgrace you as a body of gallant christian soldiery. Receive it then—rally around it. Let it teach you of God—of Erin—of Carolina. Let it teach you your duty in this life as soldiers and as christians, so that fighting the good fight of christians you may receive the reward of eternal victory from the King of Kings."[332]

In February 1862, the Irish Volunteers joined with the city's other Irish companies in an attempt to form an Irish Battalion for Confederate service. This effort was unsuccessful, and a number of Charleston militia units, including the Irish Volunteers, were then organized by the state into the First South Carolina Infantry Battalion. This unit, better known as the "Charleston Battalion," was mustered into Confederate service in April 1862 for a period of twelve months. The Irish Volunteers became Company "C" of this battalion. The Battalion Commander was Colonel P. C. Gaillard, a West Point graduate.[333]

The Charleston Battalion was stationed at Secessionville on June 2, 1862 when Union troops landed on Sol Legare Island. In the confusion that surrounded the landings, a Confederate battery had managed to get three of its guns stuck in the mud at the Rivers Causeway which connected Sol Legare Island to James Island. The next day Lieutenant Colonel Ellison Capers and several companies of the 24th South Carolina were sent to retrieve the guns. In the process, they became heavily engaged at the southern end of the causeway on Sol Legare Island with the 28th Massachusetts, an Irish unit.[334]

Capers' troops pushed the Massachusetts Irish back through a wood and had reached the edge of an open field across from the Legare House when they were reinforced by the Charleston Battalion, which had been sent to their aid from Secessionville. By the time the Charleston Battalion arrived, the 28th Massachusetts had joined with other Union units near the Legare House and were hastily forming a line of battle. The Union troops in their haste had failed to close a gap between the Irish troops and a small group of soldiers from the 100th Pennsylvania, leaving this group dangerously isolated. Capers immediately perceived the enemy's predicament and ordered the Charleston Battalion to attack the isolated group while the rest of the troops drove a wedge between it and the main body.[335]

A command was given for the Irish Volunteers to charge. "The entire company immediately sprang up, the Captain at their head waving his sword cried out, 'My brave men follow your Captain,' and all with one impulse bounded forward to the assault."[336] Captain W. H. Ryan rushed across the field, grabbed the officer in charge by the throat and ordered him to surrender. Before the Union officer could comply, a Union soldier, bayonet in hand, charged the gallant captain. Just in the nick of time, Rody Whelan of the Irish Volunteers rushed forward, locked bayonets with the Yankee, and with a quick Irish foot put him on the ground.[337] After subduing his adversary, Whelan rained down blows on him, shouting, "Blast your soul, you infernal coward! Didn't you hear your Captain surrender? Is that what you call fighting in your country? Faith I'll teach you a lesson that you won't forget in a hurry, my bold boy. Bad luck to you! Is it murder you wanted to commit this fine morning? Come along with me and I'll teach you better manners the next time."[338] The remaining Union troops immediately surrendered.[339]

The prisoners captured by the Irish Volunteers in this action were the first to be taken along the South Carolina coast during the war. Unfortunately, Private Thomas Bresnan of the Irish Volunteers, killed in the charge, became one of the first southern casualties along the coast. Captain Ryan, for his part, was awarded the sword he took from the Yankee captain.[340]

After the engagement at Sol Legare Island, the Charleston Battalion returned to Secessionville, where the Confederates were hurrying to complete their fortifications across a small peninsula. The troops worked day and night, and at 4:30 a.m. on June 16, 1862, most of them were asleep. It was at that hour that approximately 3,200 Union troops attacked the 500 Confederate defenders of the still incomplete battery.[341]

The initial wave of Union troops swept toward the left flank of the Confederate battery, and a number of them managed to climb up and over the wall. It looked for a time that the battery would fall, but Smith's 9th South Carolina Battalion arrived from its camp in time to drive the Union troops back. The situation was stabilized for the moment, but the danger had not passed. Captain Reed of Lamar's Battery, along with all of his cannoneers, had been killed in the initial assault. The guns on the battery's left front had fallen silent while thousands of Union troops continued to pour across the field in front. Captain Ryan and the Irish Volunteers, in response to a call from the battery's commander for volunteers, took over Captain Reed's guns, and they were soon raking the field with fire again. Private William Shelton of the Volunteers was noted as servicing his gun with particular fury.[342]

The fight for the battery continued and on several occasions the Volunteers ran out of ammunition. On each of these occasions, Lieutenant Alexander A. Allemong of the Irish Volunteers, exposing himself to great personal danger, went to the ammunition wagons and carried back the cartridges in his arms. Finally, the stubborn resistance of the Confederates was too much for the assaulting Union troops. After two and a half hours of fierce hand-to-hand combat, the Union commander ordered a full retreat. The Union forces had suffered around 700 casualties killed or wounded, the Confederates around 200. Private Daniel Howard of the Irish Volunteers was among those killed.[343]

The following summer, the Irish Volunteers participated in the battle for Battery Wagner, one of the fiercest engagements to take place in Charleston during the Civil War. On July 10, 1863, Union troops launched an amphibious assault against Morris Island and quickly secured the southern end. The only thing that stood between them and complete control of the island was a little sand fortification by the name of Battery Wagner, which probably did not appear too formidable. Several companies of the 7th Connecticut, followed by the 76th Pennsylvania and 9th Maine, attacked Battery Wagner on July 11th. The Connecticut troops reached the Battery's parapet, but were forced to retreat after taking heavy casualties. After this attack, the Union Army had more respect for Battery Wagner and would be better prepared next time. So would the Confederates, who reinforced the battery with the battle-hardened Charleston Battalion on July 14.[344]

The Union Army attacked again on July 18, 1863 with a much larger force. This assault was preceded by an artillery barrage from land batteries and the Union fleet, which began at 10 a.m. and lasted all day. Approximately 9,000 shells rained down on Battery Wagner during this period. Due to crowded conditions within the battery, there was not enough space in the bombproof for the entire garrison to seek shelter. Consequently, the Irish Volunteers, together with most of the remainder of the Charleston Battalion, were forced to remain on the parapets. At one point, the garrison flag was shot away and the Union troops, believing that the battery had surrendered, cheered. Their joy was short-lived, however. Sergeant William Shelton of the Irish Volunteers, along with three other soldiers, showing no concern for their personal safety, lashed the flag to a mast and raised it again.[345]

The brave Sergeant William Shelton survived the battle for Battery Wagner and also the remainder of the war. His bravery at Battery Wagner, Secessionville, and throughout the war greatly endeared him to his comrades of the Irish Volunteers, even though he was English by birth. One of his comrades was John Conroy, who was elected City Alderman after the war. One day, while Conroy was serving as Alderman, he received a visit from an Irishman who was running against William Shelton for a position in the 3rd Ward. This Irishman had claimed British protection to avoid service in the Confederate Army and Conroy informed the man that he was going to vote for Shelton. The man said, "Surely, Alderman Conroy, you would not vote for an Englishman in preference to an Irishman?" To which Conroy replied, "I would much rather vote for an Englishman who was an Irishman during the war than to vote for Irishman who was an Englishman during the same period."[346]

At dusk, 6,000 Union soldiers led by the 54th Massachusetts, a black regiment, launched a frontal assault on the shell-shocked defenders of the battery. They were met with a shower of canister and grape from Wagner's guns which cut the leading regiment to pieces. Those who survived the artillery were met by decimating musket fire from the Irish Volunteers and their comrades of Companies D and F of the Charleston Battalion, who held the right flank of the battery while the 51st North Carolina held the center. These units gallantly held their positions, driving the enemy back with staggering losses. Private Michael Toole of the Irish Volunteers was killed in the assault and Privates Callahan, Reynolds, Mannin and Hill were wounded.[347]

Things did not go as well on the left flank of Battery Wagner. The defense of this flank had been assigned to the 31st North Carolina, but these troops refused to come out of the bombproof shelter after the bombardment. As a result, a contingent of one of the attacking regiments was able to occupy the left salient of the battery. General Taliaferro, the battery's commander, called for volunteers to dislodge the enemy, and Captain William H. Ryan, along with twenty of his Irish Volunteers, immediately stepped forward. Lieutenant A. A. Allemong went to the Sumter Guards to obtain more men, but before he returned Ryan and his volunteers had charged the enemy. The gallant Captain Ryan was shot almost immediately by a Yankee soldier positioned on the slope above his head. The bullet entered Ryan near his left collarbone, passed completely through his body and exited at his right hip, killing him instantly. Shocked by the death of their seemingly invincible captain, the Irish Volunteers hesitated, and the enemy had to be dislodged by other troops.[348]

The failed attack of July 18th convinced the Union commanders that Battery Wagner could not be taken by frontal assault. Instead, the Union Army settled into a siege. The battery was subjected to constant shelling from land and sea, while parallel trenches were constructed closer and closer to it.[349]

The Confederates were determined to hold onto the battery as long as possible to allow themselves time to strengthen Fort Sumter and Charleston's other defenses. In order to do this, they garrisoned Battery

Wagner with their best troops and rotated them every few days. The Irish Volunteers served two tours at Battery Wagner during this siege. They were a part of Wagner's garrison August 4-7 and August 20-27, 1863. The duty was demanding and dangerous, but the Volunteers' only casualties during this period were Patrick Lee and Patrick Culleton, both of whom were wounded in the hand. Finally, the Confederates were forced to abandon Battery Wagner on September 7, 1863.[350]

As the Union trenches grew ever closer to Battery Wagner, the Confederates rushed to strengthen Fort Sumter. The fort was the key to Charleston's defenses, and its loss could result in the fall of the city. In addition, Fort Sumter had become the symbol of the rebellion, and its capture would be a great psychological blow to the South. It had to be held to the bitter end.[351]

On September 4, 1863, the Charleston Battalion, including the Irish Volunteers, landed at Fort Sumter. The Fort was then placed under the command of Major Stephen Elliott, a seasoned officer, who directed the completion of its defenses. Under Elliott's guidance, the Charleston Battalion turned the fort into a formidable infantry position.[352] So formidable, in fact, that when the Union forces did demand the Fort's surrender after the evacuation of Battery Wagner, Major Elliott confidently replied, "Inform Admiral Dahlgren that he may have Fort Sumter when he can take and hold it." [353]

The confidence of the Confederates in Fort Sumter's defenses was apparently not shared by the Union forces. Both the Union Army and Navy planned attacks on the fort, but could not coordinate their efforts due to inter-service rivalries. Early in the morning of September 9, 1863, the Union Navy struck first with 500 sailors and Marines who launched an amphibious assault on the fort. The Charleston Battalion was ready, and repulsed the attack, sustaining no casualties. The Union sailors and Marines, on the other hand, had 127 men either killed, wounded, or taken prisoner. The Irish Volunteers were held in reserve during the main attack, but assisted in the capture of the prisoners.[354]

On September 30, 1863 the Charleston Battalion was consolidated with the First Sharpshooters Battalion to form the 27th Regiment of South Carolina Volunteers. The Irish Volunteers became Company "H" of this regiment. The 27th Regiment in turn was combined with several others to form Hagood's Brigade. This new brigade, under the command of Colonel Johnson Hagood, served on James Island for the remainder of 1863 and the early part of 1864.[355]

The small boat attack on Fort Sumter was the Union Army's last serious offensive against Charleston, and by the spring of 1864 the pressure on Charleston had greatly decreased. The pressure on Richmond, on the other hand, was increasing daily, creating a need for more troops on both sides. In early April most of the Union troops who had fought on Morris Island moved to Virginia. Their Confederate adversaries would soon follow.[356]

Hagood's Brigade left Charleston for Virginia on April 28, 1864, and on May 4 was camped outside of Wilmington, North Carolina. On that date, General Benjamin Butler's army left Fortress Monroe and began moving up the James River, creating a menace to both Richmond and Petersburg. The next day, Hagood's Brigade was ordered to Petersburg to meet this threat while other Confederate forces were gathered. Due to a lack of adequate railroad transportation the brigade had to travel in sections.[357]

On May 6, 1864 the leading elements of Hagood's Brigade, along with a mixture of other Confederate forces, engaged one of Butler's brigades at Walthal Junction. This Union brigade, which had been pushed forward by Butler to destroy the Richmond and Petersburg Railroad, could not overcome the stubborn Confederate resistance and broke off the fight at dark. The Irish Volunteers did not participate in the battle on the first day because the 27th Regiment had not yet arrived in Petersburg, but they joined in the engagement the following morning. After an all-day battle on May 7, the Union troops withdrew, leaving the railroad and Petersburg in Confederate hands. Fortunately, none of the Irish Volunteers was killed in the battle. However, Thomas Egan was wounded and Allan Goodrich was captured.[358]

After the affair at Walthal Junction, Hagood's Brigade was moved to positions in Richmond's southern defense line at Drewry's Bluff to await an expected attack by Butler's Army. This assault, which came on May 13, 1864, had some initial success, but ultimately faltered. Several days later, General Beauregard launched a counterattack in an attempt to destroy Butler's army, but this also failed to accomplish its objective. Thereafter, Butler withdrew to his defensive lines at Bermuda Hundred, where he remained, no longer a threat to Richmond. It was during the battle at Drewry's Bluff that the Irish Volunteers suffered their first serious casualties on Virginia soil. William Dinan, Thomas Deary, Edward Ryan, and Edward Whelan were all killed. W. S. Lipscomb, John Conroy and Edward Lee were wounded. Rody Whelan, who had saved Captain Ryan's life at Secessionville, was also listed as killed, but later records show that he was captured and died in a prison camp in Elmira, New York.[359]

The containment of Butler's army within its lines at Bermuda

Hundred allowed General Beauregard to send part of his troops to the aid of General Robert E. Lee, who was being hard pressed by General Ulysses S. Grant. The Irish Voluneers were among the troops sent to join Lee and participated in his victory at the Battle of Cold Harbor. They also shared the great suffering of Lee's army in the trenches at Petersburg. During the siege at Petersburg, the Irish Volunteers lost A. A. Allemong, Thomas L. Hogan, Patrick Carroll, William Harrington, James Carroll, James Fowler, Patrick Hogan, John Maher, James McDonald, James Todd, Christopher Warren, John Warren, and Henry Wiley, killed. Thomas Connelly, James Molone, Joseph Murphy, Patrick Manion, Peter Martin and William Shelton were wounded, and Cornelius Dinan, James Flynn, Patrick Lee, Thomas Molone, John May, Martin Sullivan and James Walsh were captured.[360]

On August 21, 1864 the Irish Volunteers engaged in the Battle of Weldon Railroad. During the battle the company was surrounded by the enemy. Daniel Ward, Patrick Culleton, Thomas Carey, John Edwards, Patrick Flannigan, Thomas Hayden, T. C. James, Thomas Molone and J. Walsh were forced to surrender. Most of these men were never heard from again.[361]

What was left of the Irish Volunteers company was transferred with Hagood's Brigade to North Carolina in December 1864. After its arrival the company fought in the battle for Fort Fisher, the key to Wilmington. In this fight the unit was once again surrounded. Those who avoided capture probably remained with the 27th Regiment until its surrender with General Joseph Johnston at Durham Station, North Carolina on April 26, 1865, but the records have not survived.[362]

The defeat of the Southern Confederacy did not dampen the desire of the Irish citizens of Charleston to defend their adopted homeland, and the Irish Volunteers were reorganized in 1870. This was in the middle of the Reconstruction Era, during which southerners were discouraged from forming militia companies. Consequently, the Irish Volunteers were forced to operate first as a social organization and then as a rifle club for the first few years after reorganization. During this time the company was made up mostly of older veterans of the company who had served in the Civil War.[363]

In 1877, after the Union occupation troops were withdrawn from the state, the Irish Volunteers were able to resume their role as part of the Fourth Brigade of the South Carolina Militia. The company at that time had a total strength of 110 men armed with Springfield rifles.[364] The post-war uniform worn by the company was "a gray dress coat, and gray pants, trimmed with green, gray hat with gray and white plume."[365]

Shortly after the Union troops were withdrawn from the state, the Irish Volunteers began making plans to erect a monument at Saint Lawrence Cemetery to honor their deceased comrades and the deceased members of the Irish Volunteers for the War. A fundraiser was held at Hibernian Hall in February 1878, attended by some of Charleston's most prominent citizens and many former members of the companies. The cornerstone of the monument was laid on March 17, 1878, and the completed monument was dedicated on June 28th of that year,.[366] A description of the monument appeared in the *News and Courier* the day after its dedication:

THE MONUMENT,

which is decidedly the handsomest in the cemetery, was designed and constructed by Mr. E. T. Viett, and is thirty-three feet from the base to the tip of the cross. It is constructed entirely of Winnsboro, South Carolina, granite, and consists of a base twelve feet square, three flights of steps surmounted by another base and sub-base, upon which is inscribed in large bold polished letters, the words: 'The Irish Volunteers.' Above this comes the die block upon which appears the following inscription:

1801-1878
To the Memory of the dead of the Irish Volun-
teers
In the War of 1812
In the Florida War, 1835
Co. C Charleston Battalion,
Department of South Carolina,
Georgia and Florida, 1862-1863.
Co. K First Regiment of South Carolina Volunteers,
Army of Northern Virginia,
1861-1865.
Co. H, 27th Regiment South Carolina Volunteers, Army Northern Virginia, 1863-1865.

Above this die block is a cornice upon which rests the upper die block, into which is set a bronze *bas relief* representing the Irish harp resting beneath the shade of the palmetto, on either side of the trunk of which are stacked arms. Above this die block comes another cornice from which rises a granite shaft twelve feet six inches in height, and surmounted by a Celtic cross four feet six inches in height.[367]

Prior to the Civil War, the Irish Volunteers held most of their meetings at Military Hall on Wentworth Street between King and Meeting. The post-war company, however, initially chose to meet at Byrnes Hall on King Street near Liberty Street. Then, in 1883, the Volunteers purchased the former home of the Palmetto Fire Engine Company on Vanderhorst Street and moved their headquarters to that location. Unfortunately, this building was of masonry construction and was severely damaged in the earthquake of 1886.[368]

After the earthquake, plans were made to construct a new wooden structure to replace the masonry building. In order to raise funds for this project a Military Fair was held at Hibernian Hall during the week after Easter in 1888 at which about $4,300.00 was raised. Construction of the company's new armory began shortly thereafter and the building was formally opened in June 1889.[369] A description of the new home of the Irish Volunteers appeared in the June 19, 1889 *News and Courier*:

> The new armory of the Volunteers is a paragon of beauty, comfort and adaptability. It is two stories high, and is one of the handsomest structures of its kind in Charleston. Looking at it from the exterior, there are many striking features to be observed. The building is painted in a light drab color with dark drab trimmings and the entire prospective is set off in a very pleasing and attractive manner. The style of the architecture is Castellated Gothic. On the southeast corner of the building is a two-way tower which adds a great deal to the general appearance. Over the tower will float the new flag of the Volunteers, which will be attached to a flag staff twenty-eight feet in height. The flag, which is now being made, will be green in color with a white harp in the centre, and the name "Irish Volunteers" in white enamalled with a white border. On the reverse side will be the United States colors with forty-two stars. It will be one of the handsomest flags in the city.
> In the middle of the battlements a very pretty and appropriate design has been placed. It is a harp resting on a bed of shamrocks with the words "Erin Go Brah" and "Irish Volunteers" in gold letters just underneath it. On either side of the emblem are the dates "A.D. 1794" and "A.D. 1889". This was made to order in Salem Ohio by Beuv and Mullins. Directly under the Southwest portion of the armory is a large five point star in gold. Almost opposite this and immediately under the center window, is a handsome striking proper ornament. On a

background of green is placed a beautiful Palmetto tree with an Irish harp and American shield leaning on either side.[370]

The Irish Volunteers remained part of the Fourth Brigade until 1901, when the brigade was dissolved. The old militia companies either went out of existence or were incorporated into the South Carolina National Guard. The Irish Volunteers became Company "C" of the Third Regiment and subsequently of the Second Regiment of the South Carolina National Guard.[371]

In 1916, the Mexican bandit Pancho Villa incurred the wrath of the United States government by conducting raids along the Mexican border. United States troops under General Pershing crossed the border in pursuit of Villa, causing heightened tensions between the two countries. In order to prevent further raids by Villa, and to prepare for possible hostilities with Mexico, President Woodrow Wilson called up National Guard units from around the country for federal service along the Mexican border. The Second Regiment of the National Guard of South Carolina, which included the Irish Volunteers, was one of these units.[372]

The Second Regiment departed Charleston on June 24, 1916 for the state mobilization camp at Styx in Lexington County, South Carolina. The Irish Volunteers, always anxious, were the first to arrive at Marion Square, the point of assembly. At Styx the Second Regiment was mustered into federal service and in early August 1916 was ordered to El Paso, Texas.[373]

The Second Regiment remained in El Paso for the next seven months, always ready for action. Although it was rumored several times that the Guardsmen would be sent into Mexico to assist the regular troops, the orders never came. Finally, in early 1917 the tensions along the border had subsided to the point that the National Guard troops could be withdrawn. The Second Regiment of the South Carolina National Guard returned to Charleston on March 20, 1917 to a hero's welcome. Before being mustered out of federal service, each Guardsman was presented with a bronze medal by the mayor of Charleston in appreciation for his service.[374]

In 1918, when the United States entered World War One, the Irish Volunteers marched off to war for the last time. The company became a part of the 105th Ammunition Train and was sent to France for service. While in France, one member of the company was severely wounded and another died of disease, but fortunately no other casualties were sustained. The Volunteers returned home in March 1919. After World

War One the company did not resume its military role, but acted as a social organization until the late 1920s.[375]

THE MEAGHER GUARD

LATER KNOWN AS THE EMERALD LIGHT INFANTRY

ORGANIZED 1853

The Meagher Guard (also referred to as the Meagher Guards) was an Irish militia company organized shortly after the visit of Irish patriot Thomas Francis Meagher to Charleston in 1853. During his stay, Meagher was invited to visit the hall of the Society of United Irishmen at 90 Meeting Street. On March 23, 1853, this society formed a new militia company at the same address and named it the Meagher Rifle Guard in Meagher's honor. Eventually, the word "Rifle" was dropped and the company became known as the Meagher Guard.[376]

In December 1853, the Meagher Guard, the Washington Light Infantry, the German Rifleman, and the Moultrie Guards were organized into a rifle battalion as part of the Fourth Brigade of the South Carolina Militia. Thereafter, this battalion was combined with several other companies to form what became known as the Rifle Regiment of the Fourth Brigade of militia. The Meagher Guard remained a part of the Rifle Regiment until the Civil War.[377]

The following is a partial list of the officers of the Meagher Guard prior to the Civil War:

1854: George Sergent, Captain
1855: George Sergent, Captain; Edward Daly, 1st Lt.; M. P. Parker, 2nd Lt.
1856: George Sergent, Captain
1858: Edward Daly, Captain
1859: Edward Daly, Captain; J. Lowndes, 1st Lt.; M. P. Parker, 2nd Lt.; W. Rennett, Ensign[378]

As war clouds began to gather in the late 1850s, the Meagher Guard elected Edward McCrady, Jr. as its new Captain. An attorney in civilian life, McCrady had also been a Major in the Rifle Regiment and was well qualified for his new command. Under Captain McCrady's leadership, the Meagher Guard drilled with the other companies of the Rifle Regiment in preparing for the expected clash with Union forces. At the drill held on December 20, 1860, the Ordinance of Secession was read to the men of the regiment and thereafter they were sent home to await orders. The members of the Meagher Guard did not have to wait long.[379]

On December 26, 1860, Major Robert Anderson moved his entire garrison from Fort Moultrie to Fort Sumter. Governor Pickens demanded that they return, but Anderson refused. On December 27, the Meagher Guard, Washington Light Infantry, and Carolina Light Infantry were ordered to assemble at Citadel Square for military action. By the time the troops had assembled, the word of the occupation of Fort Sumter by the Union troops had spread throughout the city, and it was assumed that their mission was to storm Fort Sumter. Fortunately, it was not.[380]

The troops marched from Citadel Square to the waterfront, followed by tearful wives and children, where they boarded the steamer *Nina*. After leaving the dock, the steamer, instead of heading for Fort Sumter, made a straight line for Castle Pinckney. Upon arriving at the island, the Meagher Guard and their comrades ran up the dock, expecting heavy resistance. Fortunately, Castle Pinckney's garrison consisted only of Lieutenant Mede, an Ordinance Sergeant, and his family and a few workers. After a few minutes, Castle Pinckney was secured, and the state flag, which had to be borrowed from the *Nina* because the troops had not thought to bring one, was flying over the fort. The Meagher Guard had participated in the first aggressive act of the Civil War.[381]

The Meagher Guard remained at Castle Pinckney until after the repulse of the *Star of the West* on January 9, 1861, and while there, Bishop P. N. Lynch, the Catholic Bishop of Charleston, celebrated mass for the company. Thereafter, the company was stationed at Morris Island and Secessionville, where it assisted in the preparation of the city's defenses for the expected clash with the forces of the United States of America. At the time that clash came, the company was stationed at the eastern end of Sullivans Island and, although not engaged, its members were treated to a great view of the battle of Fort Sumter.[382]

On April 20, 1861, shortly after the fall of Fort Sumter, the Meagher Guard unanimously volunteered to go to Virginia to help defend that state against the Union threat. Their services were not accepted, and they were released from temporary state service. It was around this same time that the company found out that Thomas Francis Meagher had pledged his allegiance to the North.[383]

The company met on May 6, 1861 to discuss the Meagher situation. The next day the following notice was published in the *Charleston Mercury*:

At a meeting of the Meagher Guards, held at the Military Hall on the evening of the 6th inst., the following preamble and resolutions were unanimously adopted:

The report of the committee appointed to inquire into the truth of the rumor that THOMAS FRANCIS MEAGHER, Esq. (in honor of whose patriotic efforts for the liberation of Ireland this company was named) had joined the crusade against the Southern States, having been heard—

1.*Resolved*, That the same be confirmed.

And, whereas, from the said Report, it appears to be true that Mr. Meagher has been carried away by the fanaticism of the North, and has enrolled himself in the ranks of our enemies, taking arms against us in this most unholy war, insupport of usurpation and oppression, thus proving himself recreant to the sacred principles of liberty, of which he was hitherto an uncompromising an advocate; therefore,

2.*Resolved*, That, remembering the services of Mr. MEAGHER in the cause of freedom in Ireland, this Company have learned with infinite disappointment and regret that he too, should have joined the oppressors of this their adopted land.

3. *Resolved*, That under these circumstances this company can no longer, consistently with its position and dignity, bear his name, and that the same be and hereby is repudiated by them.

4.*Resolved*, That the name of THOMAS FRANCIS MEAGHER be erased from the roll of the honorary members of this Company.

5. *Resolved*, That it be referred to a Committee to suggest some suitable name by which this Company shall hereafter be known.

6. *Resolved*, That a copy of these preamble and resolutions be published in the daily papers of this city, and in the New York, *Day Book*.[384]

It did not take the company long to act. On May 10, 1861, the following notice appeared in the *Charleston Mercury*:

CHANGE OF NAME.—The fine infantry corps hitherto so well known as the "Meagher Guard," have, by a unanimous vote, changed their name to the "Emerald Light Infantry."[385]

After changing its name, the company continued under the command of Captain Edward McCrady, Jr., until early June 1861. Then on June 7th, Captain McCrady, along with all of the company's other officers and a good many of the enlisted men, joined a new Irish company being formed for service in Virginia. This new company took the name the *Irish Volunteers for the War*.[386]

The members of the Emerald Light Infantry who did not join the Irish Volunteers for the War continued to operate their company as a part of the Fourth Brigade of the South Carolina Militia. This company, like the Irish Volunteers, served along the South Carolina coast during the remainder of 1861. M. E. Rooney served as Captain during part of this time and P. E. Keating and P. Malone served as Lieutenants. The company's recruiting office was located at 43 State Street. The recruiting committee consisted of Philip Malone, Patrick Walsh, M. B. Reagan, James Ronan, and Horace McCartney.[387]

In early February 1862 the Emerald Light Infantry, which was then commanded by Captain W. A. Courtnay, led the effort to form an Irish volunteer battalion for Confederate service from Charleston's Irish companies. On February 22, 1862, the Emerald Light Infantry was combined with the Jasper Greens to form a company for Confederate service known as Company No. 6. The following April, Company No. 6 was merged into a new company known as the Montgomery Guard.[388]

THE MONTGOMERY GUARD

ORGANIZED CIRCA 1853

The Montgomery Guard (also referred to as the Montgomery Guards) was an Irish company formed in 1853 as part of the Fourth Brigade of the South Carolina Militia and held most of its drills at Military Hall on Wentworth Street. The company was named for Richard Montgomery, an Irish hero of the American Revolution. Montgomery, born in Swords, County Dublin, Ireland, was appointed a Brigadier General by the Continental Congress. He was killed while leading an assault on Quebec on December 31, 1775.[389]

Like the city's other Irish companies, the Montgomery Guard led a pretty quiet existence in the 1850s. The company's main function during this period was to drill and participate in the annual Saint Patrick's Day parade. The Captain during this time was James Conner, an able lawyer who also served as the United States Attorney. The officers serving with Captain Conner were P. F. Coogan, 1st Lieutenant; T. E. Ryan, 2nd Lieutenant; and W. J. Forsythe, 3rd Lieutenant.[390]

When South Carolina seceded from the Union, the Montgomery Guard was sent to Morris Island. Captain Conner resigned his position as United States Attorney and took command of the company on Morris Island. However, in January 1861 Conner left the Guard to accept an appointment as a member of the Secession Convention. After the Confederacy was formed, he did not rejoin the company but went to Virginia with the Hampton Legion and eventually became a Confederate general.[391]

At the time the Montgomery Guard was released from temporary state service after the fall of Fort Sumter, the governor was planning to send the Fourth Brigade's Rifle Regiment to assist in the defense of Virginia. The Montgomery Guard began organizing a company to go with the Rifle Regiment to Virginia, but the governor cancelled his plans. The company served with the state militia for the remainder of 1861.[392]

Apparently, replacing a strong leader like Captain James Conner was not an easy task, and the command of the Montgomery Guard changed hands several times during the summer and fall of 1861. The company was without a captain during part of this time, and the command fell to Lieutenant J. A. Armstrong. Finally, in September 1861, Captain R. J. Brownfield was elected Captain and led the Guard until February 1862. Benjamin Garrety was elected Lieutenant at the same time.[393]

In February 1862, the Montgomery Guard joined with the city's other Irish companies in an effort to form an Irish Battalion for Confederate service. Unfortunately, little is known about the remainder of the company's wartime service. The few details that are known are set out in the section "The Effort to Raise a an Irish Volunteer Battalion in Charleston for Confederate Service in 1862."[394]

After the war, the company was reorganized on February 21, 1874 under the name Montgomery Guards with A. G. Magrath Jr. as its captain. Unlike many of the rifle clubs being formed around the time, the Montgomery Guards adopted a military uniform and was the first company to parade in full uniform in Charleston after the war. The postwar uniform was described as follows: cadet gray swallow-tail coat with green cuffs, collar, and chest braid; sky-blue pants with a white stripe; white cross-belts; green epaulettes with white fringe; and regulation gray hat with shamrock and harp in front, surmounted by a green and white plume.[395]

The reorganized Montgomery Guards also carried a beautiful flag made for the company by women admirers. The flag was presented to the company at Hibernian Hall on November 18, 1874 by General James Conner and was described as follows:

> The flag is of green and white silk, edged with heavy bullion fringe. On the green side is painted the fall of Montgomery at Quebec, underneath are the words 'Death of Gen. Montgomery.' On the white side are an Irish harp and sunburst. Upon the top scroll is the name of the company and underneath the date of the organization.[396]

The post-war company initially established its headquarters at Byrnes Hall on King Street, which was also used by the Irish Rifle Club. It was from this hall that the members of the company fired their last shots in anger. On the night of September 7, 1876, during Wade Hampton's heated campaign for governor, several men fired into this hall and the Montgomery Guards returned their fire from the windows. One of the attackers was wounded and the others fled.[397]

After Hampton was elected governor, the Montgomery Guards rejoined the Fourth Brigade of the South Carolina Militia and moved their headquarters to Military Hall. Then in the 1880s the company's headquarters was moved to the southeast corner of King and Calhoun Streets where it remained until the company went out of existence. By 1882 the company's membership had reached seventy men, and it was incorporated by act of the Legislature under the name Montgomery Guards. The incorporators were James F. Redding, M. D. Maguire, J. B. Comar, J. J. Carey, J. Dixon and J. J. Delaney.[398]

The Montgomery Guards enjoyed a good parade and marched in Charleston's St. Patrick's Day Parade each year. The company also participated in the dedication of the Hibernian Park in 1876, and of the Irish Volunteers' monument at St. Lawrence Cemetery in 1878. In 1886 the Guards participated in the dedication of the new St Patrick's Church. As part of the ceremony a list of the company's members was placed in the church's cornerstone. The company was last listed in the Charleston City Directory in 1898 and apparently went out of existence shortly thereafter.[399]

THE EMMETT VOLUNTEERS

ORGANIZED CIRCA 1854

The Emmett Volunteers (also referred to as the Emmet Volunteers) first appeared in the Charleston newspapers in 1854. The company used

90 Meeting Street as its armory. Officers of the company for 1855 were Thomas Devine, Captain; Edward C. Anderson, First Lieutenant; P. Grace, Second Lieutenant and B. Foley, Third Lieutenant.[400]

In 1860, when the State of South Carolina seceded from the Union, the company was commanded by Captain P. Grace and served with the state militia during the siege of Fort Sumter. The Emmett Volunteers is not listed as one of the companies that joined the Confederate Army, and its members probably joined other Confederate units.[401]

THE MITCHEL GUARD

ORGANIZED CIRCA 1858

The short lived Mitchel Guard, probably named for Irish Patriot John Mitchel, participated in Charleston's 1858 St. Patrick's Day Parade. The company did not take part in St. Patrick's Day festivities the following year, or any year thereafter.[402]

THE HIBERNIAN GUARD

ORGANIZED 1860

The Hibernian Guard was organized on December 31, 1860 at Hibernian Hall. It was made up of the honorary and alarm members of the Irish Volunteers, many of whom had served with the company in the Florida Campaign of 1836 against the Seminole Indians. The Guard was formed for special city service, apparently as a back-up to the regular militia, and had seventy members. The officers of the Hibernian Guard at the time of its organization were Thomas Ryan, Captain; John Dougherty, First Lieutenant; John F. O'Neill, Second Lieutenant; John Burns, Third Lieutenant; Michael Gannon, First Sergeant; T. L. Quackenbush, Second Sergeant; Patrick Hogan, Third Sergeant; Edward Jordan, Fourth Sergeant; John O'Mara, Fifth Sergeant; Patrick Doogan, First Corporal; T. F. McManus, Second Corporal; Patrick O'Donnell, Third Corporal; and Edward Collins, Fourth Corporal. This company remained active until at least April 1862, and continued to hold its meetings at Hibernian Hall during that time.[403]

THE IRISH VOLUNTEERS FOR THE WAR

ORGANIZED 1861

After the fall of Fort Sumter, the officers of the Meagher Guard, Edward McCrady, Jr., James Armstrong, Jr., and M. P. Parker, began organizing a company for service with the Confederate Army in Virginia. On June 7, 1861, a meeting was held at the Hibernian Hall for this purpose. In order to encourage men to sign up, it was announced that the Hibernian Society and St. Patrick's Benevolent Society would help take care of the families of those who joined the company. The rolls were quickly filled.[404]

The company was mustered into Confederate service in June 1861, and immediately went into training at "Camp Erin," which was located in the Hampstead section of Charleston. The new company took the name the *Irish Volunteers for the War*. This Irish company was the first company from South Carolina that enlisted in the Confederate service for the whole war no matter what the duration.[405]

While at Camp Erin, the Irish Volunteers for the War attempted to raise an Irish Battalion for service in Virginia. As proposed, this battalion would include three Irish companies commanded by Edward McCrady, Jr. A second Irish company did begin recruitment, but ultimately this effort was unsuccessful.[406]

In July 1861, the company was sent to Richmond where it chose to join the First Regiment of South Carolina Volunteers, which was commanded by Colonel Maxcy Gregg. The Irish Volunteers for the War became Company "K" of the First Regiment of South Carolina Volunteers and was also selected the regiment's color company. The Irish Volunteers for the War retained its position as regimental color company for the entire war.[407]

On September 25, 1861, the Volunteers were camped at Suffolk, Virginia when they received a visit from James Armstrong, the father of James Armstrong, Jr., an officer of the company. The purpose of Mr. Armstrong's visit to Virginia was to bring a flag made for the company by the Sisters of Mercy of Charleston.[408] The flag was officially presented by Colonel Maxcy Gregg to Captain Edward McCrady, who upon receiving it stated on behalf of the company:

> I know, sir, it is somewhat usual upon like occasions to make pledges as to our conduct upon the battlefield, but for myself and these brave men for whom I speak, I have no words of boastfulness to utter. Such may do for the holiday orator, but would scarcely become soldiers in the presence of their enemies. We prefer, sir, to await the hour of trial, and your report of our conduct, hoping that in that hour you will not find us wanting, nor any stains disgrace these beautiful folds.[409]

The flag was described in the Charleston newspapers as:

...made of rich white and green silk, with silver fringe, and eleven silver stars on each side. In the middle, on one side, is a Cross, with an Irish harp encircled by a wreath of oak leaves, palmetto and shamrock combined. Over the Cross is the inscription *"In hoc signo Vinces"* (by this sign you shall conquer) On the reverse is a very handsomely executed painting of a palmetto tree with the rattlesnake coiled round its trunk—the whole presenting a very natural and life-like appearance. Around the palmetto is also a wreath of oak leaves, palmetto and shamrock.
Underneath is the inscription, **"Liberty or Death."** [410]

The company was still camped in Suffolk, Virginia in November 1861 when some of its members read reports in the *Charleston Daily Courier* to the effect that some English subjects in Charleston were seeking the protection of the English government to avoid Confederate service. Sergeant Alexander O'Donnell, a member of the company, immediately wrote the following letter to his fellow Irishmen in Charleston imploring them not to follow this practice:

Fellow Countrymen of Charleston:
    In looking over the Charleston Courier of the 26th ultimo, I observed it noticed that a great many English Subjects there accepting the protection of the British Consul with the view of evading to become subject to military service for the defense of the state, although that they have resided there for profit, speculation, and extortion which remark is very appropriately applied to any who would have recourse to this means to avoid bearing arms in view of the present state of affairs.
    As we unfortunately come under the heading of British subjects I hope there are none of us so forgetful of our relations with England as to accept the protection of their government after forcing us to lose sight of the cherished hearth stones of our forefathers by the galling hand of oppression and tyranny. Can any of us for a moment accept the apparent friendly grasp whilst the wounds which she has inflicted are still bleeding and will continue to do so whilst life will exist.
    Shame on the Irishman who will be so degraded. Would

Robert Emmett, would Wolf Tone, would Lord Edward Fitzgerald!

You shades of the dead, I hope you are now looking down approvingly on those who are fighting for those rights and liberties for which you sacrificed your lives on the altar of your doomed country, striving to secure to it a position amongst the nations of the earth.

They failed in their undertaking, and cheerfully died martyrs for their Country's Cause, in preference of living a life of thralldom and slavery. And in every sense of the word, the Southern people are now engaged in the same cause, but more fortunately in shaking off that form of government that was disgustful to them. If we are heedful to the teachings of the idols of our country why not take up the cause of freedom and justice and proclaim to the world by our acts that we are alive to the privileges and blessings of a free people.

I am a member of the Irish Volunteers from Charleston in Col. Greggs Regiment, now stationed at Camp Huger, near Suffolk, Va. When our company was commenced being raised I took my stand in an address to my Countrymen to rally to the standard of the Southern Cause, to identify themselves with the infant Republic, and aid in propping it up by our arms, until it would be able to stand on its own bases. To occupy a position on the grand program that was about being enacted, thereby securing to our future generations an envious legacy.

Let me say to you, show no dereliction on your part, but act with propmtitude and decision. Assist in hurling into the Sea the imbecile fanatics who yet persevere in attempting to coerce these great, glorious and free people. [411]

In December 1861, Colonel Maxcy Gregg was promoted to brigadier general and sent to South Carolina where he formed an infantry brigade known as Gregg's Brigade. This brigade was ordered to Virginia in the spring of 1862 and in June of that year the First Regiment of South Carolina Volunteers became a part of it. Gregg's Brigade in turn became a part of A. P. Hill's Light Division.[412] This division first saw action at the Battle of Cold Harbor or Gaines Mill on June 27, 1862. The following account of the battle was written by the same Sergeant O'Donnell mentioned above and appeared in the *Charleston Daily Courier* on July 9, 1862:

THE IRISH VOLUNTEERS IN THE GREAT BATTLE

Sergeant O'Donnell, of the Irish Volunteers, First Regiment South Carolina Volunteers in a private letter to his brother in this city, gives the following interesting description of what he witnessed on the battlefield:

Our army was put in motion on the evening of the 26th, marched across the Chickahominy and drove the enemy from their strong positions, with comparatively little loss of life. The enemy continued to fall back each successive day, making at times a most determined stand, but each time driven back with great slaughter. At one place, where General Ripley's brigade charged a battery, we were obliged to march down a slope of land and across a swamp of about one hundred yards. Here the road gave a sudden turn to the right, skirting the edge of the swamp, and in front of which was the enemy's breastworks. As Ripley's brigade pushed over the ridge in a gallant charge, a deadly fire from the enemy's pits opened upon them, in addition destructive discharges of grape and canister poured in upon them from the cannon mounted on the enemy's breastworks. Here, indeed, was a harrowing scene. The dead and dying were literally piled upon each other. The next morning General Gregg, by a flank movement, captured the battery, with a very slight loss.

We then followed in pursuit and came up with the enemy at Garnett's farm. At this place McClellan with four of his Generals were entrenched and fortified with about thirty thousand men. I heard that he boasted of capturing our entire army, should we be so bold to attack him in this strong position.

We did make the attack, and for a time the fortunes of the day seemed doubtful, with a prospect of McClellan's prophecy being fulfilled. Our columns had given way to the overwhelming numbers against us, and McClellan had nearly succeeded in flanking us, when Stonewall Jackson reinforced us with three brigades, and charged on the enemy. This took them by surprise. For an hour and a half the discharge of musketry was incessant and beyond description. At least twenty-five thousand men were loading and firing at the same moment.

The enemy again evacuated their positions with immense

loss of life, besides their wounded and many taken prisoners. They kept up their retreat during the night, but found to their astonishment Stonewall had outrun them, and was ten miles ahead, hemming them in completely. Our brigade (Gregg's) made a charge on the position and deployed through a swamp of underbrushes amid a shower of deadly missiles, belched from the mouths of some twenty-six cannon. We were on the edge of a copse preparing to rally and charge, when the Yankees came thundering down a slope in thousands. Our company was the first to form, the others coming up very promptly. It was here that Sergeant Taylor, color bearer of our regiment, was shot down.

Private Dominick Spellman of our Company seized the colors, wound them around his body and continued to fight with his musket, dropping one of the enemy at every shot. This bravery won for him the highest admiration from the Colonel and the men of the regiment. It was in this charge that John Rourk, Thomas Gaskins and Thomas Haggerty were killed. They met their deaths gloriously and nobly defending the sacred trust reposed in their keeping, the emblem of our adopted State. They never quailed in the hour of danger under the terrific tornado of shell, grape canister and musketry. These were the only martyrs in our company. Two more were severely and seven slightly wounded.

Capt. Boag, a brave gallant officer, the life and soul of his Company, the Richardson Guards, was also killed in the charge. Lieut. Robt Rhett of the same company was also severely wounded and died on the field.
A. O'Donnell [413]

After the Battle of Gaines Mill, General A. P. Hill's Light Division became a part of the command of General Thomas "Stonewall" Jackson. As part of this command, the Irish Volunteers for the War participated in the great Confederate victory at the Second Battle of Manassas from August 28 to 30, 1862.[414]

On the first day of the battle, Edward McCrady, Jr., who had been promoted to Major, led the First Regiment of South Carolina Volunteers across the unfinished railroad cut of the Independent Railroad from Gainesville to Alexandria in an attempt to dislodge the enemy in the woods on the other side. The enemy proved to be too strong, and much confusion ensued among the South Carolinians in the thick woods. The situation was stabilized due in large part to the efforts of Captain M. P. Parker, Lieutenant James Armstrong, Jr., and Color Sergeant Dominick Spellman of the Irish Volunteers for the War who rallied the troops around the regimental colors. Thereafter, McCrady's troops withdrew in good order and joined their comrades of the Light Division in positions along the railroad cut.[415]

During the remainder of the day, soldiers of the Union Army assaulted the defensive line of the Light Division on at least six distinct occasions, but were unable to break it. The fighting was so intense that Gregg's South Carolina troops began to run out of ammunition and General Hill inquired of General Gregg as to whether he could hold.[416] General Gregg responded, "Tell General Hill that my ammunition is exhausted, but that I will hold my position with the bayonet."[417] The federals advanced again and again, finally pushing the South Carolinians back to a ridge. At this point General Gregg attempted to rally his troops by drawing his sword and shouting, "Let us die here, my men, let us die here." [418] Fortunately, fresh reinforcements arrived at this same time and the Union forces were driven back.[419]

The following day the company's Irish-born Color Sergeant, Patrick Dominick Spellman, who had won the admiration of his comrades for his bravery and marksmanship at Cold Harbor, again demonstrated these qualities. The incident was related a number of years later by Edward McCrady, Jr., Spellman's commander during the battle:

> ...in the evening, as the regiment was lying down under a heavy fire of sharpshooters, who had possession of a wood in our front, Spellman caught a glimpse of some of the enemy's sharpshooters in the bushes, and turning over the colors to the corporal next him and seizing his musket he quietly walked out in front of the line and deliberately taking aim he fired, and turning to his regiment, called out, "I dropped that one," and, to the astonishment of his comrades, proceeded to reload his musket, standing in full view of the sharpshooters, who soon turned their entire attention to him. Again he fired, and again called that he had hit his man. The men called to him to return, but quietly he reloaded his piece and took it up to fire; but the sharpshooters on the other side, having recovered their surprise, with one ball shot away the butt of the musket from his face, and with another brought him down. [420]

Fortunately, Sergeant Spellman's wound, although serious, was not mortal. He returned to the company later in the war and was able to carry the colors on other battlefields. Spellman was seriously wounded at Jericho Ford on May 23, 1864 and again when the Union Army broke the lines at Petersburg. He returned to Charleston after the war where he died on January 4, 1883.[421]

At the Battle of Second Manassas, Daniel Coffee of the Irish Volunteers for the War was killed and Daniel Calaghan received wounds from which he later died. Among the wounded (in addition to Sergeant Spellman) were Captain Michael P. Parker, Lieutenant Thomas McCrady, Richard Hartley, John Kenefick, John Kiley, and Michael O'Neill. Major Edward McCrady, Jr. also received a serious wound to the head which caused him to miss the Maryland Campaign.[422]

On September 15, 1862, forces under Stonewall Jackson captured the Union garrison at Harper's Ferry, West Virginia as a preliminary step in Lee's first invasion of the North. A. P. Hill's Light Division was left to mop up while Jackson took the remainder of his force into Maryland to join General Lee, who was about to engage the Union Army in what has become known as the Battle of Sharpsburg, or Antietam. Prior to commencing the battle, General Lee sent for Hill's Division. The Light Division arrived on the field of battle just in time to save the Army of Northern Virginia by slamming into the Union divisions which were about to cut off the Confederate Army from its line of retreat to the Potomac River. At Sharpsburg, Peter McKeown and James Reilly of the Irish Volunteers for the War were killed, and Captain Michael P. Parker, James Brown, Michael Duffy, Michael Feeney, Patrick Holloran, and Lieutenant James Armstrong, Jr. were wounded.[423]

The next major engagement in which the company participated was the Battle of Fredericksburg in December 1862. In this battle, the beloved General Maxcy Gregg was mortally wounded. The Irish Volunteers also lost Joseph Donnelly, Michael Nowles, James Kelly, and Stephen O'Connell, killed. Several members of the company were wounded including: Michael Conway, Edmund Dillon, Michael Farrell, Nicholas J. Kane, Patrick Kelly, Michael Mahoney, Francis Manion, Michael Sullivan and Lieutenants James Armstrong, Jr. and Thomas McCrady.[424]

Edward McCrady, Jr., promoted to Lieutenant Colonel after Second Manassas, rejoined the First Regiment of South Carolina Volunteers when it returned from Maryland. He participated in the Battle of Fredericksburg where he bravely helped repulse the Union attack in which General Gregg was mortally wounded. The following month Lieutenant Colonel McCrady was injured by a falling tree, and was lost to the regiment for most of the remainder of the war. After the war, he returned to Charleston where he practiced law and served in the state legislature. Edward McCrady, Jr. died in Charleston on November 1, 1903.[425]

After the death of General Gregg, the command of his brigade was given to General Samuel McGowan and thereafter the brigade was known as McGowan's Brigade. On May 1-4, 1863, McGowan's Brigade fought in the Battle of Chancellorsville. It was during this battle that Stonewall Jackson was mistakenly shot and mortally wounded by his own Confederate forces. The Irish Volunteers for the War also lost John Casey and Joseph McNabb, killed. James McDonald and John Sweeney were wounded.[426]

On July 1, 1863, the Irish Volunteers for the War found themselves in a battle which would become the high-water mark of the Confederacy, the Battle of Gettysburg. On the first day of this battle, the company, along with the other members of A. P. Hill's Confederates, engaged the Union troops before Gettysburg, and after stiff resistance dislodged them from the town. During this engagement the color bearer was shot down and Captain James Armstrong, Jr. picked up the colors and charged with them into the town at the front of the regiment. The flag of the First South Carolina Regiment was the first Confederate banner raised in Gettysburg. Captain Armstrong was again wounded during this battle. Richard Mathews and William Fox of the company were also wounded.[427]

In May 1864, General Ulysses S. Grant began his campaign of attrition against the Confederate Army, which would ultimately bring the war to an end. During this campaign, the Irish Volunteers for the War first participated in the Battle of Wilderness, at which three members of the company were killed: G. W. Allen, L. B. Gallman and George Crabtree. In this battle Joseph Dougherty, John Gorham, Michael Sullivan, Michael Reilly and Michael McGuire were wounded.[428]

Next came the Battle of Spotsylvania Court House where McGowan's Brigade took part in the savage fight at the salient in the Confederate line. The company lost Nicholas Cain, D. P. Cameron and Michael Cunningham, killed. William Spoon and James Armstrong, Jr. were wounded. Then followed the battles of the Second Cold Harbor, Riddle's Shops, Boydton Plank Road, Weldon Railroad, Ream's Station, White Oak Road and Sutherland Station.[429]

It was at Sutherland Station that Captain James Armstrong,

Jr. received his fifth combat wound of the war. Armstrong, born in Philadelphia of Irish parents and educated in Ireland, was one of the Volunteers' original officers and served in most of their engagements. The wound sustained at Sutherland Station left him with a shattered leg, but it was not fatal. Armstrong returned to Charleston after the war, where he served as Harbor Master and as a member of the staff of the *News and Courier*. He was also the president of the Hibernian Society from 1915 to 1917. Captain Armstrong died in Charleston on August 14, 1930 at the age of eighty-seven.[430] In his obituary it was stated that on a visit to Charleston after the war, Robert E. Lee referred to Armstrong as a soldier "as brave as any in my army."[431]

The end for the Irish Volunteers for the War came at Appomattox Courthouse on April 9, 1865. The company had entered its first battle with over a hundred men. At least thirty are known to have been killed in the war, and many more died of disease or were captured. There were only seven members of the company left at the final surrender. The following four names have survived: Private Finnessee, detailed blacksmith in the brigade; Private M. Maguire, detailed ambulance driver; T. G. Martin; and C. M. Shaw.[432]

THE SARSFIELD LIGHT INFANTRY

ORGANIZED 1861

The Sarsfield Light Infantry was an Irish company which was evidently organized in the patriotic fervor which followed the fall of Fort Sumter, since its drill notices first appeared in Charleston newspapers in the summer of 1861. The company was apparently named for Patrick Sarsfield, who fought for King James against William of Orange at the Battle of the Boyne in 1690. After James was defeated, Sarsfield went to France where he served with the famous Irish Brigade of King Louis XIV. He was mortally wounded at the Battle of Landen in 1693.[433]

The Sarsfield Light Infantry was a part of the First Regiment of Rifles of the Forth Brigade of Militia, and met at Hibernian Hall. The captain of the company was W. N. Heyward, and its recruiting office was located at 20 State Street. The recruiting committee consisted of John Graham, Patrick Carroll, John J. Furlong, Timothy McCarthy and James Moran. In February 1862 the Sarsfield Light Infantry joined with Charleston's other Irish companies in an effort to form an Irish Battalion for Confederate service. In April 1862, this company was merged into a new company known as the Montgomery Guard.[434]

THE JASPER GREENS

ORGANIZED 1861

The Jasper Greens was an Irish company commanded by Captain M. P. O'Connor, and its meeting notices first appeared in Charleston newspapers in the fall of 1861. The company was probably formed around that time as the City of Charleston *Yearbook of 1883* does not list it as one of the city's militia companies serving during the siege of Fort Sumter. The Jasper Greens were probably named for Sergeant William Jasper, who rescued the flag at the Battle of Fort Moultrie during the Revolutionary War. After its formation, the company was assigned to the 17th Regiment of Infantry of the Fourth Brigade of the South Carolina Militia and served in that regiment during the fall of 1861. The company was incorporated by act of the South Carolina Legislature in December 1861.[435]

In early 1862, when it became clear that Charleston's militia companies would be required to enter Confederate service, the Jasper Greens began recruiting men for an artillery company. However, when it was suggested that an Irish Volunteer Battalion should be formed out of the city's Irish companies, the Jasper Greens joined this effort. The company's recruiting office during this effort was located at 54 Market Street, and its recruiting committee consisted of Jos. Harbeson, Jas. Torlay, F. Connor, Jas. Walsh and Jno. May. On February 22, 1862, the Jasper Greens combined with the Emerald Light Infantry to form a company for Confederate service known simply as Company No 6. This company was in turn merged into a new company known as the Montgomery Guard, in April 1862.[436]

THE IRISH RESERVE COMPANY

ORGANIZED 1861

The Irish Reserve Company was formed in Charleston at the Hibernian Hall on September 25, 1861. The officers and non-commissioned officers were John Doherty, Captain; John F. O'Neill, First Lieutenant; B. O'Neill, Second Lieutenant; H. P. Feugas, Third Lieutenant; Lors Fore, Orderly Sergeant; Patrick Hogan, Second Sergeant; E. H. Marjenhoff, Third Sergeant; T. F McManus, Forth Sergeant; Joseph Samson, First Corporal; Samuel Morrison, Second Corporal; W M. Doran, Third Corporal; John Doherty, Fourth Corporal; and Patrick Mulkai, Secretary.[437]

THE EFFORT TO RAISE AN IRISH VOLUNTEER BATTALION IN CHARLESTON FOR CONFEDERATE SERVICE IN 1862

After the fall of Fort Sumter, the South Carolina coast was fairly quiet for most of the remainder of 1861. However, this changed in November of that year when the Union fleet attacked the Confederate forts in Port Royal Sound and seized Hilton Head Island.[438] An attack on Charleston was eminent, and the fighting blood of many Irish Charlestonians was aroused. Over the next several months, some of these made efforts to encourage their countrymen to take up arms in defense of their adopted homeland. One such effort was made by Thomas Ryan, who placed the following in the *Charleston Daily Courier*:

> THE UNDERSIGNED PROPOSES TO RAISE A company of IRISH REBELS to enter Confederate Service for the defense of South Carolina. The name Rebel he prefers, because his ancestors have been so called for more than six hundred years. The fanatical Puritans have landed on our soil. Oliver Cromwell lives again in the person of Abraham Lincoln. Should they succeed in capturing Charleston the butcheries of Drogheda will be repeated in our streets. Come forward then, my countrymen, and unite with the Cavalier and the Huguenot to expel them from our beloved State, and insure to ourselves and posterity peace and happiness for ages to come. A full suit of Uniform, Clothes, Shoes and Hat will be furnished each man and rations when thirty have signed their names. Able bodied men, without regard to age, will be received. Apply at 12 State street.
> THOMAS RYAN[439]

State officials were equally alarmed at the presence of Union troops in South Carolina and passed legislation requiring most of the state's adult male population to serve in the armed forces of the Confederacy. The City of Charleston's militia companies of the Fourth Brigade, which had been protecting the city, were initially allowed to remain in state service, but this changed in February 1862. The members of these companies were given the choice of immediately enrolling in organizations of their choice consisting of at least 68 men for Confederate service, or of being involuntarily assigned to companies.[440]

Many of Charleston's Irish citizens felt that the best way for Charleston's Irish companies to enter Confederate service would be as an Irish Volunteer Battalion formed from the city's five Irish militia companies: the Irish Volunteers, the Montgomery Guard, the Emerald Light Infantry, the Jasper Greens and the Sarsfield Light Infantry. Letters to the editor supporting this idea appeared in both the *Charleston Daily Courier* and the *Charleston Mercury* in early February 1862. One even went so far as to suggest that the Irish Volunteer Battalion would be a "Darling Enterprise." [441]

The Emerald Light Infantry was in the forefront of the effort to establish the Irish Volunteer Battalion and published the following notice in the *Charleston Mercury* on February 11, 1862:

> AT A MEETING OF THIS CORPS, HELD ON THE 5th instant, the following Preamble and Resolutions were unanimously adopted:
> The EMERALD LIGHT INFANTRY have heard with pleasure the proposition to form an "IRISH VOLUNTEER BATTALION." Believing that such a corps would tend to unite the patriotic Irishmen of South Carolina in an efficient vindication of the Rights of the State, and that such an organization would possess an "*esprit du corps*," which would make it irresistible in battle, they take this early occasion to give assurance of their hearty co-operation in the good work: Be it, therefore,
> *Resolved,* That this Company will contribute its best endeavors to effect the early establishment of an "IRISH VOLUNTEER BATTALION."[442]

The other Irish companies quickly embraced the idea of an Irish Volunteer Battalion. Meetings were held at the Hibernian Hall on the evenings of February 20 and 21, 1862 for the purpose of organizing such a battalion for Confederate service. On February 22, representatives of the Irish companies met with the State Adjutant and Inspector General, who ordered the Irish Volunteers to form one company to be known as Company No. 8, the Emerald Light Infantry and Jasper Greens to combine to form another to be known as Company No. 6, and the Sarsfield Light Infantry and Montgomery Guard to combine to form a third to be known as Company No. 7. He also ordered Captain David Ramsay's company to form a fourth company for the proposed battalion. It was expected that at full strength each of the companies would include 85 men.[443]

The members of Company No. 6, created by combining the Emerald Light Infantry and Jasper Greens, were listed in the *Charleston Mercury* as follows:

J. A. Armstrong, John Andress, H. Boyle, John Bowen, W. G. Browning, W. A. Courtenay, Walter Castello, Thomas Carey, James Carlisle, H. Campbell, S. Campbell, M. Caulfield, John Corbet, Daniel Doogan, W. D. Dunn, William Davern, John Donagan, John Donahoe, Thomas Egan, P. Foley, B. Foley, James Foley, John Flaherty, John Farle, Martin Ford, J. B. Gillfeler, P. Grace, P. Gilhooly, M. Hartneet, John Hartnett, W. D. Harrioon, Joseph Harbeson, B. Kiley, A. Kiley, Thomas Kenney, M. Lehay, James Lyons, James Lorbey, M. Lacy, Thomas Marrim, John May, Thomas Magrath, P. Macken, P. May, J. A. Murray, P. Malone, John McAvoy, John McMahon, M. McSweeney, John McKenna, P. Neil, H. McCartney, B. O'Callaghan, Peter Power, John Parsons, A. Ponard, F. Riley, John Riley, M. B. Reagan, James Ronan, D. Sheehan, M. Scott, A. Stanton, John Smith, James Smith, M. Tool, James Walsh.[444]

The members of Company No. 7, created by combining the Montgomery Guard and the Sarsfield Light Infantry, were listed in the *Charleston Mercury* as follows:

R. J. Brownfield, Peter Blake, Wm. Brady, Jos. Beatty, R. Beatty, P. L. Casey, B. Conley, Wm. Cummings, M. J. Colemand, M. Canning, Dennis Cassaday, Patrick Clemy, R. Carroll, T. Cammon, T. Claffey, Dennis Canghlin, Jno. Dwyer, Jno. Doogan, Thomas Dempsey, Jno. Dunne, Chas. Enright, Jas. Fitzpatrick, T. B. Fogarty, Thos. Green, Gillfeller, T. Harrington, Jno. Harbeson, W. N. Heyward, Jno. Henley, R. J. Henry, W. G. Holmes, Jas. Kelly, Paul Keenan, Wm. Keenan, Thos. Kilroy, W. Y. Lovett, Thos. Lyons, Dennis Lyons, James Malone, Jno. Martin, Jas. Moran, James Murphy, J. M. Murray, Jas. Morris, Jas. Martin, Wm. Miller, Pat Murphy, Ed. McCaughlin, Dennis McInernay, M. McQuinlish, Jno. McCarthy, J. McCarthy, M.

F. McBride, P. McCarrel, L. McCabe, Jno. McEvoy, C. Quade, Phillip O'Keiff, Pat O'Gorman, C. Ostrch, Jas O'Gorman, P. O'Rourke, Jno. Pendergast, Ed. Pendergast, Jas. Ronan, Phillip Riley, Thomas Sheridan, M. Quinn, Thos. Quinn, J. Thompson, R. T. Thompson, Mike Toolay, George Tandy, Jas. Wallace, P. Woodlock, T. Woodlock, P. Write, D. Ward, J. Walsh, Daniel White.[445]

An election of officers for the three Irish companies was held at Hibernian Hall on February 24, 1862 and the following were selected:

Company No. 6: W. A. Courtenay, Captain; John A. Armstrong, First Lieutenant; Patrick Walsh, Second Lieutenant; Philip Malone, Third Lieutenant.
Company No. 7: W. N. Heyward, Captain; W. G. Holmes, First Lieutenant; John McCarthy, Second Lieutenant; John J. Furlong, Third Lieutenant.
Company No. 8: Edward Magrath, Captain; Wm. H. Ryan, First Lieutenant; Jas. M. Mulvaney, Second Lieutenant; A. A. Allemong, Third Lieutenant.[446]

The four companies which were to make up the Irish Volunteer Battalion were ordered to report for training at Magnolia Parade Ground on March 12, 1862. There they joined the city's other former militiamen of the Fourth Brigade who had also formed companies for Confederate service. Unfortunately, the "Darling Enterprise" began to unravel shortly thereafter.[447]

Apparently, after the troops entered the training camp the idea of forming an Irish Volunteer Battalion was quickly discarded. It was decided, instead, to form a larger "Charleston Battalion" from the former members of Charleston's militia companies who were present at the training camp. This battalion, officially known as the First South Carolina Infantry Battalion, was formed in early April 1862. It was initially made up of the Irish Volunteers, the Union Light Infantry, the Charleston Riflemen, the Sumter Guard, the Calhoun Guard and the Charleston Light Infantry.[448]

The two Irish companies of Captain W. A. Courtney and Captain W. N. Hayward were not ready when the Charleston Battalion was formed and did not join this battalion with the Irish Volunteers. These companies, made up of the former members of the Emerald Light Infantry, Jasper Greens, Sarsfield Light Infantry and Montgomery

Guard, were apparently having trouble meeting their recruiting quotas. In an attempt to field at least one full company, these remaining Irish companies agreed to merge. The new company took on the name Montgomery Guard and was commanded by Captain W. A. Courtnay.[449]

In commenting on the merger of the Irish companies, the editors of the *Charleston Daily Courier* wrote:

> THE MONTGOMERY GUARD.—We have been much gratified at seeing it announced that the name of this fine old corps—so long and so favorably known, under the command of Capt. Jas. Conner—has been revived, by the adoption of that name by the quotas of the three other Irish Companies.
>
> We venture the assertion that this happy selection of a name will go far towards uniting the membership in each of the corps—and we confidently predict that if an opportunity offers they will cover with a brighter lustre the name of the brave and chivalrous MONTGOMERY. Capt Courtenay is in command.[450]

Unfortunately, it is not known if the new Montgomery Guard had the opportunity to cover with a brighter lustre the name of Montgomery. The company was formed at a time when numerous military organizations were recruiting in Charleston for members for Confederate service. New companies were formed and disappeared every day. Captain Courtenay's Montgomery Guard apparently became one of those that disappeared. The company's name is not included in the list of city companies that entered Confederate service that was published in the 1883 Year Book of the City of Charleston. It is not known whether the company entered Confederate service under another name or if the company was dissolved and its men joined other units. In any event, it was a sad end to the idea of an Irish Volunteer Battalion which had begun with so much enthusiasm.[451]

THE EMMETT GUARDS

ORGANIZED CIRCA 1875

Perhaps the last Irish military company to be formed in Charleston was the Emmett Guards, organized sometime in 1875. On St. Patrick's Day of that year the company made its first public appearance when it participated in the St. Patrick's Day Parade. Captain P. Slattery was the company's commander and J. Corcoran was its secretary.[452] The uniform of the Guards was described in the *News and Courier* as consisting of "green cloth frock coats trimmed with green velvet, cap of same color and white pompon tipped with green, and black pants with gold bullion stripes."[453]

In 1876, the Emmett Guards again participated in Charleston's St. Patrick's Day festivities and also took part in the city's celebration of the one hundredth anniversary of the American victory over the British at Fort Moultrie in June. The company is not listed as a participant in Charleston's St. Patrick's Day activities the following year and probably went out of existence prior to March 17, 1877.[454]

CHAPTER FIVE

CHARLESTON'S CONNECTIONS WITH THE FIGHT FOR IRISH FREEDOM

Many of the Irishmen who arrived in Charleston just prior to the end of the eighteenth century had been forced to leave their homeland during the ill-fated revolution of 1798 or the British oppression which followed. These Irishmen, along with the large numbers of their countrymen who followed them to Charleston during the nineteenth century, brought with them a burning desire to see their country free. They passed this desire down to their children and grandchildren, and the advocates of freedom for Ireland could always turn to Charleston for moral and financial support. This support for the cause of Irish freedom made Charleston a popular place for visits by exiled Irish nationalists, such as Thomas Francis Meagher.[455]

Meagher was born in Waterford, Ireland, and moved as a young man to Dublin to study law. In Dublin, Meagher joined the Repeal Association of Daniel O'Connell, where he quickly gained recognition as a skilled orator. Differences arose between Meagher and O'Connell, however, as a result of Meagher's refusal to condemn the use of arms to advance the Irish cause. In July 1846, Meagher gained the nickname "Meagher of the Sword" when he made a political speech in Dublin in which he used the word "sword" eight times. Shortly thereafter, he left the Repeal Association to help form the Irish Confederation, which advocated self-government for Ireland. As an emissary of this organization he was sent to France in 1848. During this trip Meagher was given a tricolor as a gift from the people of France to the people of Ireland. The red, white and blue tricolor was later to become the green, white and orange national flag of Ireland.[456]

After his return from France, Meagher traveled throughout Ireland with William Smith O'Brien in an attempt to gain the support of the Irish people for a revolt against the British. The revolution, if it can be called that, came in July 1848, and was quickly crushed. Meagher was arrested, convicted for his part in starting the insurrection and sentenced to be hanged, drawn and quartered. This sentence was later commuted to life imprisonment, and he was transported to Van Diemen's Land. In January 1852, Meagher escaped from Van Diemen's Land. He eventually made his way to the United States where he initially earned a living as a lecturer.[457]

In March 1853 Meagher visited Charleston, where he gave lectures on Australia and patriotic Irish subjects. The Charleston Irish community extended to Meagher a hero's welcome. He was deluged at his hotel with visits from a large number of Irish Charlestonians, including the entire company of Irish Volunteers. In addition, the city's Irish organizations extended to Meagher invitations to visit their halls and meet their members. These Irish Charlestonians wanted not only to see the man that they had read so much about, but also to express to him their support for the cause of Irish freedom.[458] The following excerpt from a letter sent to Meagher by the Society of United Irishmen, along with an invitation to visit their hall at 90 Meeting Street, probably best summed up the feelings of the Irish in Charleston:

> Sir, we hail, with unfain delight your arrival in this city, some of us having the honor of being associated with you in your efforts to establish the independence of our native land. With millions of our countrymen the lovers of liberty in this great Republic, and all over the world, we felt indignant at the tyranny which expatriated you and your fellow exiles, and we sincerely hope your oft repeated wish of a re-union with them on this fine soil, will, ere long be accomplished. The principles for which you have suffered so much, we uphold, and will do so under all circumstances and in every emergency which may arise.[459]

Meagher celebrated St. Patrick's Day in Charleston by attending the banquet of the Hibernian Society, where he was seated in the place of honor at the right hand of the President. During the banquet many toasts were made in Meagher's honor, and he was made an honorary member of the Society. Shortly after St. Patrick's Day, Meagher left Charleston, but the Irish in Charleston continued to honor him. A new Irish military company was named the Meagher Rifle Guard in his honor.[460]

In 1861 Meagher pledged his allegiance to the Union and became a General in the Union Army. The Charleston Irish, who were now also Southerners, immediately began to distance themselves from Meagher. The Hibernian Society published a notice in the newspaper revoking Meagher's honorary membership. Shortly thereafter, the Meagher Guard changed its name to the Emerald Light Infantry.[461]

The central figure of the Irish Rebellion of 1848, William Smith O'Brien, also visited Charleston prior to the Civil War. O'Brien, who was a Protestant from County Clare, served in the British House of Commons, where he became known as a champion of Irish rights. He joined the Repeal Association in 1843 where he became the second man in the organization behind Daniel O'Connell. The job of running the Repeal Association fell to O'Brien while O'Connell was imprisoned. In 1846 O'Brien, like Meagher, left the Repeal Association and the following year became one of the founders of the Irish Confederation.

In 1848 the British government began arresting the leaders of the Irish Confederation, forcing O'Brien and his confederates to take action. O'Brien traveled to the south of Ireland for the purpose of organizing a revolt, but was not able to get much support. Finally, on July 29, 1848, O'Brien, with a group of poorly armed peasants, attacked a troop of police near Ballingarry in County Tipperary. The attack failed and the insurrection was over soon thereafter. O'Brien was arrested, convicted of high treason and sentenced to be hanged, drawn and quartered. The sentence was commuted, over the objection of O'Brien, to transportation to Tasmania. In 1854 he received a pardon on condition that he never return to the United Kingdom. This pardon was made unconditional in 1856.[462]

As part of a trip to America, William Smith O'Brien spent several days in Charleston in March 1859. During this visit, he received the same warm welcome from Irish Charlestonians that Thomas Francis Meagher had six years before. On the morning of St. Patrick's Day he attended Mass with Charleston's Irish citizens at Saint Finbar's Cathedral on Broad Street. That afternoon he was invited to present the awards for target shooting to the Irish military organizations at Magnolia Parade Ground. Then, in the evening, O'Brien was the guest of honor at the Hibernian Society banquet where he was serenaded by a special band from Fort Moultrie.[463]

During the American Civil War the Irish in Charleston were forced to place the cause of Irish independence aside in order to throw their full support behind the Southern cause. Irish freedom was never far from their minds, however, and one of the first new Irish organizations to be formed in Charleston after the war was a branch of the Fenian

Brotherhood. This group had been organized in the United States in 1859 as a counterpart to the Irish Revolutionary Brotherhood in Ireland, which later became known as the Irish Republican Brotherhood. Its purpose was to provide Irish American political, financial and military aid to the Irish Revolutionary Brotherhood in the British Isles to assist them in their efforts to gain independence for Ireland. Each branch was called a circle and the head of the circle was referred to as the Centre.[464]

The circle of the Fenian Brotherhood in Charleston was organized in time to participate in Charleston's St. Patrick's Day activities on March 17, 1866. That morning the Fenians marched in the St. Patrick's Day Parade with the members of the St. Patrick's Benevolent Society. In the evening the Charleston circle of the Fenian Brotherhood held a St. Patrick's Day banquet attended by approximately three hundred people at the station of the Palmetto Fire Engine Company on Anson Street. The banquet was presided over by James Power, the Centre of the Charleston circle of the brotherhood, who made the first toast, "The Day We Celebrate." This toast was responded to by John O'Brien, a member of the Irish Revolutionary Brotherhood, who educated the audience on the progress the Brotherhood had made in "Fenianizing" the English Army. More toasts followed, "The President of the United States—The man of iron will," "The F. B. and I. R. B.—The Sheet Anchor of Irish Independence" and "The Fenian Brotherhood—Ever foremost in promoting the holy cause of Irish Independence."[465]

Irish independence was as dear to the Irish women in Charleston as to the men, and a circle of the Fenian Sisterhood was established in the city by 1866. The Fenian Sisterhood was one of the first political organizations for women in the history of the country, and the members of the Charleston circle did not waste any time in exercising their new-found freedom. In April 1866, M. Burke, the secretary of the Fenian Sisterhood circle in Charleston, contacted the Hibernian Society about engaging its hall for use by the group.[466]

The Irish Revolutionary Brotherhood had planned to begin a revolution in Ireland in 1865, supported by guns from the United States and by troops who had served in the Union and Confederate armies. On November 11, 1865, however, James Stephens, the head of the Irish Revolutionary Brotherhood, was arrested by the British authorities. Stephens escaped from prison two weeks later, but at his urging the revolt in Ireland was postponed.[467]

During the delay in launching the rebellion in Ireland, a rift developed among the Fenians in America as to the best course of immediate action. One faction continued to support a revolution in Ireland while another favored an attack on British Canada to gain a foothold for the Irish Republic. James Stephens traveled to America to resolve the split, but was unsuccessful.[468] On May 31, 1866 a Fenian force of approximately eight hundred men under Colonel John O'Neill crossed the Canadian border near Buffalo, New York and occupied the village of Fort Erie. After several days of skirmishes, they were forced to withdraw and were captured by forces of the United States.[469]

After the failed Fenian invasion of Canada, James Stephens again advocated revolution in Ireland, but as 1866 wore on he once again urged postponement. Thereafter, the leadership of the Irish Revolutionary Brotherhood and the Fenians lost confidence in Stephens. In late 1866 he was replaced by Irish Civil War veteran Thomas J. Kelly as the head organizer for Ireland and England. Shortly thereafter, Kelly sailed for England to coordinate plans for a revolution in Ireland.[470]

The date of the uprising was set for March 5, 1867, and an Irish American named Godfrey Massey was appointed military commander in the field. Before the insurrection could begin, however, the Fenian plans were betrayed to the British by an informer, and Massey was arrested on March 4, 1867. A few troops did rise, but the revolution of 1867, like that of 1848, was a miserable failure. Thomas J. Kelly was arrested several months later in Manchester, England but was freed from a police van in a daring raid in which one policeman was killed. Three men were eventually hanged for taking part in the raid and these became known as the "Manchester Martyrs."[471]

The failure of the invasion of Canada in 1866 and the failure of the revolution in Ireland in 1867 did not dampen the enthusiasm of the Fenians in Charleston for the cause of Irish independence. The local circle of the Fenian Brotherhood continued to hold meetings and intensified its efforts to recruit new members. The following meeting notice of this organization appeared in the *Charleston Daily News* on February 6, 1868:

GOD SAVE IRELAND!
IRISHMEN, AWAKE, ARISE, OR BE FOREVER FALLEN!
BROTHERS—THE HOUR IS FAST APPROACHING, the long wished for day is about to dawn. The how long, O Lord, how long, of our martyred brethren of every age, is about to be heard. Haste, then, and take the first step in preparation to meet the great event that will be soon upon you, by joining

the great throng of your brothers in the Fenian ranks, thereby to be enabled to strike a blow for the Freedom of Ireland. And remember that a successful blow struck for the honor of your adopted country, is a blow struck for the salvation of your Native Land, for the honor of one is bound up with the life of the other, for is not the ruthless foe of the one the hereditary enemy of the other. Come on, then, brethren, *To-Night*, to Masonic Hall, enroll yourselves with us as brothers, for are we not brothers?
We meet *To-Night* at 7 ½ o'clock.[472]

In 1869, it was announced that General John O'Neill, the leader of the Fenian invasion of Canada, would visit Charleston. This announcement created great excitement among the Irish in the City. The Hibernian Society even called a special meeting in order to issue an invitation to O'Neill to use the Hibernian Hall for a speech. Unfortunately, O'Neill's visit had to be cancelled.[473]

There were 212 circles of the Fenian Brotherhood in good standing in the United States in 1870, including the one in Charleston. In spite of previous setbacks, these Fenians still had some fight left in them. In May, 1870, John O'Neill led a second Fenian invasion of Canada, this time from Vermont. The second invasion, like the first, was quickly repelled. O'Neill and his men were arrested for violating the American neutrality laws and given terms in prison.[474]

By the early 1870s, it was apparent that Ireland was not going to obtain its freedom from England immediately by means of physical force, and a group of Irishmen began to concentrate their efforts on obtaining at least some self-government for their country through constitutional methods. In 1873, the Home Rule League was organized with the purpose of obtaining self-government for Ireland. Fifty-nine members of the League were elected to the British Parliament in the election of 1874, and formed what has become known as the Home Rule Party, or the Irish Parliamentary Party.[475]

The following year a young Irish landowner from Meath named Charles Stewart Parnell was elected as a member of the Home Rule Party to replace a member who had died. Parnell's career began slowly, but in 1876, he drew the attention of the Fenians and of Irishmen around the world when he arose from his seat in Parliament and rebuked Sir Michael Hicks-Beach, the Chief Secretary for Ireland, for using the term "murderers" in reference to the Manchester Martyrs.[476] Thereafter, Parnell remained in the public eye and established his reputation as an advanced nationalist by joining with Joseph Biggar in a policy of obstructing the business of the English Parliament through the use of its own antiquated rules.[477]

During the late 1870s Ireland was in the midst of a serious economic crisis brought on primarily by the influx to Europe of large amounts of cheap grain from the United States. The prices for Irish farm products dropped, and to make matters worse, the Irish potato crop failed in 1877. The potato crop remained small during 1878 and 1879, raising fears of another famine. Many tenants could not pay their rent, which resulted in a large number of evictions.[478]

Two old Fenians, Michael Davitt and John Devoy, saw the crisis in Ireland as an opportunity to advance the cause of Irish freedom while at the same time helping the Irish farmer. They believed that the issue of land reform could be linked to home rule and eventual independence for Ireland and proposed that the Fenians and Constitutionalists cooperate in agitating for land reform. Charles Stewart Parnell agreed to this proposal, and a policy of cooperation on the land agitation issue, which became known as the "New Departure," was established between the two groups.[479]

The vehicle chosen to pursue the land agitation was the Irish National Land League, formed in Dublin on October 21, 1879. Parnell was elected president of the Land League, and a majority of the remaining offices were filled by Fenians or ex-Fenians.[480] The objects of the League were: "first, to bring about a reduction in rack-rents; second, to facilitate and obtain the ownership of the soil by the occupiers of the soil."[481]

Prior to the establishment of the Irish National Land League, the Irish peasants did not have any effective means of addressing grievances with their landlords. Now they had a powerful organization to support them. They flocked to the Land League in great numbers, and by the latter weeks of 1879 the organization was in operation throughout most of Ireland. Thereafter, the Land League continued to grow in strength until it became the most powerful organization in Ireland. As the Land League grew in strength, it became bolder with its demands. The British were slow to react, but finally attempted to dilute the strength of the League by arresting some of its leaders. In November 1879, Michael Davitt, James Daley, and J. B. Killen were arrested. However, no attempt was made at this time to arrest Parnell.[482]

In December 1879, Parnell made a trip to America to gain support from Irish Americans for the land agitation in Ireland and to raise money for the victims of the famine. Parnell did not visit Charleston on this trip, but this did not deter Charlestonians from supporting the causes he advocated. On January 19, 1880, a meeting was held at Hibernian Hall to initiate famine relief efforts in the city for the people of Ireland. This meeting was addressed by several prominent speakers, including Mayor William Courtenay, former Governor A. G. Magrath, and Bishop P. N. Lynch. In his speech, Mayor Courtenay criticized the Irish land laws and expressed hope that the British government would shape legislation for Ireland to enable her people to become the owners of the land they worked. After the speeches, an executive committee of eight citizens was appointed to coordinate the collection of money in the city. These were Capt. F. W. Dawson, Gen. James Conner, Hugh Ferguson, J. E. Adger, A. Johnson, Wm. Meagher, G. S. Hacker and J. H. Devereux.[483]

On February 2, 1880, Parnell was invited to address the United States House of Representatives. Charleston's Congressman, Michael Patrick O'Connor, whose father had been born in Ireland, was a member of the Committee on Reception and attended all of the events given for Parnell.[484] When asked to comment on the land agitation in Ireland and on Mr. Parnell's visit, O'Connor said:

> The word spoilation is written across every land grant in Ireland. From the date of the invasion of Ireland by Henry of England, every acre of the soil of that country has been confiscated, under some plea or pretext of English law, to enrich the invader and despoil the honest native. It is vain to say that the Irish have no substantial excuse for the wail of sorrow and distress, which now goes up from the famine-stricken land. Their starvation is not due to their improvidence, their indolence, or their thriftlessness, but because England has made the Irish peasant as degraded as the Egyptian fellah or the Indian ryot. Strip a people of the land upon which they have a natural right to live, as it is that from which they must necessarily draw their subsistence; or by legal devices, after barefaced robbery, has not accomplished its full measure, evict them from the same, can it be wondered that famine and starvation should become a periodical and epochal feature in the history of that Island.
>
> The titles of the lands in Ireland, spoiled as they have been, are in a large degree vested in the absentees, who, while the honest toiler is starving at home, are luxuriously indulging at their ease in foreign lands.

The protest which Mr. Parnell has made, should be raised by the whole civilized world, until brute power, and the more selfish greed of England's money power is compelled to abate its lust; and give back to the plundered, some of that which the laws of nature, and nature's God entitled them to.[485]

Parnell returned triumphantly to Ireland in March of 1880, but before he left the United States he organized the American Land League for the support of the Irish National Land League. This new organization quickly established branches in many American cities. The Parnell Branch of the Irish Land League of America was established in Charleston, with its headquarters at the Catholic school building on George Street. The officers of this branch were: James Ronan, president; P. Moran, first vice-president; M. F. Kennedy, second vice-president; Simon Fogarty, treasurer; M. A. Connor, financial secretary; and James Armstrong, recording secretary. The Executive committee consisted of J. Cummings, L. Cantwell, J. Cosgrove and J. Cantwell.[486]

While Parnell was in America, the land agitation in Ireland continued. The British government tried both force and promises to end the crisis, but neither worked. It was decided that the only way to destroy the Land League was to arrest its leader. On October 13, 1881, Charles Stewart Parnell was arrested after an inflammatory speech and imprisoned in Kilmainham Jail in Dublin.[487]

In retaliation for the government crackdown, Parnell and the other top leaders of the Land League issued a "no rent" manifesto, under which the tenant farmers of Ireland were instructed not to pay any rent whatsoever to the landlords. Mr. William Forster, the Lord Lieutenant of Ireland, immediately countered by issuing a decree on October 20, 1881 declaring the Irish National Land League an illegal organization and officially suppressing it.[488]

The "no rent" manifesto was not honored by a majority of the Irish tenant farmers, and jail did not agree with Charles Stewart Parnell. Both Parnell and the British government began looking for a compromise, and negotiations were opened through intermediaries. An agreement was reached in May 1882 granting Parnell his freedom. Under this agreement, known as the Kilmainham Treaty, Gladstone would introduce a satisfactory Arrears Bill and the land agitation would be slowed down. This was the final nail in the coffin of the Irish National Land League.[489]

After his release from jail, Parnell kept his agreement to slow down the land agitation. He returned to his seat in Parliament, where he renewed his quest for Irish home rule by constitutional means. On October 17, 1882, Parnell founded a new organization, the Irish National League.[490] The aims of the Irish National League were: "(1) National self-government; (2) Land Law reform; (3) Local self-government; (4) extension of the parliamentary and municipal franchise and (5) the development and encouragement of the labour and industrial resources of Ireland." By the end of 1885 the League had 1,261 branches.[491]

On the other side of the Atlantic, Irish Americans were also looking to reorganize as a result of the demise of the Irish National Land League. In April 1883, a large Irish convention was held in Philadelphia. Most of the branches of the American Land League sent representatives, including Charleston's Parnell Branch, represented by M. F. Kennedy. During the convention, the Irish National League of America was organized to cooperate with the Irish National League. The new organization would replace the American Land League. The purposes of the Irish National League of America were to support Parnell in achieving self-government for Ireland; to promote Irish industry; to injure British manufacturing by boycotting British goods; and to encourage the Irish language and arts and keep alive the flame of Irish nationality.[492]

Upon his return to Charleston, Mr. M. F. Kennedy reported to the Parnell Branch of the Irish Land League. On June 6, 1883, the Parnell Branch became a member of the Irish National League of America with F. L. McHugh as president, James Coleman as vice president, and Daniel O'Neill as treasurer. An advisory board was also appointed by the president, consisting of Hugh Ferguson, W. D. Hannifin, Thomas Flynn, James F. Redding, Dennis O'Neill, William Flynn, and Morris Quinlivan.[493]

On April 8, 1886 Gladstone introduced a Home Rule Bill which Parnell accepted. The bill was bitterly opposed, however, by the Ulster Unionists, who were allied with Churchill, and the Liberal Unionists led by Joseph Chamberlin. It was defeated on second reading on June 7, 1886. The Parnell Branch of the Irish National League of America apparently went out of existance that same year, as it does not appear in the Charleston City Directory in 1887.[494]

A little less than two years after the defeat of Gladstone's Home Rule Bill, the supporters of Irish freedom in Charleston were rejuvenated by the visit of Sir Henry Thomas Grattan Esmonde to the city. Sir Henry, like Parnell, was a member of the British House of Commons. His trip to Charleston was part of a tour of the United States in which he was seeking to increase support in this country for the cause of Irish home rule.[495]

Esmonde arrived by train at Charleston's Union Station on March 5, 1888, where he was greeted by many of Charleston's prominent Irish citizens. From the station he was taken to the Charleston Hotel, where he was welcomed to the city by Mayor William Bryan. After lunch at the hotel, Sir Henry was treated to a tour of the city, including some of its sites of Irish significance. Among the places he visited were the Hibernian Park, St. Lawrence Cemetery and the grave of Captain John Mitchel, son of Irish Patriot John Mitchel.[496]

At eight o'clock in the evening, Esmonde was escorted by the Montgomery Guards and Irish Volunteers to Hibernian Hall, where a mass meeting was scheduled. By the time Sir Henry arrived, a large crowd had gathered, and he marched triumphantly into the hall to the tune of "The Wearing of the Green." He was then escorted to the stage, where he was seated with the Mayor, the Speaker of the House of Representatives, the ex-Governor and many other dignitaries.[497]

After an appropriate introduction by Mayor Bryan, Sir Henry made an enthusiastic and informative speech, interrupted by applause and cheers at numerous points. He reminded the people of Charleston of the aid the Irish had rendered to America during its fight for freedom, and pointed out many abuses of the British system of government in Ireland which made Irish home rule essential. He then suggested that Charlestonians could now render assistance to the Irish and that the best way to do so would be for them to become a part of the Irish National League.[498]

The next speaker on the program was Mr. Sutton, the secretary of the Irish National League of America, who briefly outlined the need for relief in Ireland. He explained that the best way to help the people of Ireland would be to form a large branch of the Irish National League of America. That way they would have the support of an organization that would stretch from coast to coast.[499]

At the conclusion of the meeting the following resolutions were passed by the assembly:

> Whereas, the people of this city have been honored by the visit of a distinguished representative of home rule in Ireland in the person of Sir Thomas Henry Grattan Esmonde, the eloquent exponent of an issue which has heretofore attracted the special interest of the people of our State, and which has been successfully accomplished in South Carolina in the

restoration of a government of the people by the people, we can heartily sympathize and conscientiously extend a cordial welcome to this worthy representative, and pledge him not only our moral but substantial aid in the furtherance of the objects of his mission: therefore, be it

Resolved, That this meeting heartily endorses the cause of the Irish Parliamentary party in demanding from the British Parliament the right of home government.

Resolved further, That as a proof of this sincerity and affection of the Irishmen and friends of Ireland in this city, we pledge our entire sympathy, morally and practically, to further the cause as represented in the person of our distinguished guest.

Resolved, That a cablegram be sent by the chairman of this meeting to the Hon. William F. Gladstone and Charles Stewart Parnell expressive of these sentiments.[500]

In response to the request of Sir Henry Thomas Grattan Esmonde, a meeting was scheduled for the purpose of organizing a branch of the Irish National League of America in Charleston. This meeting was held at the Hibernian Hall on May 1, 1888 and was addressed by several prominent citizens, including ex-Governor A. G. Magrath and the powerful editor of the *News and Courier*, Captain F. W. Dawson. Captain Dawson had been born in England but was an outspoken advocate of Irish home rule.[501] In his speech, he asserted that "there need be no hesitation in declaring now and always that nothing less than national rule—the rule of the nation by the nation and for the nation—will or should satisfy the Irish people. There is no question of their right to govern themselves."[502]

At the conclusion of the speeches, the Grattan Branch of the Irish National League of America was established. The object of the new organization, according to its constitution, was "to furnish moral and material support to the cause of home rule in Ireland."[503] At the time of its establishment the officers were: President, Capt. James F. Redding; First vice president, Capt. B. F. McCabe; Second vice president, B. Boyd; Third vice president, Capt. C. A. McHugh; Corresponding secretary, P. E. Gleason; Recording secretary, H. J. McCormack; Treasurer, Simon Fogarty. The branch also had an executive committee consisting of: Thos. R. McGahan, Maj. B. H. Rutledge Jr., Maj. W. H. Brawley, Capt. Simon Hyde, Hon. J. E. Burke, Capt. Benj. Mantoue, W. H. Parker Jr., B. Callaghan, Capt. A. G. Magrath Jr., Lieut. J. D. Capplemann, F. J. McGarey, Maj. E. P. McSwiney, H. L. Cade, Capt. F. W. Dawson,

Hugh Ferguson, Dennis O'Neill, M. A. Connor, Hon. P. P. Toale, M. W. Powers, A. J. Riley, F. Q. O'Neill, William Flynn, Henry Oliver, James F. Riley, Clement S. Bissell, Anton Johnson and Frank Kressel Jr.[504]

The Charlestonians who so enthusiastically embraced the cause of Irish home rule in 1888 must have been shocked, and deeply saddened, by the events which began to unfold the following year. In December 1889, Captain William O' Shea, a Member of Parliament, sued his wife, Katherine, for divorce and named Charles Stewart Parnell as a co-respondent in the action. Parnell and Mrs. O'Shea had been conducting an affair for quite a long time, and neither contested the action. Unfortunately, a divorce action involving a popular public figure like Parnell caused quite a scandal. The Home Rule Party at first supported Parnell and re-elected him chairman on November 25, 1890. However, after both Gladstone and the Catholic Bishops expressed doubts as to his ability to lead, the party reversed its position and requested that he resign as chairman. Parnell refused, causing a split in the party, which weakened the cause of home rule for the ensuing decade. He did not live to see the full effect of his decision, however, as he died in 1891.[505]

The split in the Home Rule Party greatly disillusioned many Irish Americans with the cause of Irish home rule, and the Irish National League of America did not hold a national convention after 1891. This disillusionment was increased in 1893 when a Home Rule Bill was passed by the House of Commons only to be defeated in the House of Lords. Thereafter the funds from America began to dry up. The Grattan Branch of the Irish National League in Charleston continued to meet at Hibernian Hall until 1899, but it did not even list a president or vice president in the City Directories after 1894.[506]

The prospects for Irish home rule, which had all but disappeared during the last decade of the nineteenth century, appeared bright at the beginning of the second decade of the twentieth century. In 1912, the House of Commons passed a Home Rule Bill for Ireland. This Home Rule Bill, unlike its predecessor, could not be defeated in the House of Lords due to the passage of the Parliament Act. of 1911. Under this act, the House of Lords could only delay a bill passed by the House of Commons for about two years. Thus, it appeared that Irish home rule was inevitable.[507]

The Protestants in Ulster, however, remained opposed to Home Rule. Mass meetings were held in the northern counties at which thousands signed pledges to oppose home rule. In 1912 a military organization known as the Ulster Volunteer Force was organized for the purpose of preventing home rule by force if necessary. Arms were solicited from abroad, and 25,000 rifles, along with 2,500,000 rounds of ammunition, were smuggled into Ulster from Germany. The situation became more dangerous in 1913 when the Irish in the south formed their own military organization, the Irish Volunteers, with the express purpose of resisting any attempt to prevent home rule by force. Home rule for Ireland was signed into law on September 18, 1914, but its implementation was suspended until the end of World War One. Civil war in Ireland was thus avoided.[508]

In spite of the suspension of home rule, John Redmond, the leader of the Irish Parliamentary Party, threw his support behind the British war effort during World War One. He assured the British government that it did not need to maintain troops in Ireland and made speeches in which he encouraged Irishmen to fight for the British against the Axis powers. Redmond's support for the British recruiting effort in Ireland caused an immediate split in the Irish Volunteers. Those who supported Redmond formed a new organization called the National Volunteers. The ones who did not support him remained in the original Irish Volunteers organization under the command of Eoin MacNeill.[509]

In the United States, there were also many Irish Americans who opposed the actions of John Redmond, and a decision was made to hold an Irish Race Convention to express this opposition. The Irish Race Convention was held in New York City on March 4 and 5, 1916. At this convention a new Irish American organization was formed called the Friends of Irish Freedom.[510] The object of this group was "to encourage and assist any movement which will tend to bring about the National Independence of Ireland."[511] Branches of the Friends of Irish Freedom were established in cities throughout the United States, including Charleston. The Charleston branch of the Friends of Irish Freedom remained active through 1921.[512]

The Irish Republican Brotherhood saw Britain's preoccupation with the Great War as an opportunity for an insurrection in Ireland, and began making preparations. After much planning, the date for the rising was finally set for Easter Sunday, April 23, 1916.[513] "The purposes of such a rising was two-fold. In the first place it would revive a drooping national spirit and in the second place it would call the attention of the world to the Irish question and pave the way for favorable action at the eventual peace conference."[514]

In order for the rising to have any chance of success, the members of the Irish Republican Brotherhood, who were few in number, would need additional men and arms. The plan for the rising called for this need to be met by the eighteen thousand members of the Irish

Volunteers under the command of Eoin MacNeill and a couple of hundred members of the Irish Citizen Army under the command of James Connolly. Maneuvers of these bodies were scheduled for Easter Sunday to coincide with the rising. The German government agreed to supply the arms, and the German steamer *Aud* left Germany on April 9, 1916 for Ireland, carrying arms and ammunition for the rebels.[515]

After a treacherous journey, the *Aud* arrived in Fenit Bay on the coast of Ireland on the night of April 20, 1916. It remained there for approximately twenty hours, but was unable to make contact with the rebels. Fearing discovery, the ship's captain finally put out to sea, where the *Aud* was intercepted by a British patrol boat. In order to avoid capture, the ship was scuttled by her crew, sending it and the rebels' weapons to the bottom of the sea.[516]

The loss of the *Aud* dashed all hopes for a successful revolt. Upon hearing the news of the scuttling, Eoin MacNeill countermanded the orders for maneuvers by the Irish Volunteers on Easter Sunday. The hardcore members of the Irish Republican Brotherhood and the Irish Citizen Army in Dublin, however, refused to heed this countermand. They determined to go forward with the rising even though it would be futile.[517]

On Easter Monday, April 24, 1916, a group of seven or eight hundred rebels led by Patrick Pearse seized the General Post Office in Dublin and read a proclamation declaring the formation of the Irish Republic. At the same time, a few rebels in other parts of the country also rose, but there was no general rising as the leaders of the revolution had hoped. The rebels in Dublin held out for several days against the might of the British Army, but on April 29 they were forced to surrender unconditionally. Shortly thereafter, the remainder of the rebels surrendered and the "Easter Rising" was over.[518]

Immediately after the Easter Rising ended, hundreds of Irishmen were rounded up for questioning and a series of secret court martials were convened by the British Army. These court martials resulted in the execution of fifteen of the rebel leaders. Those executed included, among others, Patrick Pearse, James Connolly, and all of the other men who had signed the proclamation declaring the Irish Republic. Connolly, who was wounded during the rising, had to be propped up on a stretcher before the firing squad.[519]

One of the highest-ranking leaders of the Easter Rising to escape execution was Eamon de Valera, the commander the rebel position at Boland's Mills, who was sentenced to a long prison term. De Valera was born in New York in 1882 of an Irish mother and a Spanish father, and it has been suggested that his life was spared because of the possibility that he was an American citizen.[520]

The majority of Irishmen did not favor or expect the Easter Rising, and therefore, the initial reaction towards the rebels from both Ireland and America was one of hostility. This hostility quickly changed to sympathy, however, in the wake of the cruel British oppression which followed. Irish Americans had to suppress this sympathy for the cause of Irish independence after the United States entered the war as an ally of Britain in 1917. They were determined, however, to make Irish independence a part of the peace settlement.[521]

After the end of World War One, Mayor John Patrick Grace of Charleston emerged as one of America's champions of the cause of Irish freedom. Grace was elected as the city's first Irish Catholic mayor in 1911 by putting together a coalition of Irish and German voters. He was defeated in 1915, but was elected for a second term in 1919 in a hard-fought and bitter campaign. Mayor Grace approached Irish American politics with the same energy and enthusiasm as he did city politics and rose to the office of national vice president of the Friends of Irish Freedom. In this position he met and befriended many of the leaders of the Irish American movement, including its most prominent leader, Justice Daniel F. Cohalan of New York.[522]

In January 1919 the first Dail Eireann met in Ireland and ratified the establishment of the Irish Republic, which had been declared in 1916. It was felt by the Irish in America that pressure needed to be brought to bear on the participants at the Peace Conference at Versailles to recognize the Irish Republic, and it was determined to hold an Irish Race Convention in Philadelphia.[523]

A meeting of approximately five hundred people was held at the Garden Theater in Charleston on the night of February 16, 1919 to select delegates to attend the convention. The guest speaker for the evening was Reverend J. McGurk, who spoke eloquently about the cause of Irish independence.[524] After Reverend McGurk's speech, the following resolutions were passed by the assembly:

> Whereas a convention of the Irish race in America has been called to be held at Philadelphia under the auspices of the Friends of Irish Freedom, in the Second Regiment armory on February 22, and Shubert theater on February 23, 1919; and
> Whereas five delegates and five alternates have been invited to attend from Charleston, S. C.—Charleston whose two Irish sons Rutledge and Lynch signers of the American Declaration

of Independence, played such a large part at Philadelphia on that great day of American liberty; and

Whereas it is the sense of this meeting that not only as of right, but because of the sublime expression by president Wilson for the principle of "self-determination," Ireland is entitled to take her place among the nations of the earth;

Resolved, that the following gentlemen be named as sent from this gathering to the convention of the Irish Race of America, as aforesaid, with the instructions to declare it to be the sense of this meeting that Ireland be free, and to adopt there at only such measures as will insure the recognition of such a nation: Delegates to the Convention— H. A. Molony, Patrick Carter, W. Turner Logan, J. J. Furlong, W. F. Livingston, James F. Condon, T. J. Sweeney, J. I. Cosgrove, Dr. D. L. Maguire, Reverend H. W. Fleming and the Hon. J. P. Grace.[525]

The Irish Race Convention was held as scheduled in Philadelphia, Pennsylvania on February 22 and 23, 1919 under the auspices of the Friends of Irish Freedom. The Honorable John P. Grace of the City of Charleston delivered the keynote speech to the five thousand delegates in attendance, "setting the ball in motion and rousing great enthusiasm." His speech set the tone for the convention when he noted that "Ireland was a nation before Caesar was finished conquering the rude barbarians of Britain."[526] After his speech, Grace acted as temporary chairman of the convention until the permanent organization was taken over by Justice Daniel F. Cohalan of New York. The highlight of the convention was the adoption of resolutions by the delegates calling upon the Paris Peace Conference to apply to Ireland the doctrine of national self-determination and to accord to its people the right to choose their own form of government. The resolutions adopted at the convention were presented to President Wilson, but he refused to promise to bring Ireland's cause to the Peace Conference table.[527]

About the same time as the Irish in America were planning the Irish Race Convention, Eamon de Valera was making his escape from Lincoln Prison in England where he had been held since the Easter Rising. As one of the few leaders of the rising to escape execution, de Valera was immediately thrust into the leadership role of the Irish cause. In April 1919 he was elected president of the Dail Eireann, and in June of that year traveled to America to secure Irish American support for the cause of Irish independence.[528]

One of de Valera's most important reasons for coming to America was to obtain a loan for the government of the Irish Republic. Shortly after his arrival he met with Justice Daniel F. Cohalan and other members of the Friends of Irish Freedom to discuss ways to raise funds, but he did not receive much encouragement. These Irish American leaders believed that it would be illegal for the unrecognized Irish Republic to float an official loan in America. They tried to convince de Valera to abandon the idea of obtaining a loan, but he would not be deterred. Finally, a plan was agreed upon under which Irish bond certificates would be sold to raise money for the Irish Republic. These bond certificates were to be exchanged for bonds after the recognition of the Irish Republic by the international community.[529]

De Valera kicked off the campaign to sell bond certificates on January 17, 1920, and thereafter embarked on a tour of the country encouraging bond certificate sales. The expenses of this campaign were advanced by the Friends of Irish Freedom. During the next year and a half, $5,500,000 was raised for the Irish Republican Cause through the sale of these bond certificates.[530]

In June 1919, when de Valera arrived in the United States, he did not expect to stay very long. He remained until December 1920, however, and as his stay lengthened, de Valera's relations with Irish American leaders became strained. As the President of the Irish Republic, de Valera expected Irish American leaders to defer to his judgment on matters concerning Ireland. He did not seem to understand that although these were Americans of Irish descent, they were Americans first and would always put the interests of their country ahead of those of Ireland. These Irish American leaders, in turn, resented a person from a foreign country, even Ireland, telling them what to do in their own country. De Valera found that he could exercise very little control over the Friends of Irish Freedom and became increasingly frustrated.[531]

Things came to a head on March 19, 1920 at a meeting held in New York City attended by a number of prominent men identified with the Irish American movement, including the Honorable John P. Grace of Charleston. The purpose of this meeting was to discuss the strained relations between de Valera and Irish American leaders. De Valera had not been invited to attend the meeting, but after the meeting began, some of the delegates insisted that he be allowed to defend himself. At length de Valera and his supporters arrived at the meeting. Thereafter, many hours of charges and counter charges transpired in which tempers flared. Finally, both sides agreed to a truce, which was sealed by a handshake between Justice Daniel F. Cohalan and President de Valera.[532]

Mayor Grace, who had not met de Valera before the meeting in New York, did not come away with a favorable first impression of the Irish President. In a letter to Andrew Ryan describing what had occurred at the meeting, he had the following comments:

> De Valera's attitude was one of infallibility; he was right, everybody else was wrong, and he couldn't be wrong...Bishops and priests, Protestants and Catholics, aged men born in Ireland and young men born here...worked for those ten hours to bring President de Valera to the point of amenability. Justice Goff, Hon. Bourke Cockran, Judge Collins, Bishop Turner, Lindsay Crawford, and numbers of others literally begged President de Valera on our knees, in effect, not to persist in his apparent determination to have a public test of strength with Justice Cohalan...I beg to repeat that, not having seen him before, as for those ten hours he unfolded himself, I thought the man was crazy.[533]

Less than a month after the meeting in New York, Eamon de Valera was scheduled to visit Charleston as part of his national tour. The event was advertised in the *News and Courier* as a visit by "President Eamon de Valera of the Irish Republic—First Foreign Sovereign to Ever Visit Charleston."[534] Mayor Grace, inspite of his unflattering first impression of de Valera, was determined that the visit would live up to its billing. Preparatory meetings were held at the Knights of Columbus Hall on April 6, 1920 and at the Hibernian Hall on April 7, 1920 and a committee of prominent Charlestonians was formed to make sure that no detail was overlooked. The members of the committee were A. J. Riley, Jas. F. Condon, Jno. J. Furlong, W. J. O'Hagan, W. J. Storen, W. J. Condon, J. F. Riley, W. Turner Logan, James Sottile and Patrick Carter.[535]

Eamon de Valera, along with the Rev. J. A. G. Irwin, a Presbyterian minister, Mrs. Irwin, and de Valera's secretary, arrived at Charleston's Union Station on April 10, 1920 where they were greeted by a large and enthusiastic crowd. Descending from the train, the party passed through a double line of hundreds of girls and young women dressed in white and waving Irish and American flags. De Valera's motorcade, preceded by a squad of police and the Metts band, passed through Columbus Street, King Street and Broad Street on its way to City Hall.[536]

Upon his arrival at City Hall, de Valera was escorted to the City

Council Chamber where he was greeted by Mayor Grace and presented with a copy of a resolution of City Council granting him the Freedom of the City. The Mayor proclaimed:

> This is the proudest moment of my life that, as the official head of this ancient city..., I should have the honor of bestowing upon you its freedom. We welcome you with all our hearts. Words fail me, but words could add nothing to the beauty and the glory of this momentous occasion.[537]

De Valera responded by thanking Mayor Grace and the people of Charleston for his welcome. He then spoke briefly about the cause of Irish freedom, reasoning that "the people of this state would readily understand and sympathize, for it was through this port in years past that thousands of Irishmen came to escape the oppression at home and that there was no other state in America which had a larger proportion of Irish or Irish descendants in its population than South Carolina."[538] The ceremonies at City Hall were then concluded, and President de Valera was entertained at a luncheon at the Charleston Hotel.[539]

In the evening, de Valera was the guest of honor at a banquet held at the Charleston Hotel. An article in the *Charleston American* the following day reported:

> One of the most elaborate banquets ever tendered to any distinguished guest of Charleston was that given in honor of Eamonn De Valera, the first president of the Republic of Ireland at the Charleston Hotel, rivaling even the dinner held recently by the Hibernian Society at Hibernian Hall which still lingers in the memories of those who attended that affair.
>
> Addresses were made by Mayor Grace, Mr. W. J. Storen, the Rev. J. A. G. Irwin, a Presbyterian minister who is touring the country with President De Valera; Mrs. J. J. Furlong, President De Valera and Major Daniel L. Sinkler who presented Mr. De Valera with a handsome gold watch and chain as a token of affection and esteem of the people of Charleston.
>
> In accepting this gift President De Valera stated that he was very unwilling to take it as a gift to himself personally, but that he would gladly accept it in behalf of the people of the Irish Republic, and that when his term of office expired he would present it to his successor.
>
> More than two hundred ardent Irish patriots and

sympathizers attended the dinner. The symbol and atmosphere of Ireland was freely exhibited throughout the entire banquet hall its national flag being hung upon each of the four walls. The dinner itself savored of Ireland being exhibited even in the ice cream served as the last course, and which represented the new flag of the Irish republic green, white and orange[540]

On Sunday morning, President de Valera attended Mass at the Catholic Cathedral of St. John the Baptist and the Irwins attended services at the First Scots Presbyterian Church. In the afternoon de Valera held a public reception on South Battery after laying a wreath on the monument to Sergeant Jasper. That night he concluded his activities in Charleston by speaking to enthusiastic crowds, first at the Garden Theater and then at the Academy of Music.[541] In his speeches, the Irish President made a convincing plea for the freedom of Ireland, and the following resolutions were passed by those assembled at both auditoriums and sent to the President of the United States, the House of Representatives and the Senate:

RESOLUTION I

Whereas, the people of Ireland, by a general national election have established the Republic of Ireland and proclaimed its independence; and,

Whereas, the Senate and House of Representatives have on more than one occasion, supported by a general sentiment of the people, recorded their sympathy with Ireland's claim to national self-determination in the case of the reservation to the Peace Treaty; be it

RESOLVED, That we respectfully urge upon the President of the United States the propriety of recording formal recognition to the Republic of Ireland and to its duly elected government.

We urge further upon the Foreign Affairs Committee of the House of Representatives to report favorably out of committee the Mason bill, so that the house may provide appropriations for consular and diplomatic service to the new republic.

RESOLUTION II

Whereas, the British Government is spending at a rate of over $60,000,000 in its army of occupation in Ireland, which army at the present moment is persecuting the Irish people depriving them of their individual and national liberty.

Resolved, That we call upon our government and congress not to give further loans or financial accommodations to the British till she withdraws these armies of occupation and allows the peoples of these countries to choose their own way of life and obedience.[542]

At one point during the meeting at the Garden Theater, Mayor John P. Grace, acting as chairman, requested that all persons in the audience who favored Irish independence stand. Not everyone stood, and apparently Mayor Grace was determined not to adjourn the meeting until everyone was on his feet. As the evening wore on, the Mayor requested several more times that all persons in the audience who favored Irish independence stand, but each time the response was still not unanimous. The meeting continued until midnight, when the entire audience, which was exhausted by this time, stood in response to the Mayor's request and the meeting was adjourned. [543]

After de Valera left Charleston, the feud which had preceded his visit continued between him and the Irish American leaders of the Friends of Irish Freedom. During the summer of 1920 de Valera attempted to gain control of the Friends of Irish Freedom by having a person loyal to him installed as its president, but he was unsuccessful. Undeterred, he then attempted to have the Constitution of the Friends of Irish Freedom amended so that it would be easier for him to take control. De Valera's amendments were proposed at a meeting of the National Council of the Friends of Irish Freedom in New York on September 17, 1921. The adoption of these amendments was blocked, however, when they were objected to by the man who had presented de Valera with the freedom of the City of Charleston a few months before, Mayor John P. Grace. De Valera, who took offense to the tone of this objection, immediately left the meeting room with all of his followers.[544]

Frustrated in his attempts to take control of the Friends of Irish Freedom, Eamon de Valera formed a new Irish American organization on October 20, 1920 which would be loyal to him. This organization, called the American Association for the Recognition of the Irish Republic, would thereafter compete with the Friends of Irish Freedom for Irish American loyalties. Unfortunately, this competition would lead to much bitterness between the two groups. Membership in de Valera's new organization grew rapidly due to de Valera's prestige as the President of the Irish Republic. State committees quickly appeared in every state, including South Carolina, where Patrick H. Kennedy served as president for South Carolina of the American Association for the Recognition of the Irish Republic. John P. Grace remained loyal to the Friends of Irish Freedom, however, and loyalties of the Irish in Charleston continued to be divided between these two groups.[545]

During de Valera's visit to America, the situation in Ireland had steadily worsened. The war in Ireland against the British, unlike the previous attempts by the Irish people to gain their independence by force, was waged as a guerrilla war. The Irish Republican Army used the tactics of hit and run, ambush and assassination, in which they disappeared into the general population of Ireland after each attack. There were no large-scale battles, and the British became increasingly frustrated. They reacted with great cruelty against the Irish people. Hundreds of Irishmen were imprisoned, and acts of murder, torture and destruction of property were widespread throughout the country. American public opinion turned increasingly against the British.[546]

One incident which seemed to generate more sympathy for the Irish struggle than any other was the death of Terence MacSwiney. MacSwiney, the Lord Mayor of Cork, was arrested for possessing revolutionary documents and was incarcerated in Brixton Prison in London. He went on a hunger strike in protest and died on October 25, 1920. MacSwiney's willingness to starve himself to death for his beliefs captured the minds and hearts of the American people. During his ordeal, American newspapers gave more coverage to MacSwiney's hunger strike than to the American Presidential campaign, which was then in progress.[547]

On October 31, 1920, MacSwiney's name was honored in Charleston at a meeting sponsored by the Friends of Irish Freedom and attended by an overflow crowd at Hibernian Hall. The first speaker of the evening was Congressman-elect W. Turner Logan, the president of the local branch of the Friends of Irish Freedom. In his speech, Logan praised MacSwiney's heroism and predicted that Ireland would soon take its place in the world as a republic. Mr. Logan was followed on the program by the Honorable John P. Grace, who urged the audience to aid the cause of Irish freedom by boycotting all goods made in Britain. A Resolution of Sympathy was adopted at the meeting and sent to the family of Terence MacSwiney.[548]

In December 1920, de Valera was smuggled out of the United States and back to Ireland. Upon his arrival he found a very different country from the one he had left. British cruelty left thousands of people in Ireland homeless and hungry, and Americans felt a desperate need to raise funds for the relief. In 1921 the American Committee for Relief in Ireland was organized. The committee immediately went to work raising funds for the people of Ireland.[549]

On February 27, 1921, Dr. Maurice J. McCarthy, a lawyer from New York who had been deputized to organize the South, held an organizational meeting in the Charleston for the purpose of forming a state branch of the American Committee for Relief in Ireland. At this meeting Patrick Carter of Charleston was appointed state chairman. He was in turn given the task of appointing various chairmen of several subcommittees in order that the entire machinery of the fund raising campaign could be set in motion.[550]

As part of the fundraising efforts in the state, it was announced that Donal O'Callaghan, Lord Mayor of Cork, would speak at the Academy of Music in Charleston on Sunday, March 6, 1921. Lord Mayor O'Callaghan had been invited to come to this country to speak in Washington before the American Commission on Conditions in Ireland which had been created to look into the British atrocities in Ireland. The British government refused to grant him a passport to travel to America to give his testimony, so he stowed away on a ship bound for Newport News, Virginia. Upon his arrival, he was discovered by American immigration officials, but was not immediately deported due to a difference of opinion between the State Department and the Labor Department as to his status. While this difference of opinion was being worked out, Lord Mayor O'Callaghan traveled to Washington to testify before the American Commission on Conditions in Ireland and also visited several other American cities, including Charleston.[551]

O'Callaghan's visit to Charleston was almost as controversial as his entry into the United States. On Friday, March 4, 1921, the Charleston Post of the American Legion adopted a resolution protesting the visit of the Lord Mayor of Cork. The following morning, an article appeared in the *News and Courier* stating that Mr. O'Callaghan would not speak in Charleston on Sunday due to other engagements, and that the meeting at the Academy of Music had been annulled. Then on Saturday afternoon, Patrick H. Kennedy, President of the American Association for the Recognition of the Irish Republic, telegraphed the *News and Courier* from Atlanta that Mr. O'Callaghan would indeed come to Charleston.[552]

Donal O'Callaghan arrived in Charleston on Sunday, March 6, 1921 accompanied by Captain Monteith, an officer of the Irish Republican Army, and by Anna Walsh, sister-in-law of the late Lord Mayor MacCurtain of Cork. Having cancelled the event at the Academy of Music, the committee on arrangements for the Lord Mayor's visit encountered great difficulty in locating a place for O'Callaghan to speak and was rejected by most of the city's theaters and halls. In desperation, the committee applied to the pro-Irish Grace administration, which had given Eamon de Valera the freedom of the city the previous year, for a permit to allow Mr. O'Clallaghan to address a street meeting. This application was also rejected, in a move that can only be explained by the bitter rivalry between the American Association for the Recognition of the Irish Republic which was supporting O'Callaghan's visit and the Friends of Irish Freedom of which Mayor Grace was a national vice president. Finally, the Knights of Columbus Hall on Calhoun Street was obtained as a venue.[553]

On the evening of March 6, 1921 Mayor O' Callaghan addressed a small but enthusiastic crowd of three to four hundred people at the Knights of Columbus Hall. In his speech he traced the history of the struggle for Irish freedom and reminded the audience of Ireland's assistance to America during the American Revolution. Mayor O'Callaghan told his audience that he believed that there were many men and women in Charleston who desired to see Ireland free and that they were willing to do whatever was necessary to remove the barriers preventing that freedom. He implored the citizens of Charleston to answer Ireland's call for assistance in its struggle for recognition of the Irish Republic and for freedom from England.[554]

Miss Anna Walsh next addressed the audience and described the burning of the city of Cork only a short time prior to the meeting, and other atrocities which were being committed in Ireland by the British. She also described the murder of her brother-in-law, Mayor MacCurtain of Cork, who had proceeded Terence MacSwiney as mayor and had been killed by the Royal Irish Constabulary the previous year. Miss Walsh called upon the women of Charleston to join the Association for the Recognition of the Irish Republic to assist the people of Ireland. At the conclusion of the meeting, O'Callaghan and his party were treated to a reception at the home of Mrs. Julius E. Smith, the President of the Charleston chapter of the Ladies Auxiliary of the Ancient Order of Hibernians and a member of the South Carolina Association for the Recognition of the Irish Republic.[555]

Lord Mayor O'Callaghan left Charleston on March 7, 1921, but the stir caused by his visit did not immediately subside. On March 8, Patrick H. Kennedy, president of the South Carolina Association for the Recognition of the Irish Republic, announced that as a result of the refusal of various halls and theaters in the city to allow Donal O'Callaghan to speak, a national campaign was being launched to raise

$50,000 for the purpose of erecting a hall in Charleston where such meetings could be held in the future.[556] Mayor Grace also received some criticism for the part he played in the city's rejection of O'Callghan's request for a street permit. Prior to introducing Judge John W. Goff at the Hibernian Society's St. Patrick's Day banquet on March 17, 1921, Grace defended himself by explaining "that he never prohibited Lord Mayor O' Callaghan of Cork from speaking in this city, as he felt this was a given right to every man to say in speech just what he wished, but he did tell the committee that he would not grant permission for him to speak on the street, as it was Sunday after they had mentioned to him that they were unable to secure a hall."[557]

In addition to the need for organizations to raise money, there was a need for a group to see that funds raised in America were distributed to the people of Ireland. The American Red Cross was reluctant to get involved, so the Irish White Cross was formed in Ireland to fulfill this function. An American counterpart of this organization was established on December 5, 1920, and branches were quickly established in fifteen states and over a hundred cities. A branch of the Irish White Cross or Celtic Cross Association, as it was sometimes known, was established in Charleston in April 1921 by Mrs. Julius E. Smith, president of the local chapter of the Ladies Auxiliary of the Ancient Order of Hibernians. The following were also members of the Charleston branch: Mrs. William J. Condon, Mrs. James F. Condon, Mrs. D. E. Finnegan, Mrs. W. F. Livingston, Mrs. Walter F. Lewis, Mrs. Charles Dennis, Mrs. Thomas Marks, Mrs. H. J. Wan Delkin, Mrs. William Riley, Mrs. T. R. Jervey, Mrs. R. A. Torlay, Mrs. M. Fox, Miss Katie Lavelle, Mrs. M. J. Condon, Mrs. Phillip C. Doyle, Miss Mamie Cronin, Mrs. Henry Condon, Miss M. Morrissey, Mrs. P. J. Hanley, Miss Elizabeth O'Gara, Mrs. Hugh O'Gorman, Mrs. M. Harley, Mrs. George Meitzler, Mrs. John B. Comar, Miss Daisy Doran, Mrs. Charles Engle, Mrs. J. M. Cason, Miss M. J. Powers and Mrs. William J. Kennedy.[558]

By the summer of 1921, both the people of Ireland and the people of Britain had become weary of the brutality and expense of the war in Ireland. A truce was called on July 11, 1921, followed by a meeting in London between President Eamon de Valera and British Prime Minister David Lloyd George. The initial proposals from the British were rejected, but negotiations began again in London during October of that year. Finally, on December 6, 1921 a treaty was signed under which southern Ireland was to become a free state with full dominion status on the model of Canada. Charleston's long connection with the cause of Irish Freedom had finally come to an end.[559]

APPENDICES

Appendix 1: A Partial List Of The Officers And Committee Members Of The St. Patrick's Benevolent Society Of Charleston, South Carolina From 1817 Through 1922 — 149

Appendix 2: A Partial List Of The Members Of The St. Patrick's Benevolent Society Of Charleston, South Carolina In The 1880s — 163

Appendix 3: A Partial List Of The Officers Of The Ancient Order Of Hibernians In Charleston, South Carolina. From 1889 Through 1922 — 167

Appendix 4: A Partial List Of The Officers And Committee Members Of The Hibernian Society Of Charleston From 1801 Through 1922 — 181

Appendix 5: A List Of The Members Of The Hibernian Society Of Charleston From 1801 To 1868, Along With The Date Of Their Admission — 221

Appendix 6: Roll Of The Irish Volunteers Mustered Into Confederate Service As Company "C," Charleston Battalion — 231

Appendix 7: Roll Of The Irish Volunteers Company "K," First Regiment Of South Carolina Volunteers, Army Of Northern Virginia — 235

Appendix 8: Roll Of The Irish Volunteers That Served On The Mexican Border In 1916 And 1917, Company "C," Second Regiment Of The South Carolina National Guard — 241

Appendix 9: Roll Of The Irish Volunteers That Served In World War I, Company "C," 105th Ammunition Train — 243

Appendix 10: A Partial List Of The Company Commanders
Of The Irish Volunteers   245

APPENDIX 1

A PARTIAL LIST OF THE OFFICERS AND COMMITTEE MEMBERS OF THE ST. PATRICK'S BENEVOLENT SOCIETY OF CHARLESTON, SOUTH CAROLINA FROM 1817 THROUGH 1922

1817 through 1834
John Magrath, President
1835
John Magrath, President
Kerr Boyce, Vice-President
Edw. O'Neill, Treasurer
A. G. Magrath, Orator
Committee on Finance:
C. M. Furman, H. L. Pinckney and John Dougherty, Jr.
Committee on Relief:
M. Roddy, John King and James Fay.
1836 and 1837
John Magrath, President
Ker Boyce, Vice-President
John King, Treasurer
John McCormick, Secretary
A. G. Magrath, Orator
Committee on Finance:
C. M. Furman, John Dougherty, Sr. and H. L. Pinckney.
Committee on Relief:
J. L. O'Wen, A. M'Intyre and M. F. Turley.
1838
John Magrath, President
Ker Boyce, Vice-President
John King, Treasurer
Leslie O'Wen, Secretary

Committee on Finance:
C. M. Furman, H. L. Pinckney and Joseph Dougherty.
Committee on Relief:
Martin Roddy, P. Cassady and M. F. Turley
1839 through 1849
John Magrath, President
1850
Charles M. Furman, President
Ker Boyce, Vice-President
John King, Treasurer
Leslie O'Wen, Secretary
Committee on Finance:
H. L. Pinckney, John Magrath and Patrick O'Neill.
Committee on Relief:
John Dougherty, Edward Henry and Edmond O'Niell.
1851
Charles M. Furman, President
A. G. Magrath, Vice-President
Patrick O'Neill, Vice-President
Henry L. Pinckney, Treasurer
Bernard O'Neill, Secretary
Committee on Finance:
John King, Dr. Righton, William Perry, H. F. Baker and W. S. King.
Committee on Relief:
Edward Henry, Leslie O'Wen, E. O'Neill, Thomas Maher, James Browne, Patrick Nevin, Simon Kennedy, Peter O'Brien, James Armstrong, D. F. Twohill, Thomas Gannon, and John O'Sullivan.
1852
C. M. Furman, President
Rev. R. S. Baker, First Vice-President
Edmund O'Neill, Second Vice-President
H. F. Baker, Treasurer
D. L. Owen, Secretary
Orator for 1853, Rev. R. S. Baker
Committee on Finance:
J. B. O'Neill, W. Aiken, H. L. Pinckney, Jno. M. Righton, W. J. Mosimann.
Committee on Relief:
Thomas Maher, E. Henry, P. O'Brien, Thomas Gannon, W. Ellard,

B. Bross, Jno. Maher, T. W. Twohill, Jas Armstrong, R. Hasett, J. Dawson and M. Kennedy.

1853

C. M. Furman, President
Rev. R. S. Baker, First Vice-President
Edward O'Niell, Second Vice-President
H. F. Baker, Treasurer
Leslie O'Wen, Secretary
Rev. J. J. O'Connor, Orator
Committee on Finance:
B. O'Niell, Dr. Lynch, John King, A. A. Allemong and J. F. O'Neill.
Committee on Relief:
Thos. Maher, Benjn. Bross, G. Burns, Edwd. Henry, J. Feehan, Rev. J. Shanahan, Peter O'Brien,
Wm. Ellard, John Maher, Jas. Burke, Jas. Dawson and Michael Kennedy.

1854

C. M. Furman, President

1855

Rev. R. S. Baker, President
J. F. O'Neill, First Vice-President
James Browne, Second Vice-President
H. F. Baker, Treasurer
Thomas B. Fogarty, Secretary
Rev. J. T. Carr, Orator
Committee on Finance
A. A. Allemong, B. O'Neill, John Malony and Grindal O'Kane.
Committee on Relief:
P. C. Cary, M. O'Neill, M. F. O'Callaghan, M. Kennedy, F. Minahan, E. F. Sweegan and P. Boylan.

1856

Rev. R. S. Baker, President
James Brown, First Vice-President
A. A. Allemong, Second Vice President
H. F. Baker, Treasurer
Thomas B. Fogarty, Secretary
Committee on Finance
A. A. Allemong, B. O'Neill, John Molony, Daniel Twohill and Patrick O'Neill.
Committee on Relief:

P. Cleary, Michael O'Neill, M. S. Callaghan, T. Quinlivan, Michael Kennedy, Michael Feehan and Phillip Boylan.
<u>Committee on Letters</u>
Daniel F. Twohill, M. S. Callaghan and Michael O'Neill.
<u>1857</u>
John F. O'Neill, President
R. K. Payne, First Vice-President
John Burns, Second Vice-President
Leslie O'Wen, Treasurer
Thomas B. Fogarty, Secretary
Rev. R. S. Baker, Orator
<u>Committee on Finance:</u>
P. O'Donnell, Jas. Bourke, H. F. Baker and Wm. Barragan.
<u>Committee on Relief:</u>
Garrett Byrns, James Cantwell, Thomas Nolan, P. Harvey, Dan Quinn and John Smythe.
<u>Committee on Letters:</u>
A. A. Allemong, Garrett Byrnes and Thomas Nolan.
<u>1858</u>
John F. O'Neill, President
R. K. Payne, First Vice-President
John Burns, Second Vice-President
Leslie O'Wen, Treasurer
Thomas B. Fogarty, Secretary
<u>Committee on Finance:</u>
P. O'Donnell, Jas. Burke, Thomas Maher, H. F. Baker and Wm. Barragan.
<u>Committee on Relief:</u>
Garrett Byrns, Thomas Nowlan, P. Harvey, Edward Daly, Michael Kennedy and James Wallace.
<u>Committee on Letters:</u>
Thomas Quinlivan, Cornelius O'Mara and M. T. Laughran.
<u>1859</u>
J. F. O'Neill, President
John Burns, First Vice-President
P. O'Donnell, Second Vice-President
Leslie O'Wen, Treasurer
Thomas B. Fogarty, Secretary
<u>Committee on Finance:</u>
James Bourke, Thomas Maher, William Barragan, Richard Hogan and Alexander Owens.

Committee on Relief:
Garrett Burns, James Cantwell, Michael Kennedy, Jr., Patrick Harvey, Thomas Quinlivan, Cornelius O'Mara and William White.
Committee on Letters:
Philip Fogarty, C. R. Cassidy and Edward Collins.

1860
John F. O'Neill, President
John Burns, First Vice-President
Patrick O'Donnell, Second Vice-President
J. Leslie O'Wen, Treasurer
Thomas R. Fogarty, Secretary
Committee on Finance:
James Burke, Bernard O'Neill, W. P. O'Hara, H. F. Baker and Richard Hogan.
Committee on Relief:
Thomas Maher, C. R. Cassidy, Edward Collins, Wm. White, Jas. Cantwell, T. Quinlivan and M. F. Molony.
Committee on Letters:
John Molony, Lawrence Cantwell and M. J. Callahan.

1861
M. P. O'Connor, President
H. F. Baker, Vice-President
M. F. Malony, Vice-President
Leslie O'Wen, Treasurer
Thomas D. Fogarty, Secretary
Committee on Finance:
M. Gannon, John O'Mara, Thomas Maher, P. O'Donnell and B. Rodden.
Committee on Relief:
Timothy Minehan, M. Kennedy, James Melvin, P. Harvey, James Wallace, J. Barry, Garrett Byrnes, John Burke, T. Quinlivan and ED. Collins.

1862
M. F. Molony, President
T. L. Quackenbush, Vice-President
Thomas Maher, Vice-President
Dr. Leslie O'Wen, Treasurer
Dan. F. Twohill, Secretary
Committee on Finance:
P. O'Donnell, John O'Mara, M. Gannon and B. Rodden.

Committee on relief:
Garrett Byrnes, J. Barry, T. Minehan, M. Kennedy, Thomas Murphy and William Ellard.
Committee on Letters:
John Kennedy, James Wallace and M. Feehan.
1863
M. F. Molony, President
T. L. Quackenbush, Vice-President
Thomas Maher, Vice-President
Dr. Leslie O'Wen, Treasurer
Dan. F. Twohill, Secretary
Committee on Finance:
P. O'Donnell, John O'Mara, M. Gannon and B. Rodden.
Committee on Relief:
Garrett Byrnes, J. Barry, T. Minehan, M. Kennedy, Thomas Murphy and William Ellard.
Committee on Letters:
John Kennedy, James Wallace and M. Feehan.
1864
Rev. C. J. Croghan, President
Thomas Maher, Vice-President
John Barry, Vice-President
Bernard Rodden, Treasurer
D. F. Twohill, Secretary
Committee on Finance:
Garrett Byrnes, John D. Kennedy, J. M. Wolff and J. Wallace.
Committee on Relief:
P. Harvey, James O'Neill, Michael Kennedy, E. Wallace, M. Feehan, George Jaudy and J. Barry.
Committee on Letters:
Edmund Kennedy, James Shanahan and Timothy Cosgrove.
1865
Thomas Maher. President part of the year.
Rev. C. J. Croghan, President part of the year.
1866
Rev. C. J. Crogan, President
James Cosgrove, First Vice-President
Thomas Maher, Second Vice-President
B. Rodden, Treasurer
John McMahon, Secretary
Committee on Finance:

Garrett Byrnes, John D. Kennedy, A. Farley, John Barry, Joseph Dothage, Michael Feehan and Thomas Finnegan.
Committee on Relief:
Geo. Jaudy, James O'Neill, James Shannahan, John Barry, James Kennedy, W. Torlay and James Dawson.
Committee on Letters:
James Dawson and William Foley.
1867
Rev. C. J. Croghan, President
James Cosgrove, First Vice-President
Thomas Maher, Second Vice-President
James F. Slattery, Treasurer
John McMahon, Secretary
Committee on Finance:
Garrett Byrns, B. Rodden, C. D. Mulvaney, John Barry, John D. Kennedy and Joseph Dotage.
Committee on Relief:
Geo. Tandy, Thomas Finneran, Michael Kennedy, James Wallace, James Barry, P. Harvey and James Muldoon.
Committee on Letters:
Michael Feehan, James Dawson and Patrick Kennedy.
1868
Rev. C. J. Croghan, President
James Cosgrove, First Vice-President
John M. Toughey, Second Vice-President
James T. Slattery, Treasurer
William Baker, Secretary
Committee on Finance:
James J. Grace, Garrett Byrnes, Joseph Dothage, D. F. Touhill, Thomas Meager, John D. Kennedy
and D. O'Neill.
Committee on Relief:
Michael Feahan, Charles Mulraney, James Muldrow, John Edmunds and John Morrisey.
Committee on Letters:
John Barry, P. Harvey and Michael Duane.
1869
Rev. C. J. Croghan, President
James Cosgrove, First Vice-President
John M. Tuohy, Second Vice-President
James T. Slattery, Treasurer

William Baker, Secretary
Committee on Finance:
Charles D. Mulrany, Joseph Dothage, Thomas Maher, J. D. Kennedy and John Morrissey.
Committee on Relief:
Michael Feehan, John Edmonds, John Morrissey, James Muldroon and John Laval.
Committee on Letters:
John Barry, P. Harvey and Michael Duane.

1870
Rev. C. J. Croghan, President
James Cosgrove, First Vice-President
Thomas Maher, Second Vice-President
James F. Slattery, Treasurer
W. Baker, Secretary
Committee on Finance
Michael Feehan, John Barry, Jos. Dothage, J. D. Kennedy, C. D. Mulvaney, M, Canfield.
Committee on Relief
Thos. Murphy, Jas. Rahall, John Flynn, Patrick Conroy, Michael Kelly.
Committee on Letters
Patrick Kenerly, Patrick Kennedy and Michael Duane.

1871
Rev. C. J. Croghan, President
James Cosgrove, First Vice-President
James Powers, Second Vice-President
James Barry, Treasurer
Wm. Baker, Secretary
Committee on Finance
J. T. Maher, J. D. Kennedy, C. D. Mulvaney, William Corbett and Thomas Lyons.
Committee on Relief
Thos. Murphy, Stephen Maloney, James Quinn, John O'Connell, Pat Conroy, John Blake and Pat Kennerty.
Committee on Letters
John Burke, Jr., A. O'Connell and Thomas Sheahan.

1872
Rev. C. J. Croghan, President
James Cosgrove, First Vice-President
James Powers, Second Vice-President

John Barry, Treasurer
W. Baker, Secretary
Committee on Finance
John Burke, Sr., Simon Fogarty, Jas. Maloney, Michael Duane, and James Rahall.
Committee on Relief
Thomas Murphy, Patrick Knealy, J. J. Burns, Michael Fehan, Richard Murphy, Patrick Conroy and Patrick Kennedy.
Committee on Letters
Daniel Maher, Michael Hennessy and Edward O'Dea.
1873
Rev. C. J. Croghan, President
James Cosgrove, First Vice-President
James Powers, Second Vice-President
John Barry, Treasurer
W. Baker, Secretary
1874
Rev. C. J. Croghan, President
J. F. Slattery, First Vice-President
Stephen Molony, Second Vice-President
Jos. F. Redding, Secretary
Committee on Finance
Wm. Baker, Peter Fallon, John Burke, Patrick Brady and D. F. Gleason.
Committee on Relief
D. Maher, Thomas Murphy, M. Dwan, P. Canaley, Thos. Roddy and P. Flynn.
Committee on Letters
Thos. Dunn, James Martin and John Cahill.
1875
John Moore D D., President
F. Touhey, First Vice-President
John Burke, Second Vice-President
P. Fallon, Treasurer
James F. Redding, Secretary
1876
Rev. John Moore, President
John Devereux, First Vice-President
Jno. Barry, Second Vice-President
Peter Fallon, Treasurer
James F. Redding, Secretary

1877
Rev. John Moore, President
1878 through 1879
Rev. Joseph Reddington, President
1880
M. F. Kennedy, President
James Ronan, First Vice-President
Thos. Flynn, Second Vice-President
Simon Fogarty, Treasurer
M. J. Flynn, Recording Secretary
Edward Dunnler, Financial Secretary
J. W. Reed, Sergeant-at-arms
1881
M. F. Kennedy, President
James Ronan, First Vice-President
Thos. Flynn, Second Vice-President
Simon Fogarty, Treasurer
Thos. A. Murray, Recording Secretary
Wm. J. Casey, Financial Secretary
1882
M. F. Kennedy, President
Thos. Flynn, First Vice-President
F, H. Warren, Second Vice-President
Thomas A. Murray, Recording Secretary
James J. Carey, Financial Secretary
Simon Fogarty, Treasurer
1883
M. F. Kennedy, President
Thos. Flynn, First Vice-President
F. H. Warren, Second Vice-President
Simon Fogarty, Treasurer
B. P. Cunningham, Recording Secretary
James J. Carey, Financial Secretary
1884
M. F. Kennedy, President
Thos. Flynn, First Vice-President
F. H. Warren, Second Vice-President
W. E. Mulligan, Recording Secretary
B. P. Cunningham, Financial Secretary
Simon Fogarty, Treasurer
1885 and 1886

M. F. Kennedy, President
Thos. Flynn, First Vice-President
F. H. Warren, Second Vice-President
James Ronan, Recording Secretary
B. P. Cunningham, Treasurer
Board of Trustees:
Peter Lee, Patrick Moran and D. M. O'Driscoll.
Auditing Committee:
Wm. Aiken Kelly, J. O. Goutevenier and Wm. E. Milligan.
Burial Ground Committee:
Samuel Webb, Wm. Flynn and C. O'Mara.
1887
Thos. Flynn, President
W. E. Milligan, First Vice-President
J. F. Tobin, Second Vice-President
B. P. Cunningham, Treasurer
James Ronan, Recording Secretary
1888
Thos. Flynn, President
W. E. Milligan, First Vice-President
J. F. Tobin, Second Vice-President
B. P. Cunningham, Treasurer
James Ronan, Recording Secretary
1889
W. E. Milligan, President
John J. Delaney, First Vice-President
J. J. Carey, Second Vice-President
B. P. Cunningham, Treasurer
James Ronan, Recording Secretary
1890
*W. E. Milligan, President
John J. Delany, First Vice-President
Dennis McSweeney, Second Vice-President
B. P. Cunningham, Treasurer
James Ronan, Recording Secretary
*P. E. Gleason was also president in 1890 but died.
1891 and 1892
D. M. O'Driscoll, President
Jas. McAlister, First Vice-President
J. L. Rice, Second Vice-President
W. J. Casey, Treasurer

James Ronan, Recording Secretary
<u>1893</u>
D. M. O'Driscoll, President
James McAlister, First Vice-President
J. L. Rice, Second Vice-President
W. J. Casey, Treasurer
M. G. Gorman, Recording Secretary
<u>1894</u>
D. M. O'Driscoll, President
James McAlister, First Vice-President
J. L. Rice, Second Vice-President
W. J. Casey, Treasurer
M. G. Gorman, Recording Secretary
<u>1895</u>
D. M. O'Driscoll, President
Maurice Maguire, First Vice-President
John T. Donahue, Second Vice-President
W. J. Casey, Treasurer
M. G. Gorman, Recording Secretary
<u>1896</u>
D. M. O'Driscoll, President
Maurice Maguire, First Vice-President
John T. Donahue, Second Vice-President
W. J. Casey, Treasurer
M. G. Gorman, Recording Secretary
<u>1897</u>
D. M. O'Driscoll, President
Maurice Maguire, First Vice-President
John T. Donahue, Second Vice-President
W. J. Casey, Treasurer
M. G. Gorman, Recording Secretary
<u>1898, 1899, 1900 and 1901</u>
D. M. O'Driscoll, President
Maurice Maguire, First Vice-President
John T. Donahue, Second Vice-President
E. M. Barry, Treasurer
M. G. Gorman, Recording Secretary
<u>1902</u>
D. M. O'Driscoll, President
John T. Donahue, Vice-President
M. G. Gorman, Recording Secretary

J. T. Hallis, Treasurer
<u>1903</u>
D. M. O'Driscoll, President
B. P. Cunningham, Vice-President
J. T. Hallis, Treasurer
M. G. Gorman, Recording Secretary
<u>1904 through 1910</u>
B. P. Cunningham, President
J. L. Brennan, Vice-President
J. M. Walsh, Secretary/Treasurer
<u>1911-1912</u>
J. L. Brennan, President
G. M. Murphy, Vice-President
J. M. Walsh, Secretary/Treasurer
<u>1913 through 1916</u>
J. T. Hallis, President
J. C. O'Brien, Vice-President
W. B. Parsons, Secretary/Treasurer
<u>1917 through 1922</u>
J. T. Hallis, President
J. A. Goutevenier, Vice-President
W. B. Parsons, Secretary/Treasurer

The list was compiled from Charleston newspapers and city directories.

APPENDIX 2

A PARTIAL LIST OF THE MEMBERS OF THE ST. PATRICK'S BENEVOLENT SOCIETY OF CHARLESTON, SOUTH CAROLINA

IN THE 1880S*

Acilly, William, 29 America St.; Adams, C., 8 Cannon St.; Armstrong, J. A., 97 Tradd St.; Armstrong, Capt. Jas., 7 Society St.; Astle, Thomas C., 8 Minority St; Axson, A., 8 Wolfe St.

Baker, Geo. O., 8. Franklin St.; Barry, E. M., with L. Elias, Jr. King St.; Beatty, Joseph, 617 King St.; Bishop, John G., 12 Felix St.; Black, P., 617 King St.; Blank, Sol., 240 King St.; Boniface, F. J., 101 Calhoun St.; Boyce, John H., 203 Coming St.; Boyd, Bernard, 53 Elizabeth St.; Brandt, E. P., 10 Elizabeth St.; Brandt, J. F., 10 Elizabeth St.; Brandt, W. J., 10 Elizabeth St.; Brown, J. W., Cor. George & Anson; Burns, John, 221 Meeting St; Byrns, Garrett, 16 Wentworth St.; Byrns, John, 23 State St.

Callahan B., 186 Meeting St. Callahan J. J., 34 America St.; Callahan, M., 14 America St.; Cantwell, E. P., 151 St. Phillips St.; Cantwell, R., Ann Street Depot; Carey, J. J., Cor. of King and Queen Sts.; Carmody, C. M., 12 Reid St.; Cartmill, J., 12 Radcliff St.; Carwile, Thos. W., 46 Hasell St.; Casey, W. J., 22 Burns Lane; Cassidy, Paul, 197 Meeting St; Cavanagh, R., 25 Queen St., Coffey, Thos. E., 5 Montague St.; Cogan, J. J., 71 King St.; Colcolough, Jas., 25 Columbus St.; Collins, W. J., 6 South St.; Conroy, D., 32 St. Philip St; Conroy, Pat, 44 King St.; Conway, M. J., Cor. State & Chalmers; Colson, G. E., 12 Middle St.; Colson, William P., 12 Middle St.; Coogan, J. L., 5 Alexander St.; Croghan, Thos., Forks in the Road; Cosgrove, James, 37 Market St.; Croghan, J. P., Forks in the Road; Cunningham, B., 42 Tradd St.; Cunningham, B. P., 42 Tradd St.; Cunningham, Bern., 42 Tradd St.; Curly, M., 67 State St.

Detell, John, 13 John St.; Daly, Edward, 125 Meeting St.; Dalwick, T. E., 45 Coming; Darcy, J. A., 7 Drake St; Darcy M., 8 Drake St.; Delesline, W. K., Main Station House; Deveaux, John P., Fireproof Building;

Dixon, Isaac, 33 Calhoun St.; Doyle, T. F., Cor. Weims Ct. & King St.; Doyle, John C., 45 East Bay St.; Druelle, Leon, 74 Broad St.; Drew, J., 2 Middle St.; Dubos, Chas. L., 3 Gadsden St, Duffy, Andrew, 12 Montague; Dunne, J. F., Sunday Times Office; Dunne, John, 9 Liberty St.; Dunning, F. A., 326 Meeting St.; Dunning, John H., 17 Henrietta St.

Enright, John, Bag Factory John St.; Eisenhardt, E., 32 Reid St.

Ferguson, H. 48 Hasell St; Finnegan, A. F., 8 Philadelphia St.; Finnegan, J. L., 9 Chalmers St.; Finnegan, M. J., 9 Chalmers St.; Fitsgerald, Geo., 15 Mill St.; Flemming, W. J., 141 King St.; Flynn, Joseph, 7 Magazine St; Flynn, M. J., 6 Orange St.; Flynn, Thos., 93 Market St.; Flynn, William, 1 Limehouse St.; Fogarty, Phil, Military Hall; Fogarty, Simon, 96 Broad St.; Foley, B., Market St.; Frain, Thomas, Cor. Queen & Church; Freeman, R. W., 636 King St.Furlong, R. J., 79 Broad St.

Gannon, W. H., 62 Anson St.; Gaynan, John, 15 Ann St.; Garvin, Thomas, 56 Spring St.; Gilliland, D. B., 25 Broad St.; Gleason, P. E., 373 King St.; Gorman, M. G., Chas. Hotel Billiard Room; Gonzales, John, Shell Road; Grace, J. J.; Grazyck, Jos., 792 King St.; Gunning, D. R, 9 Anson St.

Hanly, P. J., 465 King St.; Hallis, Jno., 31 Beaufain St.; Halton, E. J., 10 Mary St.; Hanifan, M. D., 3 Clifford St.; Harley, J.; Harmond, J. W., Cor. State & Chalmers; Harrington, W. F., 375 King St.; Hartnett, John, 140 Calhoun St.; Hartwell, John B., 71 Broad St.; Hayden, J., 16 John St.; Heiser, Henry, 9 Liberty St.; Henneberry, J. J., 84 Spring St.; Hogan, Michael, 697 King St.; Holst, H., 37 Market St.; Howard, James, 4 Spring St.; Hughes, T. J., 25 Columbus St.; Hunt, W., Four Mile House; Hurley, J.; Hutson, S.D., 9 St. Philip St.

Irvine, Patrick, 91 Church St.

Jones, T., Pavilion Hotel; Jones, William A., Summerville; Jennings, A. T., 65 Broad St.; Jervey, J. M., 167 Calhoun St.; Jervey, W. P., 167 Calhoun St.; Johnson, W. J., 50 Reid St.

Keelan, Jno., 475 King St.; Keenan, John, Meeting St.; Kelly, W. A., 77 Beaufain St.; Kennedy, Dennis, 138 St. Phillips St.; Kennedy, John, 132 Church St.; Kennedy, A. J., 121 Meeting St.; Kennedy, M. F, 84 Anson St.; Kennedy, P. H., 132 Church St.; Kennedy, T. J., 114 Church St.; Kenney, John B., 122 Tradd St.; Kenny, John P., 358 King St.; Kerrison, Chas., Jr., 59 Smith St,; Kilroy, Jas., Central School Building

Laffan, James, Anson St.; Larousselier, E. F., East Bay St.; LeBuffe A., News and Courier; Leddy, Ber., 75 Church St.; Lee, Peter 49 Society St.; Livingston, Jacob, 58 Wentworth St.; Lord, F. A., Cor. George & King Sts.; Lynch M. J., 41 Wentworth St.

Mackin, B. P., 80 King St.; Maguire, Wm., 61 Church St.; Maher,

Kenneth, Fort Sumter; Malia, Wm. J., 59 Tradd St.; Mandeville, J. C, 122 Meeting St.; Manion, J. P., 25 Queen St.; Manion, P., 25 Queen St.; Mason C. M., 93 Church; May, P. F., 2 Columbus St.; McAlister, James, 45 St. Philip St.; McBride, Bernard, 707 King St.; McCarrell, H., 46 Coming St.; McCarrell, T. S., 2 College St.; McCarrell, W. M., Cor. Anson & Pinckney; McCormack, H. J., 75 Beaufain St.; McDonnell, E. J., Telegraph Office; McGary, T. J., 18 Tradd St.; McGary, W. P., 18 Tradd St.; McGinness, W. T., 61 King St.; McGorty, Chas., 29 Tradd St.; McKenny, Jos. W., 36 Savage St.; McHugh, C.A., 5 Friend St.; McHugh, F. L., 369 Broad St.; McInnerny, John, 5 Lamboll St.; McLoy, Alex., 108 Wentworth St.; McMahon, M., City Hospital; McManus, E. L., 16 King St.; McManus, M. J., 16 King St.; McNaughton, J., 22 Hanover St.; McPherson, John, 10 Trapman St.; McShane, James, 579 King St.; McSweeny, D., 9 Minority St.; Medison, Jacob, 112 Anson St.; Meyer, C. W., Cor. Meeting & Chalmers; Mikell, E. S, 13 Inspection St.; Miller, P. J., 9 St. Philip St.; Milligan, W. E., 22 Spring St.; Molony, James, Church & Cumberland; Molony, Thos., 214 Coming St.; Moore, E. E., 6 Beaufain St.; Moran. P., 5 Hasell St., Morello, John B., 71 Broad St.; Morrissey, John, 21 Queen St.; Murphy, L. K., 115 East Bay St.; Murphy, M., Washington St.; Murphy, Patrick, 101 Calhoun St.; Murray, John, 20 Wolfe St.; Murray, P. F., 131 Meeting St. Murray, T. A., 108 Church St.

Noah, H., 138 Meeting St,; Nunan, J. W., 71 Broad St.

Oakman, Cliff, 88 Church St.; O'Brien, Peter, Cor. King & John Sts.; O'Connell, A., 84 Meeting St.; O'Connor, M., 14 Queen St.; O'Connor, T. J. 59 Tradd St.; O'Connor, W. J., 517 King St.; O'Driscoll, D. M.; O'Gara, L. A., 34 Queen St.; O'Gorman, John, 119 Market St.; O'Gorman, Thos., 3 John St.; O'Hagan W. J.; O'Mara, Danl, 8 Wentworth St.; O'Mara, J. F., 80 Queen St.; O'Meara, C., 77 St, Philip St.; O'Neill, F. L., 80 Wentworth St.; O'Neill, John, 579 King St.; O'Neill, T. M., 52 Meeting St.; O'Shaughnessy, M., 79 Broad St.

Palmer, A. H., 13 John St.; Palmer, H. J., 13 John St.; Prince, J. E., Pye, Capt. William, 71 Broad St.

Quinlivan, John A., 43 East Bay St.; Quinn, J. E., 273 Meeting St.; Quinn, James, Chas Iron Works

Redding, James F., 15 Meeting St; Rianes, J. F., 59 Spring St; Rivers, T. E., 6 Water St.; Roddy, Thos., Cor. Church & Queen Sts.; Ronan, Jas., 56 Beaufain; Ryan, P. E., 30 Magazine St.

Sampson, Edward; Sanders. H., 71 Broad St.; Schnell, C., 100 Broad St.; Schroder, C. H., 67 ½ Cannon St.; Schulze, J. H., Express Office; Scott, G. W., 110 Church St.; Seignious, J. T., Foot of Hasell; Simons, C. L., 5 Savage St.; Simons, James, 77 Broad St.; Sherridan, P. M., 69 King

St.; Shokes, C. W., 125 Spring St.; Shokes, George M., 125 Cannon St.; Smith, W. Hampton, 64 Radcliffe St.; Storen, M., 5 Ann St.; Sullivan. P, 56 Beaufain St.; Sweeney, J. J., 27 Amherst.

Treahy, M. J., 3 Horlbeck Alley

Viett, E. T.; Vincent, W. E., 39 Ashley St.

Wallace, T. F., 17 St. Philip St.; Wallace, W. J., 17 St. Philip St.; Warren, F. H., 137 Meeting St.; Webb, Saml., 8 Friend St.; Welsh, John, 2 McKeegan's Row; Worrell, C. J., 59 Spring St. Worrell, G. M., West Point Mills; Wright, W. Harry, 29 East Bay St.

*The list is taken from a copy of old book No.1 of the St. Patrick's Benevolent Society.

APPENDIX 3

A PARTIAL LIST OF THE OFFICERS OF THE ANCIENT ORDER OF HIBERNIANS IN CHARLESTON, SOUTH CAROLINA FROM 1889 THROUGH 1922

1889 and 1890
Division No. 1
Dennis Kennedy, President; E. M. Barry, Vice President; W. J. Casey, Recording Secretary;
M. J. Danehey, Financial Secretary; B. P. Cunningham, Treasurer; and Jno. J. O'Herin, Sergeant-at-Arms
1891
Division No. 1
Dennis Kennedy, Pres.; J. C. Budds, V-Pres.; W. J. Casey, Rec. Sec.; M. J. Danehay, Cor. Sec.; W. J. Condon, Treas.
1892
Division No. 1
Jas. Ronan, Pres.; W. J. Comar, V-Pres.; J. J. Madden, Rec. Sec.; W. J. Condon, Treas.
Division No. 2
E. F. Sweegan, President; M. D. Maguire, Vice President; J. J. Corcoran, Financial Secretary and Treasurer; S. F. Dawson, Sergeant at Arms; M. P. McLaughlin, Recording Secretary; P. Devereux, Sentinel; J. F. Condon, Chairman Standing Committee; W. J. Storen, Marshal and Rev. J. J. Monaghan, Chaplin.
1893
Division No. 1
W. J. Comar, Pres.; J. W. Wallace, V-Pres.; J. P. O'Neill, Fin. Sec.; F. F. Buero, Rec. Sec.;
W. J. Condon, Treas.
Division No. 2

E. F. Sweegan, Pres.; M. Maguire, V-Pres.; M. P. McLaughlin, Rec. Sec.; J. J. Corcoran, Treas.

State Officers

F. J. Devereux, State Delegate; E. M. Barry, Secretary; B. P. Cunningham, Treas.

Charleston County Officers

J. J. Hogan, County Delegate

1894

Division No. 1

W. J. Comar, Pres.; James Laffan, V-Pres.; Jas. Mooney, Fin. Sec.; F. F. Buero, Rec. Sec.;

W. J. Condon, Treas.

Division No. 2

E. F. Sweegan, Pres.; M. Maguire, V-Pres.; M. P. McLaughlin, Rec. Sec.; J. J. Corcoran, Treas.

State Officers

F. J. Devereux, State Delegate; E, M. Barry, Secretary; B. P. Cunningham, Treas.

Charleston County Officers

J. W. Wallace, County Delegate

1895

Division No. 1

W. J. Comar, Pres.; James Laffan, V-Pres.; B. P. Carey, Fin. Sec.; F. F. Buero, Rec. Sec.;

W. J. Condon, Treas.

Division No. 2

E. F. Sweegan, Pres.; M. Maguire, V-Pres.; M. P. McLaughlin, Rec. Sec.; T. J. Sughrue, Fin. Sec.;

J. J. Corcoran, Treas.

Division No. 3

Thos. Hogan, Pres.; Jas. Cosgrove, V-Pres.; James McGrath, Fin. Sec.; J. A. Barbot, Treas.

State Officers

F. J. Devereux, State Delegate; J. J. Corcoran, Sec.; B. P. Cunningham, Treas.

Charleston County Officers

J. W. Wallace, County Delegate

1896

Division No. 1

W. J. Comar, Pres.; James Laffan, V-Pres.; B. P. Carey, Fin. Sec.; F. F. Buero, Rec. Sec.;

W. J. Condon, Treas.
Division No. 2
E. F. Sweegan, Pres.; M. Maguire, V-Pres.; M. P. McLaughlin, Rec. Sec.; T. A. Casey, Fin. Sec.;
Daniel O'Brien, Treas.
Division No. 3
D. E. F. Fortune, Pres.; J. P. Hanley, V-Pres.; F. E. Palmer, Rec. Sec.; John Quale, Fin. Sec.;
J. L. Brennan, Treas.
State Officers
F. J. Devereux, State Delegate; James Cosgrove, Sec.; B. P. Cunningham, Treas.
County Officers
E. F. Sweegan, President

1897
Division No. 1
W. J. Comar, Pres.; J. J. Henebery, V-Pres.; T. M. O'Brien, Fin. Sec.; F. F. Buero, Rec. Sec.;
W. J. Condon, Treas.
Division No. 2
E. F. Sweegan, Pres.; M. Maguire, V-Pres.; M. P. McLaughlin, Rec. Sec.; T. F. Sughrue, Fin. Sec.;
Daniel O'Brien, Treas.
Division No. 3
D. E. F. Fortune, Pres.; James Vaughan, V-Pres.; M. G. Gorman, Rec. Sec.; John Quale, Fin. Sec.;
J. L. Brennan, Treas.
State Officers
W. J. Comar, President; T. F. Sughrue, Sec.; John Quale, Treas.
County Officers
E. F. Sweegan, President

1898
Division No. 1
W. J. Comar, Pres.; J. J. Henebery, V-Pres.; T. M. O'Brien, Financial Sec.; F. F. Buero, Recording Sec.; W. J. Condon, Treas.
Division No. 2
M. Maguire, Pres.; Andrew Duffy, V-Pres.; W. F. Fleming, Recording Sec.; T. F. Sughrue, Financial Sec.; Daniel O'Brien, Treas.
Division No. 3
P. J. Hanley, Pres.; D. F. O'Brien, V-Pres.; T. P. Vaughan, Rec. Sec.; John Quale, Financial Sec.;

J. L. Brennan, Treas.
Charleston County Officers
E. F. Sweegan, Pres.
State Officers
W. J. Comar, Pres.; T. F. Sughrue, Sec.; John Quale, Treas.

1899
Division No. 1
W. J. Comar, Pres.; J. J. Henebery, V-Pres.; T. M. O'Brien, Financial Sec.; F. F. Buero, Recording Sec.; W. J. Condon, Treas.
Division No. 2
M. Maguire, Pres.; Andrew Duffy, V-Pres.; W. F. Fleming, Recording Sec.; T. F. Sughrue, Financial Sec.; Daniel O'Brien, Treas.
Division No. 3
P. J. Hanley, Pres.; D. F. O'Brien, V-Pres.; T. P. Vaughan, Recording Sec.; John Quale, Financial Sec.; J. L. Brennan, Treas.
Charleston County Officers
E. F. Sweegan, Pres.
State Officers
J. J. Henebery, Pres.; T. M. O'Brien, Sec.; T. P. Vaughan, Treas.

1900
Division No. 1
W. J. Comar, Pres.; J. J. Henebery, V-Pres.; T. M. O'Brien, Financial Sec.; F. F. Buero, Recording Sec.; W. J. Condon, Treas.
Division No. 2
M. Maguire, Pres.; Andrew Duffy, V-Pres.; W. F. Fleming, Recording Sec.; T. F. Sughrue, Financial Sec.; Daniel O'Brien, Treas.
Charleston County Officers
E. F. Sweegan, President; M. Maguire, Vice-President.
State Officers
J. J. Henebery, Pres.; T. M. O'Brien, Sec.; T. F. Sughrue, Treas.

1901
Division No. 1
W. J. Comar, Pres.; J. J. Henebery, V-Pres.; T. M. O'Brien, Financial Sec.; F. F. Buero, Recording Sec.; W. J. Condon, Treas.
Division No. 2
M. Maguire, Pres; M. P. McLaughlin, V-Pres.; W. F. Fleming, Recording Sec.; T. F. Sughrue, Financial Sec.; Daniel O'Brien, Treas.
State Officers
E. F. Sweegan, Pres.; T. R. McCarthy, Sec.; D. F. O'Brien, Treas.
Charleston County Officers

B. P. Carey, Pres.; M. P. McLaughlin, V-Pres.

1902

Division No. 1

W. J. Comar, Pres.; J. J. Henebery, V-Pres.; T. M. O'Brien, Fin. Sec.;
F. F. Buero, Rec. Sec.;
W. J. Condon, Treas.

Division No. 2

M. Maguire, Pres.; M. P. McLaughlin, V-Pres.; W. F. Fleming, Rec. Sec.; T. F. Sughrue, Fin. Sec.;
Daniel O'Brien, Treas.

Ladies Auxiliary of AOH Div. No. 1

Mrs. C. O. Schott, Pres.; Mrs. D. O'Brien, V-Pres.; Miss D. Donelan, Fin. Sec.; Miss Kate L. Sughrue, Rec. Sec.; Mrs. T. F. Sughrue, Treas.; Rev. John T. McElroy, Chaplain

Charleston County Officers

B. Carey, Pres.; M. P. McLaughlin, V-Pres.

State Officers

E. F. Sweegan, Pres.; T. B. McCarthy, Sec.; D. F. O'Brien, Treas.

1903

Division No. 1

W. J. Comar, Pres.; J. A. Noland, V-Pres.; T. M. O'Brien, Fin. Sec.;
F. F. Buero, Rec. Sec.;
T. B. McCarthy, Treas.

Division No. 2

M. Maguire, Pres.; M. J. Hanley, V-Pres.; W. F. Fleming, Rec. Sec.;
T. F. Sughrue, Fin. Sec.;
Daniel O'Brien, Treas.

Ladies' Auxiliary of AOH Div. No. 1

Mrs. C. O. Schott, Pres.; Mrs. D. O'Brien, V-Pres.; Miss D. Donelan, Fin. Sec.; Miss Kate L. Sughrue, Rec. Sec.; Mrs. T. F. Sughrue, Treas.; Rev. John T. McElroy, Chaplain.

Charleston County Officers

B. P. Carey, Pres.; Jno. J. Furlong, V-Pres.

State Officers

E. F. Sweegan, Pres.; T. F. Sughrue, V-Pres.; T. B. McCarthy, Sec.; D. F. O'Brien, Treas.

1904

Division No. 1

W. J. Comar, Pres.; J. A. Noland, V-Pres.; T. M. O'Brien, Fin. Sec.;
F. F. Buero, Rec. Sec.;
T. B. McCarthy, Treas.

Division No. 2
M. Maguire, Pres.; M. J. Hanley, V-Pres.; W. F. Fleming, Rec. Sec.; T. F. Sughrue, Fin. Sec.;
Daniel O'Brien, Treas.
Ladies' Auxiliary
Mrs. C. O. Schott, Pres.; Miss M. Dunn, V-Pres.; Miss D. Donelan, Fin. Sec.; Miss Kate L. Sughrue, Rec. Sec.; Mrs. T. F. Sughrue, Treas.; Rev. John T. McElroy, Chaplain
Charleston County Officers
B. P. Carey, Pres.; John J. Furlong, V-Pres.; F. J. Quinlivan, Sec.; J. M. Hayes, Treas.
State Officers
E. F. Sweegan, Pres.; T. F. Sughrue, V-Pres.; T. B. McCarthy, Sec.; D. F. O'Brien, Treas.
1905
Division No. 1
W. J. Comar, Pres.; J. A. Noland, V-Pres.; T. M. O'Brien, Fin. Sec.; F. F. Buero, Rec. Sec.;
T. B. McCarthy, Treas.
Division No. 2
M. Maguire, Pres.; M. J. Hanley, V-Pres; W. F. Fleming, Rec. Sec.; T. F. Sughrue, Fin. Sec.; Daniel O'Brien, Treas.
Ladies' Auxiliary
Mrs. C. O. Schott, Pres.; Miss M. Dunn, V-Pres.; Miss Kate Lucas, Fin. Sec.; Miss Kate L. Sughrue, Rec. Sec.; Mrs. T. F. Sughrue, Treas.; Rev. John T. McElroy, Chaplain
Charleston County Officers
J. J. Furlong, Pres.; T. E. Hogan, V-Pres.; M. R. Croghan, Sec.; W. J. Condon, Treas.
State Officers
T. F. Sughrue, Pres.; J. M. Hayes, V-Pres.; J. L. Kailey, Sec.; W. J. Leonard, Treas.; Rev. W. J. Wright, State Chaplain.
1906
Division No. 1
W. J. Comar, Pres.; P. H. Murphy, V-Pres.; T. M. O'Brien, Fin. Sec.; F. F. Buero, Rec. Sec.;
T. B. McCarthy, Treas.
Division No. 2
M. J. Hanley,, Pres.; T. E, Hogan, V-Pres; J. M. Hayes, Rec. Sec.; T. F. Sughrue, Fin. Sec.; J. J. Burke, Treas.
Ladies' Auxiliary

Mrs. C. O. Schott, Pres.; Miss M. Dunn, V-Pres.; Miss Kate Lucas, Fin. Sec.; Miss Kate L. Sughrue, Rec. Sec.; Mrs. T. F. Sughrue, Treas.; Rev. J. J. Hughes, Chaplain

Charleston County Officers

W. J. Comar, Pres.; T. E. Hogan, V-Pres.; M. P. Croghan, Sec.; W. J. Condon, Treas.

State Officers

T. F. Sughrue, Pres.; J. M. Hayes, V-Pres.; J. L. Kiley, Sec.; J. J. Furlong, Treas.; Rev. W. J. Wright, State Chap.

1907

Division No. 1

W. J. Comar, Pres.; P. H. Murphy, V-Pres.; T. M. O'Brien, Financial Sec.; F. F. Buero, Recording Sec.; T. B. McCarthy, Treas.

Division No. 2

M. J. Hanley, Pres.; T. E. Hogan, V-Pres.; J. M. Hayes, Rec. Sec.; T. F. Sughrue, Fin. Sec.;
J. J. Burke, Treas.

Ladies' Auxiliary

Miss Mary Delahunty, Pres.; Miss Kate Lucas, Fin. Sec.; Miss Kate L. Sughrue, Rec. Sec.; Mrs. T. F. Sughrue, Treas.

Charleston County Officers

W. P. Cullinane, Pres.; M. P. Croghan, Sec.; F. L. Torlay, Treas.

State Officers

T. B. McCarthy, Pres.; J. M. Hayes, V-Pres.; F. J. Carney, Sec.;

1908

Division No. 1

W. J. Comar, Pres.; P. H. Murphy, V-Pres.; T. M. O'Brien, Financial Sec.; F. F. Buero, Recording Sec.; M. P. Croghan, Treas.

Division No. 2

M. J. Hanley, Pres.; T. E. Hogan, V-Pres.; J. M. Hayes, Rec. Sec., T. F. Sughrue, Fin. Sec.;
J. J. Burke, Treas.

Ladies' Auxiliary

Mrs. C. O. Schott, Pres.; Miss Kate Lucas, Fin. Sec.; Miss G. Moore, Rec. Sec.; Mrs. T. F. Sughrue, Treas.

Charleston County Officers

T. M. O'Brien, Pres.; M. P. Croghan, Sec.; F. L. Torlay, Treas.

State Officers

F. J. Quinlivan, Pres.; J. M. Hayes, V-Pres.; F. J. Carney, Sec.; W. P. Cullinane, Treas.

1909

Division No. 1
W. J. Comar, Pres.; P. H. Murphy, V-Pres.; T. M. O'Brien, Fin. Sec.;
F. F. Buero, Rec. Sec.;
M. P. Croghan, Treas.

Division No. 2
M. J. Hanley, Pres.; T. E. Hogan, V-Pres.; J. M. Hayes, Rec. Sec.; T. F. Sughrue, Fin. Sec.;
J. J. Burke, Treas.

Ladies' Auxiliary
Mrs. C. O. Schott, Pres.; Miss Kate Lucas, Fin. Sec.; Mrs. A. Shoppel, Rec. Sec.; Mrs. T. F. Sughrue, Treas.

Charleston County Officers
T. M. O'Brien, Pres.; M. P. Croghan, Sec.; F. L. Torlay, Treas.

State Officers
F. J. Quinlivan, Pres.; J. M. Hayes, V-Pres.; F. J. Carney, Sec.; T. E. Hogan, Treas.

1910

Division No. 1
W. J. Comar, Pres.; B. P. Cunningham, V-Pres.; T. M. O'Brien, Fin. Sec.; F. F. Buero, Rec. Sec.;
M. P. Croghan, Treas.

Division No. 2
M. J. Hanley, Pres; T. E. Hogan, V-Pres.; J. M. Hayes, Rec. Sec.; F. J. Carney, Fin. Sec.;
W. P. Callahan, Treas.

State Officers
F. J. Quinlivan, Pres.; J. M. Hayes, V-Pres.; F. J. Carney, Sec. T. E. Hogan, Treas.

Charleston County Officers
J. J. Hogan, Pres.; M. P. Croghan, Sec.; J. J. Furlong, Treas.

1911

Division No. 1
W. J. Comar, Pres.; M. F, Kennedy, V-Pres.; T. M. O'Brien, Fin. Sec.;
F. F. Buero, Rec. Sec.;
M. P. Croghan, Treas.

Division No. 2
M. J. Hanley, Pres; T. E. Hogan, V-Pres.; J. M. Hayes, Rec. Sec.; F. J. Carney, Fin. Sec.;
W. P. Callahan, Treas.

State Officers

M. F. Kennedy, Pres.; J. M. Hayes, V-Pres.; F. J. Carney, Sec. W. J. Comar, Treas.
Charleston County Officers
W. F. Livingston, Pres.; J. J. Hogan, V-Pres.; M. P. Croghan, Sec.; J. J. Furlong, Treas.

1912
Division No. 1
W. J. Comar, Pres.; M. F. Kennedy, V-Pres.; T. M. O'Brien, Fin. Sec.; F. F. Buero, Rec. Sec.;
M. P. Croghan, Treas.
Division No. 2
M. J. Hanley, Pres.; T. E. Hogan, V-Pres.; J. M. Hayes, Rec. Sec.; F. J. Carney, Fin. Sec.;
W. P. Callahan, Treas.
Ladies Auxiliary
Mrs. W. J. Condon, Pres.; Mrs. W. P. Callahan, V-Pres.; Mrs. A. A. Schoppel, Rec. Sec.; Miss K. A. Lucas, Fin. Sec.; Mrs. T. F. Sughrue, Treas.
Charleston County Officers
W. F. Livingston, Pres.; J. J. Hogan, V-Pres.; M. P. Croghan, Sec.; J. J. Furlong, Treas.
State Officers
M. F. Kennedy, Pres.; J. M. Hayes, V-Pres.; F. J. Carney, Sec.; W. J. Comar, Treas.

1913
Division No. 1
W. J. Comar, Pres.; M. F. Kennedy, V-Pres.; T. M. O'Brien, Fin. Sec.; J. L. Kiley, Recording Secretary; M. P. Croghan, Treas.
Division No. 2
M. J. Hanley, Pres.; T. E. Hogan, V-Pres.; J. M. Hayes, Rec. Sec.; F. J. Carney, Fin. Sec.;
W. P. Callahan, Treas.
Ladies Auxiliary
Mrs. W. J. Condon, Pres.; Mrs. P. J. Heneberry, V-Pres.; Mrs. A. A. Schoppel, Rec. Sec.; Miss K. A. Lucas, Fin. Sec.; Mrs. T. F. Sughrue, Treas.
Charleston County Officers
W. F. Livingston, Pres.; J. J. Hogan, V-Pres.; M. P. Croghan, Sec.; J. J. Furlong, Treas.
State Officers

M. F. Kennedy, Pres.; J. M. Hayes, V-Pres.; F. J. Carney, Sec.; W. J. Comar, Treas.

1914
Division No. 1
W. J. Comar, Pres.; M. F. Kennedy, V-Pres.; T. M. O'Brien, Fin. Sec.; J. L. Kiley, Recording Secretary; M. P. Croghan, Treas.

Division No. 2
C. D. Budds Pres.; T. R. Garety, V-Pres.; J. M. Hayes, Rec. Sec.; F. J. Carney, Fin. Sec.;
W. P. Callahan, Treas.

Ladies Auxiliary
Mrs. P. J. Hanley, Pres.; Mrs. P. J. Heneberry, V-Pres.; Mrs. A. A. Schoppel, Rec. Sec.; Miss K. A. Lucas, Fin. Sec.; .Mrs. T. F. Sughrue, Treas.

Charleston County Officers
W. F. Livingston, Pres.; J. J. Hogan, V-Pres.; M. P. Croghan, Sec.; J. J. Furlong, Treas.

State Officers
M. F. Kennedy, Pres.; J. M. Hayes, V-Pres.; F. J. Carney, Sec.; W. J. Comar, Treas.

1915
Division No. 1
W. J. Comar, Pres.; M. F. Kennedy, V-Pres.; T. M. O'Brien, Fin. Sec.; J. L. Kiley, Rec. Sec.;
M. P. Croghan, Treas.

Division No. 2
C. D. Buds, Pres.; T. R. Garety, V-Pres.; J. M. Hayes, Rec. Sec.; F. J. Carney, Fin. Sec.;
W. P. Callahan, Treas.

Ladies Auxiliary
Mrs. P. J. Hanley, Pres.; Mrs. P. J. Heneberry, V-Pres.; Mrs. A. A. Schoppel, Rec. Sec.; Miss K. A. Lucas, Fin. Sec.; Mrs. T. F. Sughrue, Treas.

Charleston County Officers
T. J. Sheridan, Pres.; M. P. Croghan, Sec.; J. J. Furlong, Treas.

State Officers
M. F. Kennedy, Pres.; J. M. Hayes, V-Pres.; F. J. Carney, Sec.; T. R. Garety, Treas.

1916
Division No. 1

W. J. Comar, Pres.; M. F. Kennedy, V-Pres.; T. M. O'Brien, Fin. Sec.;
J. L. Kiley, Rec. Sec.;
M. P. Croghan, Treas.
Division No. 2
C. D. Budds, Pres.; T. R. Garety, V-Pres.; J. M. Hayes, Rec. Sec.; F. J. Carney, Fin. Sec.;
W. P. Callahan, Treas.
Ladies Auxiliary
Mrs. J. E. Smith, Pres.; Mrs. J. F. Condon, V-Pres.; Mrs. A. A. Schoppel, Rec. Sec.; Miss K. A. Lucas, Fin. Sec.; Mrs. T. F. Sughrue, Treas.
Charleston County Officers
T. J. Sheridan, Pres.; M. P. Croghan, Sec.; J. J. Furlong, Treas.
State Officers
M. F. Kennedy, Pres.; J. M. Hayes, V-Pres.; F. J. Carney, Sec.; T. R. Garety, Treas.
1917
Division No. 1
W. J. Comar, Pres.; M. F. Kennedy, V-Pres.; T. M. O'Brien, Fin.Sec.;
J. L. Kiley, Rec. Sec.;
M. P. Croghan, Treas.
Division No. 2
C. D. Budds, Pres.; T. R. Garety, V-Pres.; J. M. Hayes, Rec. Sec.; F. J. Carney, Fin. Sec.;
W. P. Callahan, Treas.
Ladies Auxiliary
Mrs. J. E. Smith, Pres.; Mrs. J. F. Condon, V-Pres.; Mrs. A. A. Schoppel, Rec. Sec.; Mrs. W. P. Callahan, Fin. Sec.; Mrs. T. F. Sughrue, Treas.
Charleston County Officers
T. J. Sheridan, Pres.; M. P. Croghan, Sec.; J. J. Furlong, Treas.
State Officers
M. F. Kennedy, Pres.; C. D. Budds, V-Pres.; F. J. Carney, Sec.; T. R. Garety, Treas.
1918
Division No. 1
W. J. Comar, Pres.; M. F. Kennedy, V-Pres.; T. M. O'Brien, Fin. Sec.;
J. L. Kiley, Rec. Sec.;
M. P. Croghan, Treas.
Division No. 2

C. D. Budds, Pres; T. R. Garety, V-Pres.; J. M. Hayes, Rec. Sec.; D. F. O'Brien, Financial Sec.;
W. P. Callahan, Treas.
Ladies Auxiliary
Mrs. J. E. Smith, Pres.; Mrs. J. F. Condon, V-Pres.; Mrs. A. A. Schoppel, Rec. Sec.; Mrs. W. P. Callahan, Fin. Sec.; Mrs. T. F. Sughrue, Treas.
State Officers
M. F. Kennedy, Pres.; C. D. Budds, V-Pres.; F. J. Carney, Sec.; T. R. Garety, Treas.
Charleston County Officers
T. J. Sheridan, Pres.; M. P. Croghan, Sec.; J. J. Furlong, Treas.
1919
Division No. 1
W. J. Comar, Pres.; M. F. Kennedy, V-Pres.; T. M. O'Brien, Fin. Sec.; J. L. Kiley, Rec. Sec.;
M. P. Croghan, Treas.
Division No. 2
C. D. Budds, Pres.; J. J. Hogan, V-Pres.; J. M. Hayes, Rec. Sec.; D. F. O'Brien, Fin. Sec.;
W. P. Callahan, Treas.
Ladies Auxiliary
Mrs. J. E. Smith, Pres.; Mrs. J. F. Condon, V-Pres.; Mrs. A. A. Schoppel, Rec. Sec.; Mrs. W. P. Callahan, Fin. Sec.; Mrs. T. F. Sughrue, Treas.
Charleston County Officers
T. J. Sheridan, Pres.; M. P. Croghan, Sec.; J. J. Furlong, Treas.
State Officers
M. F. Kennedy, Pres.; C. D. Budds, V-Pres.; F. J. Carney, Sec.; T. R. Garety, Treas.
1920
Division No. 1
J. J. Furlong, Pres.; M. F. Kennedy, V-Pres.; T. M. O'Brien, Fin. Sec.; J. L. Kiley, Rec. Sec.;
M. P. Croghan, Treas.
Division No. 2
C. D. Budds, Pres.; J. J. Hogan, V-Pres.; J. M. Hayes, Rec. Sec.; D. F. O'Brien, Fin. Sec.;
W. P. Callahan, Treas.
Ladies Auxiliary
Mrs. J. E. Smith, Pres.; Mrs. J. F. Condon, V-Pres.; Mrs. A. A.

Schoppel, Rec. Sec.; Mrs. W. P. Callahan, Fin. Sec.; Mrs. T. F. Sughrue, Treas.
State Officers
M. F. Kennedy, Pres.; C. D. Budds, V-Pres.; F. J. Carney, Sec.; T. R. Garety, Treas.
Charleston County Officers
T. J. Sheridan, Pres.; M. P. Croghan, Sec.; J. J. Furlong, Treas.
1921
Division No. 1
J. J. Furlong, Pres.; M. F. Kennedy, V-Pres.; T. M. O'Brien, Fin. Sec.; J. L. Kiley, Rec. Sec.;
M. P. Croghan, Treas.
Division No. 2
C. D. Budds, Pres.; J. J. Hogan, V-Pres; D. F. O'Brien, Fin. Sec.; W. P. Callahan, Treas.
Ladies Auxiliary
Mrs. J. E. Smith, Pres.; Mrs. J. F. Condon, V-Pres.; Mrs. A. A. Schoppel, Rec. Sec.; Mrs. W. P. Callahan, Fin. Sec.; Mrs. T. F. Sughrue, Treas.
Charleston County Officers
T. J. Sheridan, Pres.; M. P. Croghan, Sec.; J. J. Furlong, Treas.
State Officers
M. F. Kennedy, Pres.; C. D. Budds, V-Pres.; F. J. Carney, Sec.; T. R. Garety, Treas.
1922
Division No. 2
C. D. Budds, Pres.; M. J. Hanley, V-Pres.; D. F. O'Brien, Fin. Sec.; W. P. Callahan, Treas.
Ladies Auxiliary
Mrs. J. E. Smith, Pres.; Mrs. P. J. Hanley, V-Pres.; Mrs. A. A. Schoppel, Rec. Sec.; Mrs. W. P. Callahan, Fin. Sec.; Mrs. T. F. Sughrue, Treas.

The list was compiled from Charleston newspapers and city directories.

APPENDIX 4

A PARTIAL LIST OF THE OFFICERS AND COMMITTEE MEMBERS OF THE HIBERNIAN SOCIETY OF CHARLESTON FROM 1801 THROUGH 1922

1801

Officers
Rev. Simon F. Gallagher, D. D., President.
John S. Adams. Vice President
Thomas Malcom, Treasurer
Charles M'Kenna, Secretary

1802 to 1803

Officers
Rev. Simon F. Gallagher, D. D., President.
Dominick Hall, Vice-President.
Edmund M. Phelon, Treasurer.
John Boyd, Secretary.

1803 to 1804

Officers
O'Brien Smith, President.
Simon Magwood, Vice-President.
John Query, Treasurer.
Peter T. Marchant, Secretary.

1804 to 1805

Officers
O'Brien Smith, President.
Simon Magwood, Vice-President.
Thomas Malcom, Treasurer.
John Langton, Secretary.

1805 to 1808

Officers

Simon Magwood, President.
Edmund M. Phelon, Vice-President.
Thomas Malcom, Treasurer.
John Langton, Secretary.

1808 to 1825

Officers
Simon Magwood, President.
Edmund M. Phelon, Vice-President.
Thomas Malcom, Treasurer.
Thomas Stephens, Secretary.

1825 to 1826

Officers
Col. S. Magwood, President
Col. E. M. Phelon, Vice-President
Thos. Malcom, Treasurer
Thos. Stephens, Secretary
Committee on Charity
E. M. Phelon, J. Adger, J. Gordon, T. Milliken and T. Flemming.
Committee on Finance
Ker Boyce and Thomas Flemming.

1826 to 1828

Officers
Simon Magwood, President.
Edmund M. Phelon, Vice-President.
Thomas Stephens, Treasurer.
George Henry, Secretary.

1828 to 1829

Officers
Simon Magwood, President
E. M. Phelon, Vice-President
Thomas Stephens, Treasurer
George Henry, Secretary
Committee on Charity
James Black, Wm. A. Caldwell, John Gordon, O. L. Dobson and James Ross.
Committee on Finance
William Aiken, R. Wotherspoon, R. Birney, James Adger and Sam. Patterson.

1829 to 1830

Officers
Simon Magwood, President

William Aiken, Vice-President
Thomas Stephens, Treasurer
George Henry, Secretary
<u>Committee on Charity</u>
E. M. Phelon, James Black, Wm. A. Caldwell, James Ross and John Gordon.
<u>Committee on Finance</u>
James Adger, R. Wotherspoon, R. Birney, Saml. Patterson and Alexr. Black.

1830 to 1831

<u>Officers</u>
Simon Magwood, President
William Aiken, Vice-President
Thomas Stephens, Treasurer
George Henry, Secretary
<u>Committee on Charity</u>
Edward M. Phelon, James Black, W. A. Caldwell, James Ross and James Gordon.
<u>Committee on Finance</u>
James Adger, Robert Birney, Saml. Patterson, Alex. Black and Chas. Brenan.

1831 to 1832

<u>Officers</u>
Simon Magwood, President.
Samuel Patterson, Vice-President.
Thomas Stephens, Treasurer.
George Henry, Secretary.
<u>Committee on Charity</u>
E. M. Phelon, Jas. Black, W. A. Caldwell, James Ross and John Gordon.
<u>Committee on Finance</u>
James Adger, Robert Birney, Saml. Patterson, Alex. Black, Chas. Brenan and Robert Patterson.
<u>Committee on Building</u>
Thomas Flemming, James Adger, Saml. Patterson, John Gordon and Henry O'Hara.

1832 to 1833

<u>Officers</u>
Simon Magwood, President
Saml. Patterson, Vice-President
Thomas Stephens, Treasurer

George Henry, Secretary
<u>Committee on Charity</u>
W. A. Caldwell, Jas. Black, Jas. Ross, John Gordon and Henry O'Hara.
<u>Committee on Finance</u>
James Adger, Robert Birney, Alex. Black, Chas. Brenan and Jos. Johnson.
<u>Committee on Building</u>
Thomas F. Flemming, James Adger, John Gordon, John Stoney and Thomas Bennett.

<u>1833 to 1834</u>

<u>Officers</u>
Simon Magwood, President
Samuel Patterson, Vice-President
Thomas Stephens, Treasurer
George Henry, Secretary
<u>Committee on Relief</u>
William A. Caldwell, John Gordon, James Black, James Ross and Henry O'Hara.
<u>Committee on Finance</u>
James Adger, Jos. Johnson, Alex. Black, Robert Birney and Chas. Brenan.
<u>Committee on Building</u>
James Adger, Thos. Bennett, Thos. Flemming, John Stoney and John Gordon.

<u>1834 to 1835</u>

<u>Officers</u>
Simon Magwood, President
Samuel Patterson, Vice-President
Thomas Stephens, Treasurer
Alexr Robinson, Secretary
<u>Committee on Relief</u>
Wm. A. Caldwell, John Gordon, James Black, James Ross and George Hervey.
<u>Committee on Finance</u>
James Adger, Jos. Johnson, Alexr. Black, Robert Birney and Chas. Brenan.
<u>Committee on Building</u>
Thos. Bennett, Thos. Flemming, John Stoney, John Gordon and James Adger.

1835 to 1836

Officers

Simon Magwood, President
Samuel Patterson, Vice-President
Thomas Stephens, Treasurer
Alexr. Robinson, Secretary

Committee on Relief

Wm. A. Caldwell, James Black, James Ross, George Hervey and Thomas Milliken.

Committee on Finance

James Adger, Jos. Johnson, Alexr. Black, Chas. Brenan and Thos. Blackwood.

Committee on Building

Thos. Bennett, James Adger, John Stoney, Joel R. Poinsett and Alexr. Black.

1836 to 1837

Officers

*Simon Magwood, President
Saml. Patterson, Vice-President
Thomas Stephens, Treasurer
Alexr. Robinson, Secretary

*Simon Magwood died on August 4, 1836, and Samuel Patterson became president.

Committee on Relief

Wm. A. Caldwell, James Black, James Ross, George Hervey and Alexr. McDonald.

Committee on Finance

James Adger, Jos. Johnson, Alexr. Black, Chas. Brenan and Thos. Blackwood.

Committee on Building

Thos. Bennett, James Adger, John Stoney, Joel R. Poinsett and Alexr. Black.

1837 to 1838

Officers

Samuel Patterson, President
James Adger, Vice-President
Thomas Stephens, Treasurer
Alexr. Robinson, Secretary

Committee on Relief

Wm. A. Caldwell, James Black, James Ross, George Hervey and Alexr. McDonald.

<u>Committee on Finance</u>

Jos. Johnson, Alexr. Black, Chas. Brenan, Robt. Martin and George Henry.

<u>Committee on Building</u>

Thos. Bennett, John Stoney, Alexr. Black, William Aiken and John Robinson.

1838 to 1839

<u>Officers</u>

*Samuel Patterson, President

James Adger, Vice-President

Thomas Stephens, Treasurer

Alexander. Robinson, Secretary

*Samuel Patterson died in December 1838, and James Adger became president.

<u>Committee on Relief</u>

Wm. A. Caldwell, James Black, James Ross, George Hervey and Alexander McDonald.

<u>Committee on Finance</u>

Dr. Joseph Johnson, Chas. Brenan, Robt. Martin and Dr. J. E. McDonald.

<u>Committee on Building</u>

Thos. Bennett, John Stoney, Alexr. Black, William Aiken and John Robinson.

1839 to 1840

<u>Officers</u>

James Adger, President

William A. Caldwell, Vice-President

Thomas Stephens, Treasurer

Alexr. Robinson, Secretary

<u>Committee on Relief</u>

George Hervey, Charles Brenan, Alexr. McDonald, Robert Pennal and Oliver L. Dobson.

<u>Committee on Finance</u>

Jos. Johnson, Alexr. Black, Chas. Brenan, Robt. Martin and Dr. J. E. McDonald.

<u>Committee on Building</u>

Thos. Bennett, John Robinson, Alex. Black, William Aiken and John Hunter.

1840 to 1841

<u>Officers</u>

James Adger, President

Wm. A. Caldwell, Vice-President
Thomas Stephens, Treasurer
Alexr. Robinson, Secretary
Committee on Relief
George Hervey, Charles Brenan, Alexr. McDonald, Robert Pennal and Oliver L. Dobson.
Committee on Finance
Dr. Jos. Johnson, Alexr. Black, Chas. Brenan, Robt. Martin and Thomas Cormick.
Committee on Building
Thos. Bennett, John Robinson, Alexr. Black, Wm. Aiken and John Hunter.

1841 to 1842

Officers
*James Adger, President
Wm. A. Caldwell, Vice-President
Thomas Stephens, Treasurer
Alexr. Robinson, Secretary
*James Adger resigned as president in 1841, and William a. Caldwell became president.
Committee on Relief
Charles Brenan, Alexr. McDonald, Oliver L. Dobson, Thomas Cormick and Robert Pennal.
Committee on Finance
Dr. Jos. Johnson, Alexr. Black, Chas. Brenan, Robt. Martin and Thomas Cormick.

1842 to 1843

Officers
William A. Caldwell, President
Thomas Stephens, Vice President
Alexander Robinson, Treasurer
William N. Hamilton, Secretary
Committee on Relief
Charles Brenan, Alexr. McDonald, Robert Pennal, Oliver L. Dobson and Robert C. Smith.
Committee on Finance
James Adger, Robert Martin, Thomas Cormick, Joel Stevens and Alexander Black.

1843 to 1844

Officers
William A. Caldwell, President

Thomas Stephens, Vice-President
Alexander Robinson, Treasurer
William N. Hamilton, Secretary
<u>Committee on Finance</u>
James Adger, Robert Martin, Thomas Cormick, Joel Stevens and Alexander Black.
<u>Committee on Relief</u>
Charles Brenan, Alexr. McDonald, Robert Pennal, Oliver L. Dobson and Robert C. Smith.
<u>Hall keeper</u>
Thomas Ryan

1844 to 1845

<u>Officers</u>
William A. Caldwell, President
Thomas Stephens, Vice-President
Alexander Robinson, Treasurer
William N. Hamilton, Secretary
<u>Committee on Finance</u>
James Adger, Robert Martin, Hall T. McGee, Joel Stevens and Alexander Black.
<u>Committee on Relief</u>
Charles Brenan, Alexr. McDonald, Robert Pennal, Oliver L. Dobson and E. M. Carey.
<u>Hall keeper</u>
Thomas Ryan

1845 to 1846

<u>Officers</u>
*William A. Caldwell, President
Thomas Stephens, Vice-President
Alexander Robinson, Treasurer
Thomas Reilly, Secretary
*William A. Caldwell resigned as president in November 1845, and Thomas Stephens became president.
<u>Committee on Finance</u>
James Adger, Robert Martin, H. T. McGee, Joel Stevens and Alexander Black.
<u>Committee on Relief</u>
C. Brenan, R. Pennal, O. L. Dobson, W. H. Gilliland and M. Roddy.
<u>Hall keeper</u>
Thomas Ryan

1846 to 1847

Officers
*Thomas Stephens, President
James Adger, Vice-President
Alex Robinson, Treasurer
Thomas Reilly, Secretary
*Thomas Stephens resigned as president in January 1847, and H. W. Conner became president.

Committee on Finance
H. W. Conner, R. Martin, H. T. McGee, Joel Stevens and Alex Black.

Committee on Relief
C. Brenan, R. Pennal, O. L. Dobson, W. H. Gilliland and M. Roddy.

Hall keeper
Thomas Ryan

1847 to 1848

Officers
H. W. Conner, President.
James Adger, Vice-President.
Alexander Robinson, Treasurer.
Thomas Reilly, Secretary.

Committee on Finance
C. Brenan, A. Black, R. Martin, Joel Stevens and H. T. McGee.

Committee on Charity
C. Brenan, R. Pennal, O. L. Dobson, W. H. Gilliland and M. Roddy

Keeper of the Hall
W. N. Hamilton

1848 to 1849

Officers
H. W. Conner, President.
James Adger, Vice-President.
*Alexander Robinson, Treasurer.
Thomas Reilly, Secretary.

Committee on Relief
C. Brenan, W. H. Gilliland, O. L. Dobson, M. Roddy and W. M'Burney

Committee on Charity
C. Brenan, Alex. Black, R. Martin, H. T. M'Gee and W. H. Houston

Keeper of the Hall
W. N. Hamilton

*Treasurer Alexander Robinson resigned, and J. W. Caldwell elected instead.

1849 to 1850

Officers
H. W. Conner, President.
James Adger, Vice-President.
Alexander Robinson, Treasurer.
W. P. O'Hara, Secretary.

Committee on Relief
C. Brenan, W. H. Gilliland, O. L. Dobson, M. Roddy and W. McBurney

Committee on Finance
C. Brenan, R. Martin, H. T. McGee, Alex. Black and W. H. Houston.

Keeper of the Hall
W. N. Hamilton

1850 to 1851

Officers
Henry W. Conner, President
James Adger, Vice-President
J. W. Caldwell, Treasurer
W. P. O'Hara, Secretary

Committee on Relief
C. Brenan, O. L. Dobson, W. H. Gilliland, W. M'Burney and J. P. Stewart.

Committee on Finance
Robert Martin, W. H. Houston, J. L. Patterson, A. M'Kensie and J. H. Robinson.

1851 to 1852

Officers
Henry W. Conner, President
James Adger, Vice-President
J. W. Caldwell, Treasurer
W. P. O'Hara, Secretary

Committee on Finance
Robert Martin, W. H. Houston, J. L. Patterson, J. K. Robinson and A. McKenzie.

Committee on Relief

C. Brenan, W. H. Gilliland, W. McBurney, J. P. Stuart and E. M. Carey.

<u>Keeper of Hall</u>
Wm. N. Hamilton

1852 to 1853

<u>Officers</u>
Henry W. Conner, President
James Adger, Vice-President
Alexander Robinson, Treasurer
W. P. O'Hara, Secretary
<u>Committee on Finance</u>
Robert Martin, W. H. Houston, J. L. Patterson, J. R. Robinson and A. McKenzie.

<u>Committee on Relief</u>
W. H. Gilliland, W. McBurney, J. P. Stuart, E. M. Carey and Charles Brenan.

<u>Hall Keeper</u>

W. N. Hamilton

1853 to 1854

<u>Officers</u>
H. W. Conner, President
James Adger, Vice-President
Alexander Robinson, Treasurer
W. P. O'Hara, Secretary
<u>Committee on Finance</u>
W. H. Houston, J. L. Patterson, A. McKensie, R. Robinson and W. M. Martin.

<u>Committee on Relief</u>
W. H. Gilliland, Wm. McBurney, J. P. Stuart, E. M. Carey and Charles Brenan.

<u>Hall keeper</u>
W. N. Hamilton

1854 to 1855

<u>Officers</u>
H. W. Conner, President
J. Adger, Vice-President
Alexander Robinson, Treasurer
W. P. O'Hara, Secretary
<u>Committee on Finance</u>
W. H. Houston, J. L. Patterson, A. McKensie, J. K. Robinson and William M. Martin.

Committee on Relief

W. H. Gilliland, Wm. McBurney, J. P. Stuart, E. M. Carey and Charles Brenan.

Hall keeper

W. N. Hamilton

1855 to 1856

Officers

Henry W. Conner, President

James Adger, Vice-President

John W. Caldwell, Treasurer

W. P. O'Hara, Secretary

Committee on Finance

W. H. Houston, J. L. Patterson, A. McKensie, J. K. Robinson and William M. Martin.

Committee on Relief

W. H. Gilliland, Wm. McBurney, J. P. Stuart, E. M. Carey and Charles Brenan.

Hall keeper

W. N. Hamilton

1856 to 1857

Officers

*H. W. Conner, President

J. Adger, Vice-President

J. W. Caldwell, Treasurer

W. P. O'Hara, Secretary

*President H. W. Conner resigned March 30, 1856, and A. G. Magrath elected instead, February 3, 1857.

Committee on Finance

W. H. Houston, J. L. Patterson, A. McKenzie, J. K. Robinson and William M. Martin.

Committee on Relief

W. H. Gilliland, Wm. McBurney, J. P. Stuart, Thomas Ryan and B. M. Carey.

Hall keeper

W. N. Hamilton

1857 to 1858

Officers

A. G. Magrath, President

James Adger, Vice-President

A. A. Allemong, Secretary

William P. O'Hara, Treasurer

Committee on Finance
John W. Caldwell, J. L. Patterson, J. K. Robinson, A. McKensie and W. M. Martin.

Committee on Relief
W. H. Gilliland, Wm. McBurney, E. M. Carey, W. H. Houston and Thomas Ryan.

1858 to 1859

Officers
*A. G. Magrath, President
**James Adger, Vice-President
W. P. O'Hara, Treasurer
A. A. Allemong, Secretary

* President A. G. Magrath resigned March 30, 1858, and J. K. Robinson elected July 6, 1858.

** James Adger died September 1858, and W. H. Gilliland elected Vice-President December 7, 1858.

Committee on Finance
J. W. Caldwell, J. L. Patterson, J. K. Robinson, A. McKensie and Wm. Martin.

Committee on Relief
W. H. Gilliland, Wm. McBurney, E. M. Carey, W. H. Houston and Thomas Ryan.

Hall keeper
W. N. Hamilton

1859 to 1860

Officers
James K. Robinson, President
W. H. Gilliland, Vice-President
W. P. O'Hara, Treasurer
A. A. Allemong, Secretary

Committee on Finance
J. W. Caldwell, J. L. Patterson, A. McKensie, Wm. M. Martin and E. P. Milliken.

Committee on Relief
W. H. Gilliland, Wm. McBurney, E. M. Carey, Wm. H. Houston and John O'Neill.

Hall keeper
W. N. Hamilton

1860 to 1861

Officers
James K. Robinson, President

W. H. Gilliland, Vice-President
W. P. O'Hara, Treasurer
A. A. Allemong, Secretary

Committee on Finance

J. W. Caldwell, J. L. Patterson, A. McKensie, Wm. M. Martin and E. P. Milliken.

Committee on Relief

W. H. Gilliland, Wm. McBurney, W. H. Houston, E. M. Carey and John F. O'Neill.

Committee on Hall and Grounds

Thomas Ryan, J. McConkey and A. Cunningham.

Hall keeper

W. N. Hamilton

1861 to 1862

Officers

James K. Robinson, President
W. H. Gilliland, Vice-President
W. P. O'Hara, Treasurer
A. A. Allemong, Secretary

Committee on Finance

J. W. Caldwell, J. L. Patterson, A. McKenzie, Wm. Martin and E. P. Milliken.

Committee on Relief

W. H. Gilliland, W. H. Houston, Wm. McBurney, E. M. Carey and John F. O'Neill.

Committee on Grounds

Thomas Ryan, C. H. Simonton and Andrew Cunningham.

Hall keeper

J. J. Fenall

1862 to 1863

Officers

James K. Robinson, President
W. H. Gilliland, Vice-President
W. P. O'Hara, Treasurer
A. A. Allemong, Secretary

Committee on Finance

J. W. Caldwell, A. McKenzie, J. L. Patterson, J. W. Brownfield and E. P. Milliken.

Committee on Relief

W. H. Gilliland, E. M. Carey, Wm. McBurney, W. H. Houston and J. F. O'Neill.

Committee on Grounds
Thomas Ryan, C. H. Simonton and A. Cunningham.
Hall keeper
J. J. Fenall

1863 to 1864

Officers
James K. Robinson, President
W. H. Gilliland, Vice-President
W. P. O'Hara, Treasurer
A. A. Allemong, Secretary
Committee on Finance
J. W. Caldwell, A. McKenzie, J. L. Patterson, J. W. Brownfield and E. P. Milliken.
Committee on Relief
W. H. Gilliland, E. M. Carey, Wm. McBurney, W. H. Houston and J. F. O'Neill.
Committee on Grounds
Thomas Ryan, C. H. Simonton and G. A. Bowman.
Hall keeper
John J. Fenall

1864 to 1865

Officers
James K. Robinson, President
Wm. H. Gilliland, Vice-President
*W. P. O'Hara, Treasurer
**A. A. Allemong, Secretary

*Treasurer W. P. O'Hara died April 1864 and J. L. Patterson was elected, June 7, 1864.

** Secretary A. A. Allemong was killed at the siege of Petersburg on June 22, 1864, and Thomas O'Brien elected instead.

Committee on Finance
J. W. Caldwell, A. McKenzie, J. L. Patterson, J. W. Brownfield and E. P. Milliken.
Committee on Relief
W. H. Gilliland, E. M. Carey, W. H. Houston, Wm. McBurney and J. F. O'Neill.
Committee on Grounds
Thomas Ryan, C. H. Simonton and G. A. Bowman.
Hall keeper
John. J. Fenall

1865 to 1866

Officers
James K. Robinson, President
Wm. H. Gilliland, Vice-President
James L. Patterson, treasurer
Thomas O'Brien, Secretary

1866 to 1867

Officers
J. K. Robinson, President
Wm. H. Gilliland, Vice-President
James L. Patterson, Treasurer
Thomas O'Brien, Secretary

Committee on Finance
C. H. Simonton, J. W. Brownfield, E. P. Milliken, A. P. Caldwell and A. R. Taft.

Committee on Relief
W. H. Gilliland, W. H. Houston, Jn. F. O'Neill, W. A. Courtenay and W. M. McBurney.

Committee on Hall and Grounds
Thomas Ryan, G. A. Bowman and James McConkey.

Hall keeper
J. J. Fenall

1867 to 1868

Officers
*James K. Robinson, President
**Wm. H. Gilliland, Vice-President
***James L. Patterson, Treasurer
Thos. O'Brien, Secretary

*J. K. Robinson died July 1867, and W. H. Gilliland elected in his place.

** W. H. Gilliland died March 15, 1868.

***Treasurer James L. Patterson died February 10, 1868.

Committee on Finance
C. H. Simonton, J. W. Brownfield, A. P. Caldwell, Bernard O'Neill and Adam B. Glover.

Committee on Relief
M. P. O'Connor, W. H. Houston, J. M. Mulvaney, William White and George A. Bowman.

Committee on Hall and Grounds
Jno. F. O'Neill, C. C. Trumbo and James McConkey.

Hall keeper

John Burns

1868 to 1869

Officers

John F. O'Neill, President

James Conner, Vice-President

Thomas O'Brien, Treasurer

W. A. Kelly, Secretary

Committee on Finance

B. O'Neill, C. H. Simonton, A. P. Caldwell, James McConkey and Edward Daly.

Committee on Relief

M. P. O'Connor, W. H. Houston, G. A. Bowman, J. M. Mulvaney and C. C. Trumbo.

Committee on Letters

James Cantwell, J. H. Murrell, John Kenny, W. Howland and W. Knox.

Hall keeper

John Burns

1869 to 1870

Officers

John F. O'Neill, President

General James Conner, Vice-President

Thomas O'Brien, Treasurer

Wm. Aiken Kelly, Secretary

Committee on Finance

B. O'Neill, A. P. Caldwell, James McConkey, T. S. O'Brien And H. J. Baker.

Committee on Relief

M. P. O'Connor, W. H. Houston, G. A. Bowman, J. W. Mulvaney and C. C. Trumbo.

Committee on Letters

James Cantwell, John Kenny, W. Howland and W. Knox.

Hall keeper

John Burns

1870 to 1871

Officers

Jno. F. O'Neill, President

General James Conner, Vice-President

Thomas O'Brien, Treasurer

Captain James Armstrong, Jr., Secretary

Committee on Finance

B. O'Neill, A. P. Caldwell, James McConkey, T. S. O'Brien and H. F. Baker.

Committee on Relief

M. P. O'Connor, W. H. Houston, G. A. Bowman, J. M. Mulvaney and C. C. Trumbo.

Committee on Letters

James Cantwell, J. H. Murrell, John Kenny, W. Howland and W. Knox.

Hall keeper

John Burns

1871 to 1872

Officers

General James Conner, President

Bernard O'Neill, Vice-President

Thomas O'Brien, Treasurer

James Armstrong, Jr., Secretary

Committee on Finance

A. P. Caldwell, James McConkey, T. S. O'Brien, H. F. Baker and F. L. O'Neill.

Committee on Relief

M. P. O'Connor, W. H. Houston, G. A. Bowman, J. M. Mulvaney and C. C. Trumbo.

Committee on Letters

James Cantwell, J. R. Murrell, John Kenny, W. Howland and James F. Slattery.

Hall keeper

John Burns

1872 to 1873

Officers

General James Conner, President

Bernard O'Neill, Vice-President

Thomas O'Brien, Treasurer

James Armstrong, Secretary

Committee on Finance

A. P. Caldwell, James McConkey, T. S. O'Brien, H. F. Baker, F. L. O'Neill.

Committee on Relief

M. P. O'Connor, W. H. Houston, G. A. Bowman, C. C. Trumbo, J. M. Mulvaney.

Committee on Letters

James Cantwell, J. S. Murrell, John Kenny, James F. Slattery and W. E. Howland.

Hall keeper
John Burns

1873 to 1874

Officers
General James Conner, President
Bernard O'Neill, Vice-President
Thomas O'Brien, Treasurer
James Armstrong, Secretary

Committee on Finance
A. P. Caldwell, James McConkey, T. S. O'Brien, H. F. Baker, F. L. O'Neill.

Committee on Relief
M. P. O'Connor, W. H. Houston, G. A. Bowman, C. C. Trumbo, A. McLoy.

Committee on Letters
J. H. Murrell, John Kenny, James F. Slattery, James Cosgrove.

Hall keeper
John Burns

1874 to 1875

Officers
M. P. O'Connor, President
W. A. Courtenay, Vice-President
A. P. Caldwell, Treasurer
James Armstrong, Secretary

Committee on Finance
James McConkey, T. S. O'Brien, H. F. Baker, F. L. O'Neill and E. Daly.

Committee on Relief
W. H. Houston, G. A. Bowman, C. C. Trumbo, A. McLoy and John Burke.

Committee on Letters
J. S. Murrell, John Kenny, James F. Slattery, James Cosgrove and H. J. O'Neill.

Hall keeper
John Burns

1875 to 1876

Officers
M. P. O'Connor, President
George A. Bowman, Vice-President

A. P. Caldwell, Treasurer

James Armstrong, Secretary

Committee on Finance

James McConkey, T. S. O'Brien, H. F. Baker, F. L. O'Neill and E. Daly.

Committee on Relief

W. H. Houston, C. C. Trumbo, A. McLoy, John Burke and John H. Devereux.

Committee on Letters

J. H. Murrell, John Kenny, James F. Slattery, James Cosgrove And H. J. O'Neill.

Hall keeper

John Burns

1876 to 1877

Officers

M. P. O'Connor, President

George A. Bowman, Vice-President

A. P. Caldwell, Treasurer

James Armstrong, Secretary

Committee on Finance

H. F. Baker, T. S. O'Brien, F. L. O'Neill, E. Daly and T. R. McGahan.

Committee on Relief

W. H. Houston, C. C. Trumbo, A. McLoy, John Burke and John H. Devereux.

Committee on Letters

J. H. Murrell, John Kenny, James Cosgrove, H. J. O'Neill and Hugh Ferguson.

Hall keeper

John Burns

1877 to 1878

Officers

M. P. O'Connor, President

Geo. A. Bowman, Vice-President

A. P. Caldwell, Treasurer

James Armstrong, Secretary

Committee on Finance

H. F. Baker, T. S. O'Brien, F. L. O'Neill, E. Daly and T. R. McGahan.

Committee on Relief

John Burke, C. C. Trumbo, A. McLoy, John H. Devereux, John H. Houston.

Committee on Letters

J. H. Murrell, John Kennedy, James Cosgrove, H. J. O'Neill and Hugh Ferguson.

Hall keeper

John Burns

1878 to 1879

Officers

M. P. O'Connor, President

A. T. Smythe, Vice-President

A. P. Caldwell, Treasurer

James Armstrong, Secretary

Committee on Finance

H. F. Baker, T. S. O'Brien, F. L. O'Neill, E. Daly and T. R. McGahan.

Committee on Relief

John Burke, A. McLoy, John H. Devereux, W. L. Daggett and P. P. Toale.

Committee on Letters

James Cosgrove, Hugh Ferguson, B. Boyd, H. J. O'Neill and J. J. Dunning.

Hall keeper

John Burns

1879 to 1880

Officers

A. T. Smythe, President

E. F. Sweegan, Vice-President

A. P. Caldwell, Treasurer

James Armstrong, Secretary

Committee on Finance

H. F. Baker, T. S. O'Brien, F. L. O'Neill, E. Daly and T. R. McGahan.

Committee on Relief

John Burke, A. McLoy, John H. Devereux, W. L. Daggett and P. P. Toale.

Committee on Letters

James Cosgrove, B. Boyd, J. H. Murrell, J. Clark Houston and J. J. Dunning.

Hall keeper

John Burns

1880 to 1881

Officers

A. T. Smythe, President
E. F. Sweegan, Vice-President
A. P. Caldwell, Treasurer
James Armstrong, Secretary

Committee on Finance

H. F. Baker, T. S. O'Brien, F. L. O'Neill, E. Daly and T. R. McGahan.

Committee on Relief

A. McLoy, John H. Devereux, James Cantwell, J. E. Burke and P. P. Toale.

Committee on Letters

James Cosgrove, B. Boyd, J. H. Murrell, J. Clark Houston and J. J. Dunning.

Hall keeper
John Burns

1881 to 1882

Officers

A. T. Smythe, President
E. F. Sweegan, Vice President
James Armstrong, Secretary
A. P. Caldwell, Treasurer

Committee on Finance

H. F. Baker, T. S. O'Brien, F. L. O'Neill, Edward Daly and T. R. McGahan.

Committee on Relief

Alex. McLoy, John H. Devereux, James Cantwell, J. E. Burke and P. P. Toale.

Committee on Letters

James Cosgrove, B. Boyd, A. Moroso, J. Adger Smythe and W. Gayer.

Hall keeper
John Burns

1882 to 1883

Officers

A. T. Smythe, President
E. F. Sweegan, Vice President
James Armstrong, Secretary
A. P. Caldwell, Treasurer

Committee on Finance

H. F. Baker, T. S. O'Brien, F. L. O'Neill, E. Daly and T. R. McGahan.

Committee on Relief

A. McLoy, John H. Devereux, James Cantwell, J. E. Burke and P. P. Toale.

Committee on Letters

James Cosgrove, B. Boyd, A. Moroso, J. Adger Smythe and W. Gayer.

Hall keeper

John Burns

1883 to 1884

Officers

E. F. Sweegan, President

George D. Bryan, Vice-President

A. P. Caldwell, Treasurer

James Armstrong, Secretary

Committee on Finance

H. F. Baker, F. L. O'Neill, T. S. O'Brien, E. Daly and T. R. McGahan.

Committee on Relief

A. McLoy, Jno. H. Devereux, P. P. Toale, James Cantwell and J. E. Burke.

Committee on Letters

James Cosgrove, B. Boyd, W. J. Gayer, J. Adger Smythe and C. W. Stiles.

Hall Keeper

John E. Burns

1884 to 1885

Officers

E. F. Sweegan, President

George D. Bryan, Vice-President

William Aiken Kelly, Secretary

James Armstrong, Treasurer

Committee on Finance

H. F. Baker, F. L. O'Neill, T. S. O'Brien, E. Daly and T. R. McGahan.

Committee on Relief

A. McLoy, Jno. H. Devereux, P. P. Toale, James Cantwell and J. E. Burke.

Committee on Letters

James Cosgrove, B. Boyd, W. J. Gayer, J. Adger Smythe and C. W. Stiles.

<u>Hall Keeper</u>
John E. Burns

1885 to 1886

<u>Officers</u>
E. F. Sweegan, President
George D. Bryan, Vice-President
James Armstrong, Treasurer
W. A. Kelly, Secretary

<u>Committee on Finance</u>
H. F. Baker, F. L. O'Neill, T. S. O'Brien, E. Daley and T. R. McGahan.

<u>Committee on Relief</u>
A. McLoy, John H. Devereux, P. P. Toale, James Cantwell and J. E. Burke.

<u>Committee on Letters</u>
James Cosgrove, B. Boyd, W. J. Gayer, J. Adger Smythe and C. W. Stiles.

<u>Hall keeper</u>
John Burns

1886 to 1887

<u>Officers</u>
George D. Bryan, President
James F. Redding, Vice-President
James Armstrong, Treasurer
Wm. Aiken Kelly, Secretary

<u>Committee on Finance</u>
H. F. Baker, F. L. O'Neill, T. S. O'Brien, T. R. McGahan and D. B. Gilliland.

<u>Committee on Relief</u>
A. McLoy, John H. Devereux, P. P. Toale, James Cantwell and J. E. Burke.

<u>Committee on Letters</u>
James Cosgrove, Bernard Boyd, Wm. J. Gayer, J. Adger Smythe and C. W. Stiles

<u>Hall Keeper</u>
John Burns

1887 to 1888

<u>Officers</u>
George D. Bryan, President

James F. Redding, Vice-President
James Armstrong, Treasurer
Wm. Aiken Kelly, Secretary
Committee on Finance
T. R. McGahan, D. B. Gilliland, P. P. Toale, H. F. Baker and F. L. O'Neill
Committee on Relief
John H. Devereux, James Cantwell, J. E. Burke, Jas. Riley and T. A. Huguenin
Committee on Letters
Jas. Cosgrove, Bernard Boyd, W. J. Gayer,, J Adger Smythe and C. W. Stiles
Hall Keeper
B. P. Cunningham

1888 to 1889

Officers
G. D. Bryan, President
James F. Redding, Vice-President
James Armstrong, Treasurer
W. Aiken Kelly, Secretary
Committee on Finance
T. R. McGahan, D. B. Gilliland, P. P. Toale, H. F. Baker and F. L. O'Neill.
Committee on Relief
John H. Devereux, James Cantwell, J. E. Burke, Jas. Riley and T. A. Huguenin
Committee on Letters
Jas. Cosgrove, Bernard Boyd, W. J. Gayer, J Adger Smythe and C. W. Stiles
Hall Keeper
B. P. Cunningham

1889 to 1890

Officers
James F. Redding, President
B. F. MaCabe, Vice-President
P. E. Gleason, Secretary
L. Arthur O'Neill, Treasurer
Managing Committee
F. J. McGarvey, B. Boyd, B. Mantoue, F. Kressel Jr. and D. A. J. Sullivan.
Committee on Finance

T. R. McGahan, J. Adger Smyth, H. Oliver, S. Fogarty and E. P. McSwiney.

Committee on Relief

J. E. Burke, J. Cantwell, P. P. Toale, P. Darcy and T. Young.

Committee on Letters

C. W. Stiles, W. J. Gayer, J. D. Murphy, W. F. Harragan and M. A. Connor.

Hall Keeper

B. P. Cunningham

1890 to 1891

Officers

James F. Redding, President
B. F. MaCabe, Vice-President
P. E. Gleason, Secretary
Simon Fogarty, Treasurer

Managing Committee

F. J. McGarvey, E. P. McSwiney, Joseph Book and E. P. Huger.

Committee on Finance

T. R. McGahan, J. Adger Smyth, H. Oliver, M. Kelly, and E. P. McSwiney.

Committee on Relief

J. E. Burke, J. Cantwell, James Walsh, P. Darcy and T. Young.

Committee on Letters

C. W. Stiles, W. J. Gayer, J. D. Murphy, W. F. Harragan and M. A. Connor.

Hall Keeper

B. P. Cunningham

1891 to 1892

Officers

James F. Redding, President
B. F. MaCabe, Vice-President
L. C. Ferrall, Secretary
Simon Fogarty, Treasurer

Managing Committee

J. W. Book, E. P. Huger, I. E. Brown, K. S. Tupper and Frank Boyd.

Committee on Finance

J. Adger Smyth, A. Johnson, Henry Oliver, E. P. McSwiney and D. A. J. Sullivan.

Committee on Relief

J. E. Burke, J. J. Regan, M. D. Maguire, J. Cantwell and Thomas Young.

Committee on Letters

C. W. Stiles, W. J. Gayer, J. D. Murphy, W. F. Harragan and M. A. Connor.

Hall Keeper

B. P. Cunningham

1892 to 1893

Officers

B. F. McCabe, President

Wm. F. Barragan, Vice-President

S. Fogarty, Treasurer

F. J. Devereux, Secretary

Managing Commission

J. A. Barbot, T. F. McGarey, H. L. P. Bolger, T. J. Hennessy and T. J. Delaney.

Committee on Finance

J. A. Smythe, Henry Oliver, F. P. McSwiney, L. A. O'Neill and T. R. McGahan.

Committee on Relief

J. E. Burke, B. Mantoue, J. L. Webber, M. D. Maguire and A. J. Riley.

Committee on Letters

C. W. Stiles, W. J. Gayer, M. A. Connor, J. D. Murphy and J. H. Thayer.

1893 to 1894

Officers

B. F. McCabe, President

William Barragan, Vice President

S. Fogarty, Treasurer

F. J. Devereux, Secretary

Managing Committee

J. A. Barbot, T. F. McGarey, H. L. P. Bogler, T. J. Hennessy and T. J. Delaney.

Committee on Finance

J. A. Smythe, Henry Oliver, E. P. McSwiney, L. A. O'Neill And T. R. McGahan.

Committee on Relief

J. E. Burke, B. Mantoue, J. L. Weber, M. D. Maguire and A. J. Riley.

Committee on Letters

G. W. Stiles, W. J. Gayer, M. A. Connor, J. D. Murphy and J. H. Thayer.

1894 to 1895

<u>Officers</u>
Thomas R. McGahan, President
George W. Egan, Vice-President
Simon Fogarty, Treasurer
F. J. Devereux, Secretary
<u>Managing Committee</u>
A. J. Riley, J. H. Thayer, T. J. Delany, A. F. C. Cramer and T. F. McGarey.
<u>Committee on Finance</u>
J. Adger Smythe, Henry Oliver, E. P. McSwiney, L. A. O'Neill and E. F. Sweegan.
<u>Committee on Relief</u>
J. E. Burke, M. D. Maguire, Edward Perry, J. E. Brown and James Armstrong.
<u>Committee on Letters</u>
C. W. Stiles, J. D. Murphy, B. P. Cunningham, J. H. Perrine and Leon C. Ferrall.

1895 to 1896

<u>Officers</u>
Thomas R. McGahan, President
George W. Egan, Vice-President
Simon Fogarty, Treasurer
F. J. Devereux, Secretary
<u>Managing Committee</u>
A. J. Riley, J. H. Thayer, T. J. Delaney, A. F. C. Cramer and T. F. McGarey.
<u>Committee on Finance</u>
J. Adger Smythe, Henry Oliver, W. J. Storen, W. H. Dunkin and H. L. P. Bogler.
<u>Committee on Relief</u>
J. E. Burke, M. D. Maguire, Edward Perry, J. E. Brown and James Armstrong.
<u>Committee on Letters</u>
J. D. Murphy, B. P. Cunningham, J. H. Perrine, Leon C. Ferrall and J. B. Davin.

1896 to 1897

<u>Officers</u>
Thomas R. McGahan, President
George W. Egan, Vice-President

Simon Fogarty, Treasurer
F. J. Devereux, Secretary
Managing Committee
A. J. Riley, J. H. Thayer, T. J. Delaney, A. F. C. Cramer and T. F. McGarey.
Committee on Finance
J. Adger Smythe, Henry Oliver, W. J. Storen, W. H. Dunkins and H. L. P. Bogler.
Committee on Relief
J. E. Burke, M. D. Maguire, Edward Perry, Dr. Lane Mullally and James Armstrong.
Committee on Letters
J. D. Murphy, B. P. Cunningham, J. H. Perrine, Leon C. Ferrall and J. B. Davin.

1897 to 1898

Officers
Thomas R. McGahan, President
George W. Egan, Vice-President
Simon Fogarty, Treasurer
W. E. Duffus, Secretary
Managing Committee
A. J. Riley, W. H. Dunkin, E. P. McSwiney, H. L. P. Bolger and J. H. Thayer.
Committee on Finance
J. F. Redding, Henry Oliver, W. J. Storen, James M. Seignious and H. A. Molony.
Committee on Relief
J. E. Burke, M. D. Maguire, Edward Perry, Dr. Lane Mullally and James Armstrong.
Committee on Letters
J. D. Murphy, B. P. Cunningham, J. H. Perrine, Leon C. Ferrall and J. B. Davin.

1898 to 1899

Officers
T. R. McGahan, President
George W. Egan, Vice-President
Simon Fogarty, Treasurer
W. E. Duffus, Secretary
Managing Committee
A. J. Riley, W. H. Dunkin, E. P. McSwiney, H. L. P. Bolger and J. H. Thayer.

<u>Committee on Finance</u>

J. F. Redding, Henry Oliver, W. J. Storen, James Seignious and H. A. Molony.

<u>Committee on Relief</u>

J. E. Burke, M. Maguire, P. Carter, T. H. Reynolds and James Armstrong.

1899 to 1900

<u>Officers</u>

Thomas R. McGahan, President
George W. Egan, Vice-President
John T. Roddy, Treasurer
W. E. Duffus, Secretary

<u>Managing Committee</u>

W. J. Storen, L. A. O'Neill, P. Carter, T. H. Reynolds and E. W. Wynne.

<u>Committee on Finance</u>

J. F. Redding, Henry Oliver, J. Adger Smythe, J. M. Seignious and H. A. Molony.

<u>Committee on Relief</u>

J. E. Burke, M. D. Maguire, L. M. Pinckney, C. J. Redding and James Armstrong.

<u>Committee on Letters</u>

J. H. Perrine, J. D. Murphy B. P. Cunningham, W. H. Gannon and W. F. Barragan.

1900 to 1901

<u>Officers</u>

T. R. McGahan, President
George W. Egan, Vice-President
John T. Roddy, Treasurer
W. E. Duffus, Secretary

<u>Managing Committee</u>

Henry Oliver, T. H. Reynolds, George S. Legare, C. J. Redding and J. E. Fallin.

<u>Committee on Finance</u>

J. F. Redding, J. Adger Smythe, J. M. Seignious, H. A. Molony and F. Q. O'Neill.

<u>Committee on Relief</u>

J. E. Burke, L. M. Pinckney, James Armstrong and C. J. Redding.

<u>Committee on Letters</u>

J. H. Perrine, B. P. Cunningham, W. H. Gannon, J. D. Murphy and D. L. Sinkler.

1901 to 1902

Officers
Thomas R. McGahan, President
George W. Egan, Vice-President
John T. Roddy, Treasurer
W. E. Duffus, Secretary

Managing Committee
James M. Seignious, Thomas F. O'Donnell, W. M. Fitch, L. M. Pinckney and H. F. Bremer.

Committee on Finance
Jas. F. Redding, James H. Thayer, J. Adger Smythe, H. A. Molony and F. Q. O'Neill.

Committee on Relief
J. E. Burke, H. W. Mitchell, Jr., M. D. Maguire, C. Julius Redding and James Armstrong.

Committee on Letters
B. P. Cunningham, D. L. Sinkler, W. H. Gannon, M. F. Kennedy and W. P. Cantwell.

1902 to 1903

Officers
James H. Thayer, President
William J. Storen, Vice-President
C. Julius Redding, Secretary
John T. Roddy, Treasurer

Managing Committee
H. F. Bremer, T. F. O'Donnell, B. P. Cunningham, M. Triest and J. S. Farnum.

Committee on Finance
James F. Redding, J. Adger Smythe, James Seignious, H. A. Molony and F. Q. O'Neill.

Committee on Relief
J. E. Burke, H. W. Mitchell, Jr., M. D. Maguire, Simon Fogarty and James Armstrong.

Committee on Letters
B. P. Cunningham, D. L. Sinkler, W. H. Gannon, M. F. Kennedy and W. P. Cantwell.

1903 to 1904

Officers
James H. Thayer, President
William J. Storen, Vice-President
C. Julius Redding, Secretary

John T. Roddy, Treasurer
Managing Committee
H. F. Bremer, T. F. O'Donnell, W. H. Dunkin, M. Triest and J. S. Farnum.
Committee on Finance
James F. Redding, J. Adger Smythe, R. G. Rhett, H. A. Molony and F. Q. O'Neill.
Committee on Relief
J. E. Burke, J. B. Keckeley, M. D. Maguire, Simon Fogarty and James Armstrong.
Committee on Letters
B. P. Cunningham, D. L. Sinkler, W. H. Gannon, M. F. Kennedy and W. P. Cantwell.

1904 to 1905

Officers
James H. Thayer, President
William J. Storen, Vice-President
C. Julius Redding, Secretary
John T. Roddy, Treasurer
Managing Committee
H. F. Bremer, Thomas F. O'Donnell, William H. Dunkin, M. Triest and J. S. Farnum.
Committee on Finance
F. Q. O'Neill, J. Adger Smythe, R. G. Rhett, H. A. Molony and H. W. Conner.
Committee on Relief
J. E. Burke, J. B. Keckeley, M. D. Maguire, Simon Fogarty and James Armstrong.
Committee on Letters
B. P. Cunningham, Daniel L. Sinkler, W. H. Gannon, M. F. Kennedy and W. P. Cantwell.

1905 to 1906

Officers
James H. Thayer, President
William J. Storen, Vice-President
C. Julius Redding, Secretary
John T, Roddy, Treasurer
Managing Committee
William H. Dunkin, M. Triest, James P. Magrath, Hugh Ferguson and J. S. Farnum.
Committee on Finance

F. Q. O'Neill, W. E. Hughes, R. G. Rhett, H. A. Molony and H. W. Conner, Jr.

Committee on Relief

J. E. Burke, J. B. Keckeley, M. D. Maguire, Simon Fogarty and James Armstrong.

Committee on Letters

B. P. Cunningham, C. J. Murphy, W. H. Gannon, M. F. Fogarty and W. P. Cantwell.

1906 to 1907

Officers

W. J. Storen, President

E. W. Hughes, Vice President

C. J. Redding, Secretary

John T. Roddy, Treasurer

Managing Committee

H. W. Conner, Jr., C. J. Murphy, J. Herman Ostendorff, J. Burns and W. J. O'Hagan.

Committee on Finance

F. Q. O'Neill, H. Thayer, R. G. Rhett, H. A. Molony and H. W. Mitchell Jr.

Committee on Relief

J. E. Burke, J. B. Keckeley, M. D. Maguire, Simon Fogarty and James Armstrong.

Committee on Letters

B. P. Cunningham, E. F. Connor, W. H. Gannon, M. F. Kennedy and W. P. Cantwell.

1907 to 1908

Officers

W. J. Storen, President

E. W. Hughes, Vice President

C. J. Redding, Secretary

John T. Roddy, Treasurer

Managing Committee

H. W. Conner, Jr., C. J. Murphy, J. Herman Ostendorff, J. Burns and W. J. O'Hagan.

Committee on Finance

F. Q. O'Neill, William H. Dunkin, R. G. Rhett, H. A. Molony and H. W. Mitchell Jr.

Committee on Relief

J. E. Burke, J. B. Keckeley, M. D. Maguire, Simon Fogarty and James Armstrong.

Committee on Letters

B. P. Cunningham, E. F. Connor, W. H. Gannon, M. F. Kennedy and W. P. Cantwell.

1908 to 1909

Officers

Edward Hughes, President

H. A. Molony, Vice President

D. M. O'Driscoll, Secretary

John T. Roddy, Treasurer

Managing Committee

H. W. Conner, C. J. Murphy, Thos. S. Sinkler, John J. Furlong and Henry F. Hayne.

Committee on Finance

F. Q. O'Neill, W. H. Dunkin, R. G. Rhett, H. W. Mitchell Jr. and H. F. Bremer.

Committee on Relief

J. E. Burke, James Armstrong, S, Fogarty, J. K. Follin and M. D. Maguire.

Committee on Letters

B. P. Cunningham, E. F. Conner, W. H. Gannon, M. F. Kennedy and W. P. Cantwell.

1909 to 1910

Officers

Edward Hughes, President

H. A. Molony, Vice President

D. M. O'Driscoll, Secretary

John T. Roddy, Treasurer

Managing Committee

C. J. Murphy, J. J. Furlong, E. S. Dingle, J. D. Adams and A. C. Tobias.

Committee on Finance

F. Q. O'Neill, R. G. Rhett, William Dunkin, H. W. Conner and H. F. Bremer.

Committee on Relief

J. E. Burke, James Armstrong, S. Fogarty, J. E. Follin and H. W. Mitchell Jr.

Committee on Letters

B. P. Cunningham, W. H. Cannon, E. P. Conner, M. F. Kennedy and W. P. Cantwell.

1910 to 1911

Officers

H. A. Molony, President
H. W. Conner, Vice President
D. M. O'Driscoll, Secretary
John T. Roddy, Treasurer
Managing Committee
E. S. Dingle, J. D. Adams, A. C. Tobias Jr., W. J. Leonard and J. P. DeVaux.
Committee on Finance
F. Q. O'Neill, R. G. Rhett, William H. Dunkin, C. J. Murphy and H. F. Bremer.
Committee on Relief
J. E. Burke, James Armstrong, M. F. Kennedy, S. Fogarty, J. E. Follin and W. Mitchell Jr.
Committee on letters
B. P. Cunningham, W. H. Gannon, E. F. Conner, M. F. Kennedy and W. P. Cantwell.

1911 to 1912

Officers
H. A. Molony, President
H. W. Conner, Vice President
D. M. O'Driscoll, Secretary
John T. Roddy, Treasurer
J. E. Burke, Solicitor
Managing Committee
J. D. Adams, A. C. Tobias Jr., A. Marion Stone, W. J. Leonard and G. J. McDowell.
Committee on Finance
F. Q. O'Neill, R. G. Rhett, William H. Dunkin, C. J. Murphy and H. F. Bremer.
Committee on Relief
James Armstrong, M. F. Kennedy, S. Fogarty, J. E. Follin and W. Mitchell Jr.
Committee on Letters
W. H. Gannon, T. F. O'Donnell, H. F. Hayne, E. F. Connor, and W. P. Cantwell.

1912 to 1913

Officers
H. A. Molony, President
H. W. Conner, Vice President
D. M. O'Driscoll, Secretary
John T. Roddy, Treasurer

J. E. Burke, Solicitor

<u>Managing Committee</u>

A. C. Tobias Jr., A. Marion Stone, W. J. Leonard, G. J. McDowell and T. J. Sweeney.

<u>Committee on Finance</u>

F. Q. O'Neill, R. G. Rhett, William H. Dunkin, C. J. Murphy and H. F. Bremer.

<u>Committee on Relief</u>

James Armstrong, M. F. Kennedy, S. Fogarty, J. E. Follin and John P. DeVeaux.

<u>Committee on Letters</u>

W. H. Gannon, T. F. O'Donnell, H. F. Hayne, E. F. Connor, and W. P. Cantwell.

1913 to 1914

<u>Officers</u>

H. W. Conner, President

James Armstrong, Vice President

D. M. O'Driscoll, Secretary

John T. Roddy, Treasurer

J. E. Burke, Solicitor

<u>Managing Committee</u>

T. J. Sweeney. W. J. Leonard, G. J. McDowell, A. Marion Stone and Lawrence W. Whiting.

<u>Committee on Finance</u>

F. Q. O'Neill, R. G. Rhett, William H. Dunkin, H. A. Molony, C. J. Murphy and H. F. Bremer.

<u>Committee on Relief</u>

M. F. Kennedy, S. Fogarty, J. E. Follin, T. H. Reynolds and John P. DeVeaux.

<u>Committee on Letters</u>

W. H. Gannon, T. F. O'Donnell, H. F. Hayne, E. F. Conner, and W. P. Cantwell.

1914 to 1915

<u>Officers</u>

H. W. Conner, President

James Armstrong, Vice President

D. M. O'Driscoll, Secretary

John T. Roddy, Treasurer

J. E. Burke, Solicitor

<u>Managing Committee</u>

T. J. Sweeney, W. J. Leonard, G. J. McDowell, A. Marion Stone and W. F. Livingston.

Committee on Finance

F. Q. O'Neill, R. G. Rhett, William H. Dunkin, H. A. Molony, C. J. Murphy and H. F. Bremer.

Committee on Relief

M. F. Kennedy, S. Fogarty, J. E. Follin, T. H. Reynolds and John P. DeVeaux.

Committee on Letters

W. H. Gannon, H. F. Hayne, E. F. Conner, M. O'Shaughnessy and W. P. Cantwell.

1915 to 1916

Officers

Col. James Armstrong, President

W. Turner Logan, Vice-President

G. J. McDowell, Secretary

John T. Roddy, Treasurer

J. E. Burke, Solicitor

Managing Committee

T. J. Sweeney, A. Marion Stone, George W. Bremer, John P. Michel and John I. Cosgrove.

Committee on Finance

Mayor John P. Grace, H. A. Molony, R. G. Rhett, C. J. Murphy, H. F. Bremmer and W. K. McDowell.

Committee on Relief

A. J. Riley, H. W. Conner, John McAlister, M. F. Kennedy, T. H. Reynolds and John P. DeVeaux.

Committee on Letters

W. P. Cantwell, W. H. Gannon, E. F. Conner, H. F. Hayne and M. O'Shaughnessy.

1916 to 1917

Officers

James Armstrong, President

W. Turner Logan, Vice President

J. W. Molony, Secretary

John T. Roddy, Treasurer

Managing Committee

T. J. Sweeney, A. Marion Stone, George W. Bremer, John P. Michel and John I. Cosgrove.

Committee on Finance

John P. Grace, W. K. McDowell, W. J. O'Hagan, H. A. Molony, R. G. Rhett and C. J. Murphy.

<u>Committee on Relief</u>

A. J. Riley, John McAlister, M. F. Kennedy, T. H. Reynolds and John P. DeVeaux.

<u>Committee on Letters</u>

W. P. Cantwell, W. H. Gannon, E. F. Conner, H. F. Hayne and M. O'Shaughnessy.

1917 to 1918

<u>Officers</u>

W. Turner Logan, President

Thomas J. Sweeney, Vice-President

J. Vincent Price, Secretary

J. Roddy, Treasurer

<u>Managing Committee</u>

John I. Cosgrove, A. M. Stone, George W. Bremer, J. P. Michel and R. H. Brown.

<u>Committee on Finance</u>

J. P. Grace, W. K. McDowell, W. J. O'Hagan, H. A. Molony, R. G. Rhett and C. J. Murphy.

<u>Committee on Relief</u>

A. J. Riley, John McAlister, F. M. Bryan, M. F. Kennedy, T. H. Reynolds and J. F. Condon.

<u>Committee on Letters</u>

W. P. Cantwell, C. C. Kanapaux, M. O'Shaughnessy, H. F. Hayne, E. F. Conner, and D. L. Sinkler.

1918 to 1919

<u>Officers</u>

W. Turner Logan, President

Thomas J. Sweeney, Vice-President

J. Vincent Price Secretary

John T. Roddy, Treasurer

<u>Managing Committee</u>

John I. Cosgrove, A. M. Stone, George W. Bremer, J. P. Michel and R. H. Brown.

<u>Committee on Finance</u>

J. P. Grace, W. K. McDowell, W. J. O'Hagan, H. A. Molony, R. G. Rhett and C. J. Murphy.

<u>Committee on Relief</u>

A. J. Riley, John McAlister, F. M. Bryan, M. F. Kennedy, T. H. Reynolds and J. F. Condon.

Committee on Letters

W. P. Cantwell, C. C. Kanapaux, M. O'Shaughnessy, H. F. Hayne, E. P. Connor, and D. L. Sinkler.

1919 to 1920

Officers

W. Turner Logan, President

Thomas J. Sweeney, Vice-President

J. Vincent Price, Secretary

John T. Roddy, Treasurer

Managing Committee

John I. Cosgrove, A. M. Stone, George W. Bremer, J. P. Michel, D. F. Craig and R. H. Brown.

Committee on Finance

J. P. Grace, W. K. McDowell, W. J. O'Hagan, H. A. Molony, R. G. Rhett and C. J. Murphy.

Committee on Relief

A. J. Riley, John McAlister, F. M. Bryan, M. F. Kennedy, T. H. Reynolds and J. F. Condon.

Committee on Letters

W. P. Cantwell, C. C. Kanapaux, M. O'Shaughnessy, H. F. Hayne, E. F. Conner, and M. S. Stoppelbein.

1920 to 1921

Officers

Thomas J. Sweeney, President

A. Marion Stone, Vice-President

J. Vincent Price Secretary

John T. Roddy, Treasurer

Managing Committee

John I. Cosgrove, R. H. Brown, J. P. Michel, D. F. Craig and W. A. O'Brien.

Committee on Finance

J. P. Grace, W. King McDowell, W. J. O'Hagan, Daniel Sinkler, R. G. Rhett and C. J. Murphy.

Committee on Relief

A. J. Riley, F. M. Bryan, Isaac Marks, M. F. Kennedy, W. A. O'Hagan and J. F. Condon.

Committee on Letters

W. P. Cantwell, C. C. Kanapaux, E. F. Connor, J. J. Comar, A. W. Weiters and M. S. Stoppelbein.

1921 to 1922

Officers
Thomas J. Sweeney, President
A. M. Stone, Vice President
J. V. Price Secretary
J. Roddy, Treasurer

Managing Committee
John I. Cosgrove, George W. Bremer, R. H. Brown, John P. Michel, D. F. Craig and W. A. O'Brien.

1922

Officers
A. Marion Stone, President
John I. Cosgrove, Vice-President
Martin T. Powers Secretary
J. Vincent Price, Treasurer

Managing Committee
George W. Bremer, J. P. Michel, D. F. Craig, R. H. Brown, Daniel L. Sinkler and W. A. O'Brien.

Committee on Finance
John P. Grace, T. W. Passailaigue, W. O'D. Langley, W. K. McDowell, W. J. O'Hagan and C. M. Gibson.

Committee on Relief
A. J. Riley, F. M. Bryan, Isaac Marks, M. F. Kennedy, W. A. O'Hagan and J. F. Condon.

Committee on Letters
W. P. Cantwell, W. J. Hanlon, N. S. Lea, Arnoldus Vanderhorst, J. J. Comar and August W. Weiters.

*The list was compiled from Charleston newspapers and city directories.

APPENDIX 5

A LIST OF THE MEMBER OF THE HIBERNIAN SOCIETY OF CHARLESTON FROM 1801 TO 1868 ALONG WITH THE DATE OF THEIR ADMISSION*

John S. Adam, March 17, 1801; W. S. Adams, January 7, 1855; Thomas E. Addy, March 2, 1840;James Adger, March 17, 1813; William Aiken, February 1, 1814; William Aiken, Jr., March 2, 1830;John J. Alexander, May 6, 1822; A. A. Allemong, April 4, 1854; Joseph Anthony, March 17, 1801; James Archer, March 19, 1868; James Armstrong, March 17, 1849; James Armstrong, Jr., March 19, 1868; C. M. Arnold, January 4, 1848; P.A. Aveilhe, January 4, 1848; P. A. Aveilhe, Jr. April 3, 1849; and Chas. H. Axson, April 3, 1849.

W. R. Babcock, April 1, 1845; Jas. G. Bailie, March 17, 1854; H. F. Baker, March 17, 1849;H. F. Baker, November 5, 1867; Rev. R. S. Baker, April 2, 1839; Thomas E. Baker, April 4, 1848; F. C. Barber, January 4, 1848; Theo. G. Barker, March 17, 1866; William Barker, March 6, 1838; Samuel Barnet, April 25, 1801; E. L. Barre, March 19, 1868; Thomas G. Bashford, November 1, 1803; E. M. Beach, March 5, 1839; Jas. Beattie, March 17, 1849; Jonathan Beatty, January 2, 1816; Joseph Beatty, March 6, 1866; John Bellinger, M.D., March 1, 1836; Thomas Bennett, March 3, 1829; Thos. B. Bennett, March 17, 1853; W. J. Bennett, August 3, 1847; S. B. Bernard, April 2, 1850; Capt. M. Berry, March 17, 1847; Alexander Black, May 6, 1817; Geo. C. Black, April 3, 1866; Geo. W. Black, February 2, 1847; James Black, April 4, 1820; John Blackwood, April 7, 1818; Thomas Blackwood, October 4, 1814; John Blair, January 2, 1816; William Blair, March 7, 1837; Daniel Boinest, March 6, 1866; John Bones, April 3, 1838; Wm. Bones, March 17, 1849; Thomas Bourke, August 4, 1801; J. W. Bowen, April 7, 1840; Geo. A. Bowman, October 4, 1853; Ker Boyce, March 2, 1841; John D. Boyd, June 2, 1801; Dennis Boyle, March 17, 1804; J. W. Bradley, April 3, 1849; Hugh Brady, July 5, 1859; John Brady, March

7, 1848; Patrick Brady, March 19, 1868; Thomas Braley, July 6, 1802; Charles Brenan, April 1, 1828; A. Brown, June 5, 1855; Geo. W. Brown, June 6, 1843; Geo. W. Brown, March 17, 1853; S. W. Brown, March 17, 1867; Julius P. Browne, March 3, 1868; J. W. Brownfield, April 1, 1856; A. F. Browning, February 6, 1855; R. S. Bruns, November 4, 1856; R. S. Bruns, December 3, 1867; H. C. Bryan, January 2, 1851; Thos. G. Budd, April 3, 1849; Jas. S. Burgess, March 2, 1841; Rev. Wm. Burke, March 3, 1840; Thos. Burke, March 17, 1848; A. W. Burnett, December 3, 1850; Jno. Burns, March 17, 1860; and Geo. W. Busby, January 2, 1855.

Hugh Cahill, September 7, 1802; A. P. Caldwell, May 4, 1847; James Caldwell, March 3, 1868; Jas. M. Caldwell, March 5, 1839; John W. Caldwell, March 7, 1837; Robert Caldwell, March 5, 1839; William A. Caldwell, March 3, 1807; W. R. Caldwell, April 3, 1866; Geo. S. Cameron, February 1, 1848; J. B. Campbell, April 2, 1850; James Campbell, October 1, 1816; James T. Campbell, March 19, 1868; Patrick Campbell, April 4, 1826; A. Cannady, March 1, 1853; James Cantwell, February 6, 1866; Laurence Cantwell, February 6, 1866; Patrick Cantwell, October 3, 1843; J. N. Cardozo, April 1, 1845; John E. Carew, October 1, 1844; W. B. Carlisle, April 4, 1854; C. D. Carr, September 7, 1847; H. W. Carr, April 6, 1858; Eugene M. Carey, April 2, 1839; B. R. Carroll, March 6, 1860; E. M. Carroll, March 6, 1860; George H. Carroll, April 5, 1831; James P. Carroll, March 5, 1811; David A. Carson, February 3, 1852; Elisha Carson, March 17, 1830; Samuel Carson, March 17, 1804; Geo. R. Cathcart, August 7, 1866; R. S. Cathcart, March 17, 1867; M. Caulfield, March 3, 1868; James Chapman, April 4, 1837; Richard Clabby, March 17, 1809; W. D. Clancy, April 7, 1857; Michael Clansey, November 1, 1803; Samuel Clarke, April 3, 1838; John Clarken, January 2, 1844; Finlater Clements, March 17, 1812; L. C. Clifford, February 5, 1839; Mathew Coan, March 2, 1802; John Coburn, March 2, 1802; W. S. Cochran, November 4, 1851; C. S. Cogdell, February 6, 1849; J. W. Cogdell, January 4, 1848; John J. Cohen, February 4, 1854; J. W. Cogdell, January 4, 1848; John J. Cohen, February 4, 1854; N. A. Cohen, March 1, 1842; C. J. Colcock, February 6, 1855; Nicholas Colleton, April 3, 1866; John Commins, March 3, 1867; Thos. D. Condy, January 4, 1848; Henry W. Conner, April 1, 1845; James Conner, April 4, 1854; P. J. Coogan, March 6, 1860; John M. Corcoran, March 17, 1842; Thomas Cormick, October 6, 1801; S. G. Courtenay, February 3, 1852; S. G. Courtenay, March 17, 1866; W. A. Courtenay, March 4, 1862; Edward Courtney, March 17, 1801; W. C. Courtney, February 3, 1852; James Cosgrove, October 4, 1864; J. R. E. Coutrier, Dr. March 5, 1850; Capt. L. M. Coxetter, March 7, 1867; William Crafts, Jr., September 22, 1814; Lemuel Crane, March 6, 1866; Daniel Crawford, February 4, 1854;

Joseph Crombie, March 17, 1801; John Crow, March 17, 1801; Andrew Cunningham, February 5, 1828; J. G. Cunningham, September 3, 1867; and John Cunningham, July 6, 1847.

Joseph D. Daley, March 1, 1853; Edward Daly, April 1, 1856; J. J. Darrell, June 2, 1818; William Davidson, March 17, 1835; J. S. Davies, April 1, 1856; George Y. Davis, March 17, 1835; James B. Davis, April 2, 1850; Thomas G. Davis, April 3, 1849; W. H. Davis, December 3, 1850; Francis Dawson, January 2, 1855; Francis W. Dawson, March 19, 1868; F. G. DeFontain, March 19, 1868; John Deighen, March 6, 1866; Thomas Denny, M.D., March 17, 1801; John H. Devereaux, March 17, 1867; W. S. Dewar, March 17, 1849; William S. Dewar, April 3, 1832; John Dickey, March 2, 1802; Thomas Dixon, November 3, 1840; O. L. Dobson, April 3, 1838; Francis W. Donlevy, December 2, 1817; T. Doonan, March 17, 1849; John Dougherty, February 2, 1841; Miles Drake, February 6, 1866; Leon Druelle, November 5, 1867; Henry Duffey, July 6, 1802; A. W. Duffus, June 7, 1864; G. H. S. Duffus, March 7, 1848; Thomas Duggan, October 6, 1818; Joseph H. Dukes, March 17, 1847; T. C. H. Dukes, April 3, 1866; William C. Dukes, March 17, 1837; Rice Dulin, January 4, 1848; James Duncan, June 2, 1801; John Duncan, November 3, 1801; A. H. Dunkin, April 4, 1848; Benjamin F. Dunkin, October 3, 1820; W. C. Dunlap, April 2, 1839; Robert Dunlop, M.D., December 1, 1801; George Dunn, March 3, 1839; and R. S. Duryea, March 17, 1867.

J. F. Early, March 17, 1867; E. W. Edgerton, March 2, 1841; Charles Edmonston, April 7, 1840; George Edwards, March 18, 1833; Albert Elfe, February 1, 1848; Barnard Elliott, October 6, 1818; W. S. Elliott, April 2, 1861; Henry Ellison, January 5, 1802; E. J. England, March 17, 1867; Right Rev. John England, D. D., June 4, 1821; E. D. Enston, March 6, 1866; and David Ewart, July 2, 1833.

Richard Fair, March 17, 1813; Andrew Farrelly, October 4, 1864; S. S. Farrer, April 3, 1849; John Ferguson, March 4, 1862; J. J. Ferrall, April 6, 1858; William Ferres, March 17, 1815; John Finley, June 2, 1801; Christopher Fitzsimons, January 6, 1818; Christopher Fitzsimons, Jr., February 1, 1825; D. F. Flemming, April 7, 1840; Joseph Flemming, April 6, 1824; Mathias Flemming, December 1, 1801; Robert Flemming, February 3, 1818; C. H. Flynn, March 6, 1866; Thos. Flynn, July 5, 1859; Thomas Flynn, May 3, 1814; Thomas Flynn, April 3, 1866; Philip Fogarty, February 6, 1866; John J. Foran, April 17, 1841; Edward Forgartie, February 4, 1851; Rev. John Forrest, March 17, 1849; William B. Foster, March 17, 1838; John Fox, January 6, 1818; George Fryer, July 5, 1842; C. M. Furman, October 1, 1844; and J. K. Furman, Dr., March 17, 1852.

James Gadsden, June 1, 1847; G. Gaetjens, March 2, 1841; P. C.

Gaillard, January 4, 1848; John W. Gallagher, June 4, 1839; Rev. Simon Felix Gallagher, D. D. March 17, 1801; J. W. Gamble, December 2, 1856; Thomas J. Gantt, March 2, 1841; William Garnon, March 17, 1802; Thomas Garrity, March 3, 1852; W. C. Gatewood, April 1, 1845; Wm. J. Gayer, March 17, 1866; G. C. Geddes, December 6, 1843; John Geddes, May 3, 1814; E. Geddings, Dr., August 6, 1839; James George, August 4, 1818; Archibald Getty, February 6, 1866; Alexander Gilfillen, March 7, 1837; D. B. Gilliland, March 6, 1866; W. D. Gilliland, March 2, 1841; William H. Gilliland, March 17, 1814; George Girity, March 18, 1811; A. B. Glover, September 6, 1859; Geo. M. Goodwin, April 6, 1852; Walter Goodman, January 4, 1814; James Gordon, June 6, 1809; John Gordon, June 6, 1809; Thomas Gough, February 2, 1802; Henry Gourdin, March 5, 1833; James J Grace, March 19, 1868; S. Colleton Graves, June 4, 1816; Alexander Gray, October 4, 1814; Christopher Gray, April 4, 1848; Francis J. Green, March 19, 1868; James F. Green, March 3, 1867; William Greer, May 1, 1849; Wm. Gregg, February 2, 1841; W. H. Gruver, January 2, 1855; Dr. J. G. Guignard, March 17, 1848; and John Gyles, September 1, 1818.

Dominick A. Hall, March 17, 1801; John R. Hamilton, March 1, 1836; William N. Hamilton, March 17, 1838; O. H. Hart, January 7, 1868; John Haslett, Sr., May 5, 1801; Dr. A. P. Hayne, March 6, 1850; Isaac Hayne, March 17, 1867; J. W. Hayne, January 4, 1848; J. W. Hayne, June 2, 1863; John Heart, April 3, 1849; George Henry, June 1, 1819; Robert F. Henry, April 1, 1834; O. B. Heriot, March 17, 1851; George Herron, April 3, 1850; Samuel Herron, March 3, 1818; George Hervey, March 2, 1830; Patrick Hogan, March 6, 1866; James Holmes, March 17, 1816; John H. Holmes, January 4, 1848; James A. Hopkins, April 2, 1844; Francis D. Hort, March 2, 1841; James Houston, March 17, 1812; William H. Houston, November 7, 1837; Richard F. Howard, January 5, 1808; W. E. Howland, March 17, 1866; C. N. Hubert, March 17, 1847; John R. Hudson, February 3, 1852; B. F. Hunt, May 6, 1851; Benjamin F. Hunt, April 4, 1820; James Hunter, March 17, 1801; John Hunter, May 5, 1818; William Hunter, March 17. 1801; E. Hutchet, March 17, 1867; E. A. Hutchinson, May 5, 1807; H. Hutchinson, February 6, 1850; Hugh Hutchinson, December 1, 1807; T. L. Hutchinson, April 3, 1849; and Joseph Hyde, March 17, 1837.

H. L. Jeffers, March 17. 1866 and Joseph Johnson, M. D., March 17, 1832.

C. E. Kanapaux, February 6, 1855; Charles Kanapaux, January 2, 1855; Michael Keating, September 3, 1816; P. E. Keating, October 4, 1864; E. C. Keckeley, April 7, 1840; James Keily, January 7, 1868; Col. L.

M. Keitt, April 3, 1852; Marcus Nelson Kelly, March 17, 1818; Patrick C. Kelly, March 17, 1812; T. Kelly, March 17. 1855; Wm. Aiken Kelly, March 17, 1867; George H. Kelsey, March 17, 1838; John Kenifick, March 17, 1866; John C. Kennon, March 2, 1841; John Kenny, February 6, 1866; James Parsons Kennedy, February 6, 1821; John Kennedy, March 19, 1868; Peter Kennedy, March 17, 1801; Thomas W. Kennedy, February 3, 1852; John Cessford Ker, March 17, 1837; George Kerr, March 5, 1839; Thomas J. Kerr, May 4, 1847; P. C. Kerrigan, March 6, 1866; Henry C. King, February 1, 1848; John King, December 6, 1842; Mitchell King, March 18, 1833; R. E. King, November 4, 1858; S. H. King, August 6, 1867; Wm. A. King, March 7, 1848; W. L. King, August 6, 1867; W. S. King, April 3, 1844; T. W. Kingman, March 6, 1866; Thos. J. Knauff, February 5, 1867; and William Knox, March 6, 1866.

William Laidler, April 4, 1854; Charles Lambert, March 17, 1849; Walter Lambert, March 17, 1855; James Lamont, May 5, 1801; William Lance, March 17, 1827; John Langton, December 7, 1802; F. Lanneau, January 2, 1855; Edward R. Laurens, October 3, 1826; Joshua Lazarus, January 4, 1848; C. C. Leary, March 5, 1867; Dr. Robert Lebby, February 6, 1855; David Leckie, April 3, 1838; James Legare, Jr., March 18, 1833; George Leghorn, December 2, 1817; Vincent Leseigneur, M.D., May 3, 1831; Elias Levy, March 17, 1837; Thomas P. Lockwood, June 7, 1864; John Loggan, March 17, 1801; Robert A. Long, January 1, 1841; H. G. Loper, March 17, 1845; David Lopez, January 4, 1848; Samuel H. Lothrop, July 7, 1818; John C. Lozier, November 6, 1838; Benjamin Lucas, January 2, 1855; C. C. Lynch, March 7, 1854; and P. N. Lynch, D. D., March 17, 1846.

Charles Macbeth, April 1, 1846; James Macbeth, May 6, 1851; Robert Macbeth, April 7, 1840; Neil MacNeal, April 7, 1818; Arthur Magee, April 1, 1845; John Magee, March 1, 1842; J. H. Maggett, April 1, 1846; A. G. Magrath, April 3, 1838; W. J. Magrath, March 17, 1842; Charles A Magwood, January 4, 1825; Simon Magwood, November 3, 1801; Simon J. Magwood, April 3, 1838; James J. Maher, February 5, 1867; John Mahoney, Jr., August 6, 1867; John Makky, May 5, 1801; Thomas Malcom, March 17, 1801; Rev. James Malcomson, July 5, 1803; John L. Manning, January 4, 1848; Lawrence Manning, June 2, 1801; Thomas Marshall, November 7, 1848; John C. Martin, March 17, 1849; Robert Martin, September 1, 1818; W. E. Martin, March 5, 1850; William M. Martin, February 5, 1839; F. W. Mathiesen, March 19, 1868; James McBride, October 6, 1801; William McBurney, March 7, 1837; B. F. McCabe, March 3, 1867, James McCarey, May 6, 1851; Joseph R. McCay, November 1, 1814; James McConkey, February 1, 1853; James McCormick, June 2, 1863; Richard McCormick, August 6, 1811; John McCready, December 1, 1801; Charles McCulloch,

March 17, 1817; Francis McCully, February 7, 1832; Alexander McDonald, May 3, 1831; J. E. W. McDonald, M.D., March 17, 1837; Andrew McDowell, June 2, 1829; Davidson McDowell, April 2, 1839; John McDowell, April 6, 1819; R. H. McDowell, April 5, 1853; Hall T. McGee, March 5, 1839; J. McCreery, April 1, 1856; Thomas R. McGhan, April 1, 1856; G. McGlenaghen, March 17, 1849; Dennis McGowan, March 17, 1801; Francis Q. McHugh, April 5, 1836; D. L. McKay, February 6, 1855; John McKee, April 5, 1836; John McKeegan, March 7, 1837; John McKeegan, May 6, 1851; David McKelvy, May 5, 1801; William P. McKelvey, March 17, 1801; Charles McKenna, March 17, 1801; Archibald McKensie, February 5, 1839; William McLean, March 5, 1861; Archibald McLeish, February 4, 1851; James McLeish, March 3, 1840; Alexander McLoy, July 5, 1859; John McMaster, March 7, 1837; J. R. McMillan, March 5, 1839; John McMillan, March 17, 1837; J. McNamara, April 3, 1866; Neill McNeill, July 7, 1818; Neill McNeill, January 4, 1848; R. H. McOwen, March 2, 1841; S. L. McOwen, June 7, 1864; William Meeds, March 6, 1810; C. G. Memminger, April 6, 1830; William Menagh, April 5, 1803; M. T. Mendenhall, March 17, 1845; Jacob F. Mentzing, February 1, 1842; William E. Mikell, March 6, 1860; Robert Miller, April 4, 1837; William Miller, January 4, 1848; Adam T. Milliken, April 5, 1859; E. P. Milliken, February 2, 1841; Edward Milliken, January 5, 1808; John B. Milliken, April 7, 1840; Thomas Milliken, July 3, 1804; Wm. Milliken, April 2, 1839; Andrew Milne, May 1, 1838; Vincent Milnor, March 6, 1866; Otis Mills, December 1, 1840; Humphrey Minchin, March 17, 1801; Henry Missroon, April 3, 1849; C. T. Mitchell, March 17, 1849; Daniel Mixer, February 3, 1852; A. Moise, January 4, 1848; W. S. Monefeldt, February 1, 1848; Henry H. Moore, April 2, 1811; John Moore, April 7, 1818; Stephen West Moore, March 4, 1817; James Moorhead, February 6, 1840; Patrick Moran, August 6, 1867; William Moran, March 19, 1868; M. C. Mordecai, May 4, 1847; Andrew Moreland, March 17, 1827; Thomas Morris, March 19, 1868; J. W. Motte, January 4, 1848; Patrick Mulkai, October 2, 1860; T. D. Mulkai, February 6, 1866; John Mulligan, October 6, 1801; James M. Mulvaney, March 6, 1866; James Murdoch, November 7, 1841; William C. Murray, May 2, 1837; and James H. Murrell, February 6, 1866.

M. H. Nathans, January 2, 1850; C. C. Neill, February 5, 1867; James C. Norris, April 2, 1839; and C. B. Northrop, March 17, 1845.

A. F. O'Brien, March 17, 1867; Thomas O'Brien, November 3, 1840; Thomas S. O'Brien, February 6, 1866; W. E. O'Conner, March 6, 1866; M. P. O'Connor, March 17, 1857; Thomas O'Connor, March 17, 1810; John E. O'Denna, March 3, 1839; Michael O'Donovan, February 4, 1806; Cornelius O'Driscoll, March 17, 1801; Matthew O'Driscoll, M.

D., March 18, 1816; Charles O'Hanlon, May 4, 1830; Arthur O'Hara, February 3, 1818; Charles O'Hara, April 6, 1802; Henry O'Hara, March 17, 1801; Oliver O'Hara, March 17, 1838; William P. O'Hara, April 4, 1843; David O'Keeffe, April 3, 1866; Henry O'Loane, March 17, 1827; Cornelius O'Mara, April 3, 1866; Thomas P. O'Neale, July 3, 1866; Bernard O'Neill, December 3, 1850; Edmond O'Neill, June 4, 1844; F. L. O'Neill, February 6, 1866;John O'Neill, March 3, 1839; John F. O'Neill, January 3, 1843;John J. O'Neill, March 3, 1868, Rev. Patrick O'Neill, July 5, 1842; Israel Ottolengui, March 17, 1867; William Overstreet, March 17. 1825; Alexander Owens, March 17, 1849; and C. D. Owens, April 3, 1866.

James L. Patterson, March 2, 1841; Samuel Patterson, March 17, 1806; William Patton, January 6, 1824; John William Payne, March 3, 1818; Josiah Smith Payne, May 6, 1822; Robert K. Payne, April 2, 1839; William Payne, April 7, 1818; N. A. Peery, December 3, 1844; R. E. Pennal, April 1, 1866; Robert Pennal, March 17, 1835; W. K. Pennall, February 6, 1866; George Perman, March 17, 1814; Henry Peyton, March 17, 1801; Edmund M. Phelon, March 17, 1801; James H. Poag, April 2, 1839; Joel R. Poinsett, February 2, 1833; Francis Y. Porcher, M. D., March 17, 1835; L. T. Potter, February 6, 1850; Edward Power, March 6, 1804; James Preston, April 2, 1839; George Pringle, March 17, 1837; Dr. C. C. Pritchard, February 1, 1842; William Pritchard, Jr., June 4, 1811; N. B. Prothro, April 3, 1849; Joseph   Purcell, June 4, 1867; Thomas F. Purse, May 1, 1838; Patrick Pursell, January 3, 1804; and John Pyne, February 6, 1810.

James Quale, February 6, 1866; Cornelius S. Quigly, May 3, 1808; Rev. Edward Quigly, April 3, 1849; James Quin, March 17, 1801; and William Quirk, April 1, 1845.

Patrick   Rahall, April 3, 1849; David Ramsay, February 2, 1858; H. H. Raymond, June 1, 1847; William S. Redmond, March 17, 1837; Thomas Reedy, February 4, 1822; John T. Reid, March 17, 1841; Thomas Reilly, March 2, 1841; Thomas Reilly, M. D., March 17, 1801; James Smith Rhett, April 7, 1840; Frederick Richards, March 2, 1841; C. Y. Richardson, March 17, 1840; F. D. Richardson, April 1, 1845; B. R. Riordan, March 19, 1868; Alexander Robertson, February 7, 1841; Dr. F. M. Robertson, February 6, 1855; James Robertson, March 7, 1837; Alexander Robinson, January 6, 1818; James K. Robinson, March 7, 1837; John Robinson, May 4, 1813; Joseph A. Robinson, April 2, 1839; Murray Robinson, November 1, 1859; Randal Robinson, May 6, 1817; S. T. Robinson, February 3, 1852; Samuel Robinson, March 18, 1839; E. L. Roche, March 6, 1866; Bernard Roddin, February 6, 1866; John A. Roddy, March 17, 1841; Martin Roddy,

Jr., April 2, 1844; James Ross, April 6, 1813; James Ross, April 4, 1848; James L. Ross, March 5, 1839; N. A. Roye, January 3, 1865; John Russell, March 7, 1837; John Russell, April 3, 1849; A. J. Rutjes, June 7, 1853; John Ryan, April 2, 1839; Lawrence Ryan, May 6, 1817; Peter Thomas Ryan, February 4, 1812; Thomas Ryan, April 7, 1835; Thomas E. Ryan, July 5, 1859; William Ryan, March 17, 1845; William B. Ryan, January 4, 1848; and William K. Ryan, July 5, 1859.

Frank Sanders, March 1, 1853; John W. Sawner, January 7, 1868; C. A. Scanlon, November 1, 1853; F. J. Schaffer, March 17, 1852; John Schnierle, April 5, 1842: H. H. Schultz, January 4, 1848; William Scott, November 3, 1818; J. W. Scruggs, February 6, 1855; F. P. Seignous, January 2, 1855; J. M. Seixas, February 3, 1852; George Sergeant, April 1, 1846; William D. Shaw, March 1, 1814; George Shegog, April 4, 1837; Joseph Shegog, April 4, 1837; John Sherer, November 3, 1801; William Shirtliff, March 17, 1810 Jeremiah; James Short, April 5, 1836; Eden Shotwell, March 2, 1802; Jeremiah Shrewsbury, December 5, 1814; Thomas Y. Simons, M. D., April 7, 1835; C. H. Simonton, April 4, 1854; William Gilmore Sims, March 17, 1849; Samuel H. Skinner, January 6, 1818; James F. Slattery, January 7, 1868; Nathaniel Slawson, April 3, 1827; O'Brien Smith, March 17, 1801; Robert C. Smith, March 5, 1839; William Smith, March 17, 1801; Sen. William Smith, April 5, 1836; William H. Smith, March 19, 1868; William J. Smith, April 3, 1838; Andrew Smylie, March 17, 1801; Aug. T. Smythe, March 17, 1867; William E. Snowden, March 5, 1839; Archibald Spears, March 17, 1830; L. W. Spratt, May 6, 1851; James Steadman, December 4, 1838; Thomas Steadman, December 4, 1838; Charles John Steedman, March 17, 1825; Thomas Stephens, August 4, 1801; Joel Stevens, March 17, 1838; Alexander Stewart, January 5, 1802; Angus Stewart, March 17, 1821; John Y. Stock, April 3, 1849; Albert O. Stone, December 3, 1867; John Stoney, March 17, 1832; P. Gillard Stoney, April 2, 1839; S. D. Stoney, April 3, 1849; S. G. Stoney, February 6, 1855; Thaddeus Street, April 4, 1837; James P. Stuart, April 1, 1846; E. F. Sweegan, March 3, 1867; Bryan Sweeny, March 1, 1803; and W. H. Swift, March 17, 1867.

William R. Taber, Jr., May 4, 1854; A. R. Taft, March 3, 1839; Patrick Telvin, February 3, 1845; T. Heyward Thayer, January 4, 1848; Thomas Heyward Thayer, April 5, 1836; A. W. Thompson, March 3, 1839; George Thompson, April 2, 1839; W. L. Timmons, March 3, 1839; Joseph L. Tobias, March 17, 1867; Peter Della Torre, January 4, 1848; Lewis Trapmann, March 17, 1818; A. S. Trumbo, January 3, 1863; C. C. Trumbo, May 4, 1854; C. O. Trumbo, March 3, 1867; R. H. Tucker, Jr.,

April 4, 1848; Adam Tunno, March 17, 1820; John M. Tuohy, January 7, 1868; James Tupper, April 2, 1850; and James M. Tyrrell, April 6, 1852.

James Usher, Jr., March 4, 1822.

William J. Vincent, March 17, 1835.

Robert Waddel, May 2, 1837; Theodore D. Wagner, April 4, 1854; James M. Walker, April 3, 1838; John Falls Walker, March 5, 1833; Joseph Walker, March 2, 1841; R. T. Walker, March 17, 1845; W. H. Walker, April 3, 1849; John Wallace, May 5, 1801; Edward Walsh, November 5, 1805; John T. Walsh, April 3, 1866; E. W. Walter, February 5, 1839; George H. Walter, February 3, 1852; John Ward, February 2, 1841; W. A. Wardlaw, March 1, 1853; D. G. Wayne, January 2, 1855; Walter Webb, March 3, 1867; William Whaley, March 17, 1867; E. John White, March 6, 1866; E. R. White, March 17, 1867; J. H. White, February 3, 1852; James White, December 3, 1839; John White, April 2, 1833; Dr. O. A. White, April 5, 1853; William White, June 7, 1864; E. M. Whiting, April 3, 1866; Theodore A. Whitney, March 1, 1853; M. W. Wigg, March 19, 1868; William B. Wilkie, April 6, 1830; A. S. Willington, March 2, 1824; James Wilson, November 6, 1838; Robert Wotherspoon, June 2, 1818; and Thomas Wylie, March 3, 1807.

Legare J. Yates, June 7, 1864 and Richard Yeadon, Jr., December 3, 1833.

*The list is from a list in the possession of the Hibernian Society.

APPENDIX 6

ROLL OF THE IRISH VOLUNTEERS MUSTERED INTO CONFEDERATE SERVICE AS COMPANY "C," CHARLESTON BATTALION*

W. H. Ryan, Captain—Killed July 18, 1863 at Battery Wagner
James M. Mulvaney, First Lieutenant.
A. A. Allemong, Second Lieutenant—Killed at Petersburg, Va.
John Burke, Third Lieutenant,
F. L. O'Neil, First Sergeant.
P. R. Hogan, Second Sergeant.
Edward Lee, Third Sergeant.
Lawrence Madigan, Fourth Sergeant.
Michael Moran, Fifth Sergeant.
John Conroy, First Corporal.
Patrick Culleton, Second Corporal.
Thomas L. Hogan, Third Corporal—Killed at Petersburg, Va.
Wm. Harrington, Fourth Corporal—Killed at Petersburg, Va.
Daniel Ward, Fifth Corporal.
Bresnan, T., Killed at Legare's Point, S.C.
Brooks, Robert
Callagher, Jas., Killed at Battery Wagner, S.C.
Carey, Thomas
Carroll, James, Killed at Petersburg, Va.
Carroll, Patrick
Conley, Thomas
Cavanah, Thomas
Deary, Thos., Killed at Drury's Bluff, Va.
Devine, John
Dinan, Wm., Killed at Drury's Bluff, Va.
Dodds, George
Doherty, Luke

Driscoll, Timothy
Dunn, John
Edmunds, John
Egan, Thomas
Ellis, Daniel
Fitzgerald, Stephen
Flanigan, E., Killed at Petersburg, Va.
Flynn, James
Fowler, Thos., Killed at Petersburg, Va.
Goodrich, Henry
Goodrich, Thomas
Gralton, Daniel
Hartnett, Michael
Hayden, Thomas
Hogan, P., Killed at Petersburg, Va.
Holcombe
Howard, D., Killed at Secessionville, S.C.
Hughes, Thomas
Jager, J.
Kenny, Peter, Killed in North Carolina
Lanigan, Edward
Lee, Patrick
Lipscombe, W. L.
Maher, John, Killed at Petersburg, Va.
Manion, Patrick
Manion, Thomas
Martin, Thomas
Martin, William
May, John
McDonald, T., Killed at Petersburg, Va.
McMahon, John
McManigle, John
Murphy, J. P.
Nunan, John
O'Neil, Henry
Phillips———
Preston, John F.
Shelton, William
Sullivan, Martin
Reynolds, Samuel
Ryan, Edward, Killed at Drury's Bluff, Va.

Thompson, Henry
Toole, Michael, Killed at Battery Wagner, S.C.
Todd, Jas. R., Killed at Petersburg, Va.
Walsh, James
Warren, Chris., Killed at Petersburg, Va
Warren, John, Killed at Petersburg, Va.
Whelan, E., Killed at Drury's Bluff Va.
Whelan, Rody, Killed at Drury's Bluff Va.
Wiley, Henry, Killed at Petersburg, Va.
Wise, Edward
Wise, Thomas
*The list was printed in the *News and Courier* on June 19, 1889.

APPENDIX 7

ROLL OF THE IRISH VOLUNTEERS, COMPANY "K," FIRST REGIMENT OF SOUTH CAROLINA VOLUNTEERS, ARMY OF NORTHERN VIRGINIA*

Edward McCrady, Jr., Captain; Promoted to Lieutenant-Colonel, Wounded.

M. P. Parker, Lieutenant; Promoted to Captain, Disabled at the Battle of Sharpsburg—Died from wounds or disease contracted in service.

Thomas P. Ryan, Second Lieutenant—Resigned.

James Armstrong, Jr., Second Lieutenant; Promoted to Captain—Wounded.

Thomas McCrady, Second Lieutenant; Promoted to First Lieutenant—Wounded.

John Sweeney, First Sergeant; Promoted to Second Lieutenant—Wounded.

Alex. O'Donnell, Second Sergeant; Promoted to First Sergeant—Died from wounds or disease contracted in service.

M. McDermott, Third Sergeant—Killed

R. Mathews, Fourth Sergeant—Wounded.

Peter McKeon, Fifth Sergeant—Killed.

Daniel Miller, Corporal; Promoted to Sergeant—Wounded.

M. M. Dunn, Corporal—Wounded.

John Kilroy, Corporal—Killed.

William Fox, Corporal; Promoted to Sergeant—Wounded.

John Bateman, Corporal; Promoted to Sergeant—Died from wounds or disease contracted in service.

Alexander, Wm.

Allen, G. W.—Killed

Anderson, Robert

Brerton, Daniel, Promoted to corporal—Wounded.

Brown, James—Wounded
Burns, James—Killed.
Burns, Robert—Wounded
Byrd, Michael—Wounded.
Callahan, Owen—Wounded.
Callaghan, Daniel—Killed.
Cameron, D. P.—Killed.
Carroll, John J., Promoted to Sergeant—Died from wounds or disease contracted in service.
Carten, Charles J.—Promoted to Sergeant—Wounded.
Casey, John—Killed.
Carroll, John—Died from wounds or disease contracted in service.
Clancy, J.—Died from wounds or disease contracted in service.
Coffee, Daniel—Killed.
Collier, George
Conway, Michael—Wounded.
Crabtree, George—Killed.
Cronan, Patrick—Died from wounds or disease contracted in service.
Cummings, Patrick—Killed.
Cunningham, M.—Killed
Curran, John—Wounded.
Daly, T.—Discharged, physical disability.
Delany, John
Dillon, Edward—Wounded.
Donnelly, Joseph—Killed.
Donohoe, Henry—Died from wounds or disease contracted in service.
Doogan, Martin
Dougherty, J., Promoted to Sergeant—Died from wounds or disease contracted in service.
Duffy, Michael—Wounded.
Dunn, J. M.
Ellis, W. J.—Wounded.
Farrell, Michael—Wounded.
Feeney, Michael—Wounded.
Finessy, John
Fitzpatrick, John—Killed.
Fleming, John—Killed.
Gallman, L. B.—Killed.

Gascons, Thomas—Killed.
Gleaton, D. B.—Killed.
Gorman, John
Gully, Michael—Died from wounds or disease contracted in service.
Hagan, J.—Died from wounds, or disease contracted in service.
Haggerty, Thomas—Killed
Hartley, Richard—Died from wounds or disease contracted in service.
Hickey, Paul—Transferred to the Navy.
Holleran, Patrick—Died from wounds, or disease contracted in service.
Hynes, M.
Jones, D.—Discharged, physical disability.
Kane, Nicholas J.—Killed
Kelly, James—Killed.
Kiley, James—Died from wounds, or disease contracted in service.
Kelly, John
Kelly, Patrick—Died from wounds or disease contracted in service.
Kennedy, Edward—Wounded.
Kenney, Thomas
Kennifick, John—Wounded
Lally, M.—Killed.
Leddy, Bernard
Looney, Dennis—Died from wounds or disease contracted in service.
Mahony, Michael—Died from wounds or disease contracted in service.
Manion, Francis—Killed.
May, Michael—Died from wounds or disease contracted in service.
Motes, J. B.—Killed.
McDonald, James—Died from wounds or disease contracted in service.
McGill, Jas.—Died from wounds or disease contracted in service.
McGuire, Michael—Wounded.
McGuire, Thos.—Died from wounds or disease contracted in service.

McNabb, John—Died from wounds or disease contracted in service.
McNabb, Joseph—Killed
Mitchell, Michael—Killed.
Morris, Patrick—Wounded.
Nolan, James
Nowles, Michael—Killed.
O'Brien, James—Died from wounds or disease contracted in service.
O'Brien, Michael
O'Connell, Stephen—Killed
O'Neill, Michael
O'Rourke, John—Killed
Quintin, James—Killed.
Reilly, G. S.—Died from wounds or disease contracted in service.
Reilly, James—Killed.
Reilly, Jeremiah—Wounded.
Reilly, Michael—Died from wounds or disease contracted in service.
Rivett, B. J.—Promoted to Corporal.
Roach, Patrick—wounded.
Ryan, Thomas—Died from wounds or disease contracted in service.
Shaw, C. M.—Killed
Sinott, Arthur—Died from wounds or disease contracted in service.
Spellman, Dominick, Promoted to color sergeant—Wounded.
Spoon, William—Wounded.
Sullivan, Daniel
Sullivan, Dennis—Died from wounds or disease contracted in service.
Sullivan, Michael—Killed.
Sullivan, John
Sullivan, Thomas—Wounded.
Sweeney, James—Died from wounds or disease contracted in service.
Tobin, William—Killed.
Tracy, W., Promoted to Sergeant—Participated in every engagement.
Welch, Maurice C., Promoted to Commissary Sergeant.
Welch, Michael

Whipple, E.—Died from wounds or disease contracted in service.
Wilson, John—Died from wounds or disease contracted in service.
Wright, James M.

* The list was printed in the *News and Courier* on June 19, 1889.

APPENDIX 8

ROLL OF THE IRISH VOLUNTEERS THAT SERVED ON THE MEXICAN BORDER IN 1916 AND 1917, COMPANY "C," SECOND REGIMENT OF THE SOUTH CAROLINA NATIONAL GUARD*

Captain Thomas R. Garety, First Lieutenant John P. Sullivan, Second Lieutenant William E. King.

First Sergeant John J. Powers, Mess Sergeant Harry A. Dewey, Supply Sergeant Laurence A. Clair.

Sergeants: John F. W. Tiedman, Louis E. Burmester, James J. Gorman, Cornellus A. Heneberry, John F. Boniface, Marvin Neese.

Corporals: Charles F. Fogarty, Thomas J. Smith, Harold J. Fortune, William P. Teague, John J. Conlon, Carl W. T. Prause, Charles J. Moore, Louis E. Lamkin.

Corporal (company clerk) Raymond L. Conroy.

Buglers: Arthur B. Moore and Roscoe Turner,

Mechanic: John P. Jellicoe.

Cooks: Charles E. Libenrood and Charles L. Savarese.

Privates (first class): Ernest B. Altman, Clarence L. Barrineau, Loran M. Belvin, George W. Brittle, Frank E. Condon, Percy L. Daniels, Samuel J. Dixon, John F. Hesse, Barney L. Jones, Vicent J. McDermott, Alexander Moore, Thomas M. O'Neill, Frank E. Priester, Frederick E. Sommer, Henry N. Stause, Edward A. VanDelken, Andrew Webber, Harry J. VanDelken.

Privates: Joseph Blocker, George M. Casifield, Henry Harley, Albert Hodge, Jullian F. King, Claude P. Landers, Joseph A. Leopold, William McClain, William B. McCoy, John A. McDonald, Arthur McFayden, John M. Moore, Bnajamin F. Passilaigue, Harry A. Peeples, Adrian D. Salters, Ernest D. Shriver, James W. Sineath, Percy W. Smith,

John E. Stutts, John F. Sweat, Joseph F. Tolley, Carl B. Tuten, Andrew D. Watkins, Theodore A. Watkins and John A. Harrell.

*The list was printed in the *News and Courier* on April 20, 1917. The names are spelled as set out in the newspaper.

APPENDIX 9

ROLL OF THE IRISH VOLUNTEERS THAT SERVED IN WORLD WAR I, COMPANY "C," 105TH AMMUNITION TRAIN*

Captain Thos. R. Garety
First Lieut. J. J. Powers
Second Lieut. L. A. Clair
First Sergt. William P. Teague
Supply Sergt. R. I. Conroy
Mess Sergts. John P. Jellico, L. E. Bermester, Jno. F. Bonniface, Harry A. Dewey, Marvin Neese, Charles J. Moore and Claude Planders.
Corporals: Louis E. Lamkin, Carl W. T. Prause, Harold J. Fortune, Alex. Moore, Edward Wan Delkin, Vincent McDermott, Wm. B. Rose, John M. Moore, Walter Saye.
Mechanic: Joseph A. Leopold
Buglers: Arthur B. Moore and Roscoe Turner,
Cooks: John F. Sweat and Chas. J. Savarese
Privates first-class, Ernest B. Altman, Robert L. Arms, Clarence L. Barrineau, Laurence M. Belvin, Samuel J. Dixon, Robert C. Garland, William H. Horn, Barney Jones, Keneth F. Lee, Harry A. Peeples, Frank E. Priester, William B. McCoy, George C. Nauful, Percy Smith, Henry N. Strauss, Ernest E. Seyle, John J. Teague, Harry J. Wan Delkin, Andrew Webber.
Privates, Henry B. Ayers, Leon C. Barrineau, Wm. T. Barrineau, Bernard A. Bolchoz, William Brunson, Chas. A. Brown, John T. Buckheister, Marion H. Cole, William R. Davis, Robert M. Dunlap, Pierce F. Easterling, William Edwards, Frank L. Fleming, Charles Griffin, Henry Harley, Hugo Hill, Hamp H. Hilton, Albert Hodge, Wm. M. Hogan, Henry La Coste, Charles Loury, John A. McDonald, Walter J. Melfi, Virtes M. Mizzell, Harry C. Musselman, Edward T. Owen, Robert O'Brien, Benjamin Franklin Passailaigue, Abe H. Peeples, Percy L. Prince, A. C. Salvo, James W. Sineath, Uble Singletary, Harold A.

Smart, John H. Strange, Gussie H. Sweatman, John R. Tillman, Frank B. Wilkinson, Robert Williams, James R. Wilson, George L. Winn.

*The list was printed in the *Charleston American* on March 27, 1919. The names are spelled as set out in the newspaper.

APPENDIX 10

A PARTIAL LIST OF THE COMPANY COMMANDERS OF THE IRISH VOLUNTEERS

(All held the rank of captain unless otherwise indicated)*

COMPANY COMMANDERS 1794-1815:

1794-1799 Charles Crowley
1799-1805 O'Brien Smith (later served in the United States Congress)
1805-1812 E. M. Phelan (promoted to major)
1812-1813 Peter Kennedy
1813-1815 — — Kelly

COMPANY COMMANDERS 1827-1919:

1827-1829 Alex. Black (promoted to major)
1829-1832 P. Cantwell
1832-1835 John Magrath
1835-1848 George Henry (Company Commander during the Florida campaign)
1848-1854 A. G. Magrath (later served as Governor of South Carolina)
1854-1862 Edward Magrath (Company Commander at the time of the firing on Fort Sumter)
1862-1863 William H. Ryan (Company Commander at Legareville, Secessionville and Battery Wagner)
1863-1865 James M. Mulvaney (Company Commander during the Virginia campaign of 1864-1865)
1870-1873 John Burke
1873-1874 F. Q. O'Neill
1874-1877 Philip Fogarty

1877-1880 B. F. McCabe
1880-1883 Patrick O'Neill
1883-1886 William F. Breese
1886-1887 Michael Quinlivan
1887-1891 Charles A. McCue
1891-1893 B. P. Cunningham
1893-1898 James F. O'Gara
1898-1899 James F. Walsh (held the rank of Lieutenant during this period of time)
1899-1903 D. F. Kerney
1903-1908 James F. Walsh (retired with the rank of major because of ill health)
1908-1912 John J. Burke
1912-1915 W. C. O'Driscoll
1915-1916 John P. Sullivan
1916-1919 Thomas R. Garety (Company Commander on the Mexican border and in France during World War I)

*The list was taken from a list printed in the *Charleston American* on March 27, 1919 and from city directories. The spelling of the names is the same as set out in the newspaper.

(Endnotes)

CHAPTER NOTES

CHAPTER ONE
[1] Bob Considine, *It's The Irish* (New York: Doubleday & Company, 1961), 30; Augustine T. Smythe, *Centennial Address Delivered before the Hibernian Society of Charleston, S C. on its One Hundredth Anniversary 18th March 1902* (Charleston: Walker, Evans & Cogswell Co., 1902), 6-7.

[2] Patrick Melvin, "Captain Florence O'Sullivan and the Origins of Carolina," *South Carolina Historical Magazine*, Vol. 76 (October 1975), 235-239 (here after cited as Melvin, "Captain Florence O'Sullivan," *SCHM, 76)*; Edward McCrady, *The History of South Carolina Under The Proprietary Government, 1670-1719* (1897; reprint, New York: Russell & Russell, 1969), 120-126 (Hereinafter cited as McCrady, *South Carolina Proprietary Government*).

[3] Melvin, "Captain Florence O'Sullivan," *SCHM*, 76: 236-238; McCrady, *South Carolina Proprietary Government*, 122.

[4] Melvin, "Captain Florence O'Sullivan," *SCHM*, 76: 235, 240, 245 and 246.

[5] Samuel A. Cothran and others, *Charleston Murders* (New York: Duell, Sloan and Pearce,1947), 4.

[6] Michael J. O'Brien, "The Irish in Charleston, South Carolina," *Journal of the American Irish Historical Society*, Vol. 25 (1926), 137 (hereinafter cited as O'Brien, "The Irish in Charleston, South Carolina," *JAIHS, 25)*.

[7] Thomas Pettigrue Lesesne, *History of Charleston County, South Carolina* (Charleston: A. H. Cawston, 1931), 40.

[8] O'Brien, "The Irish in Charleston, South Carolina," *JAIHS*, 25: 137-138; McCrady, *South Carolina Proprietary Government*, 367.

[9] William A. Tobin, *The Irish in South Carolina* (Florence, S. C.: W. J. Stricklin Company, n. d.), 7.

[10] *Year Book-1883 City of Charleston, So. Ca.* (Charleston: The News and Courier Book Presses, 1883), 389. Hereinafter cited as *City of Charleston*

Year Book-1883; Arthur Mitchell, *The History of the Hibernian Society of Charleston, South Carolina, 1799-1981*, (Charleston: n. p., 1981), 5; Audrey Lockhart, *Some Aspects of Emigration from Ireland to the North American Colonies Between 1660 and 1775* (New York: Arno Press, 1976), 61-65.

[11] McCrady, *South Carolina Proprietary Government*, 556-557; Richard C. Madden, *Catholics in South Carolina* (New York: University Press of America, 1985), 9.

[12] Thomas Cooper and David J. McCord, eds., *The Statutes at Large of South Carolina [1682-1838]*, 10 vols. (Columbia: A. S. Johnson, 1836-1841), 2: 647-648 (hereinafter cited as Cooper and McCord, *Statutes*); McCrady, *South Carolina Proprietary Government*, 556-557; Madden, *Catholics in South Carolina*, 9.

[13] McCrady, *South Carolina Proprietary Government*, 557.

[14] Kerby A. Miller, *Emigrants and Exiles: Ireland and the Irish Exodus to North America* (New York, Oxford: Oxford University Press, 1985), 137; Peter Guilday, *The Life and Times of John England*, 2 vols. (New York: The American Press, 1927), 1: 135; Madden, *Catholics in South Carolina*, 8; *City of Charleston Year Book-1883*, 389.

[15] J. J. O'Connell, *Catholicity in the Carolinas and Georgia* (Westminister, Maryland: ARS SACRA, 1964), 140.

[16] Robert Meriwether, *The Expansion of South Carolina, 1729-1765* (Kingsport, Tenn.: Southern Publishers, 1940), 6 and 17-20; Jean Stephenson, *Scotch-Irish Migration to South Carolina 1772* (Strausburg: Shenandoah Publishing House, 1971), 6.

[17] Edward McCrady, *The History of South Carolina Under the Royal Government, 1719-1776* (1899; reprint, New York: Russell & Russell, 1969), 132-133; Stephenson, *Scotch-Irish Migration to South Carolina 1772*, 6; Meriwether, *The Expansion of South Carolina*, 79-81; Robert K. Ackerman, *South Carolina Colonial Land Policies* (Columbia: University of South Carolina Press, 1977), 85; Walter B. Edgar, *South Carolina: A History* (Columbia: University of South Carolina Press, 1998), 57-58.

[18] Meriwether, *The Expansion of South Carolina*, 26, 82; David Duncan Wallace, *The History of South Carolina*, 2 vols. (New York: The American Historical Society, Inc., 1934), 1: 341.

[19] Ibid., 29; Cooper and McCord, *Statutes*, 3: 781-782, 4: 10-12; .Stephenson, *Scotch-Irish Migration to South Carolina 1772*, 6, 7 and 10.

[20] Stephenson, *Scotch-Irish Migration to South Carolina 1772*, 7.

[21] Edgar, *South Carolina: A History*, 58-59; Stephenson, *Scotch-Irish Migration to South Carolina 1772*, 10; David Ramsey, *Ramsey's History of South Carolina*, 2 vols. (Newberry: W. J. Duffie, 1858) 1: 11; Mitchell, *The History of the Hibernian Society*, 5.

[22] Alexander Hewatt, *An Historical Account of the Rise and Progress of South Carolina and Georgia*, 2 vols. (London: Alexander Donaldson, 1778), 2: 272-273.

[23] George C. Rodgers, *Charleston in the Age of the Pinckneys* (Columbia: University of South Carolina Press, 1984), 7

[24] Wallace, *The History of South Carolina*, 1: 341.

[25] Lockhart, *Some Aspects of Emigration from Ireland to the North American Colonies*, 150; Mitchell, *The History of the Hibernian Society*, 5.

[26] Mitchell, *The History of the Hibernian Society*, 5.

[27] Henning Cohen, *The South Carolina Gazette, 1732-1775* (Columbia: University of South Carolina Press, 1953), 5. *South Carolina Gazette,* June 24 to July 1, 1751.

[28] *South Carolina Gazette,* January 5-12, 1767.

[29] Miller, *Emigrants and Exiles*, 146.

[30] Cohen, *The South Carolina Gazette,* 23; *South Carolina Gazette,* March 21, 1771.

[31] James Haw, *John & Edward Rutledge of South Carolina* (Athens: University of Georgia Press, 1997), 1-3; David Ramsay, *Ramsay's History of South Carolina from its First Settlement in 1670 to the Year 1808*, 2 vols. (Newberry, S.C.: W. J. Duffie, 1858), 2: 269-272.

[32] Haw, *John & Edward Rutledge of South Carolina*, 81, 93; Ramsay, *Ramsay's History of South Carolina* 2: 269-272.

[33] Ramsay, *Ramsay's History of South Carolina*, 2: 269-270; Haw, *John & Edward Rutledge of South Carolina*, 87.

[34] Miller, *Emigrants and Exiles*, 169.

[35] P. C. Coker, *Charleston's Maritime History, 1670-1865* (Charleston: Coker Craft Press, 1987),127; Petition for the Incorporation of the Friendly Brothers of Ireland, General Assembly Papers, Petitions, 1787, no. 4. In the collection of the South Carolina Department of Archives and History.

[36] Agatha Aimar Simmons, *Brief History of St. Mary's Roman Catholic Church Charleston, South Carolina* (Charleston: John J. Furlong & Company, Inc., 1961), 6-7; O'Connell, *Catholicity in the Carolinas and Georgia*, 141.

[37] Madden, *Catholics in South Carolina,* 18-19.

[38] *City Gazette or the Daily Advertiser,* August 8, 1788; Madden, *Catholics in South Carolina,*18-19.

[39] Madden, *Catholics in South Carolina,* 20

[40] Madden, *Catholics in South Carolina,* 20; Simons, *Brief History of St. Mary's Roman Catholic Church,* 5-6; Guilday, *The Life and Times of John England,* 1: 142.

⁴¹Guilday, *The Life and Times of John England,* 1: 142; Madden, *Catholics in South Carolina,* 21.

⁴²Smythe, *Centennial Address,* 9-10; R. F. Foster, *Modern Ireland* (New York: Penguin Books, 1988), 278-282; Mitchell, *The History of the Hibernian Society,* 13.

⁴³Col. James Armstrong, *Portrayal of Eventful Past as Recounted at Centennial of St. Patrick's Benevolent Society March 17, 1917,* 13. South Carolina Historical Society.

⁴⁴*Constitution and Rules of the Hibernian Society Unanimously Approved and Adopted, At an Anniversary Meeting. Held at Mr. Burger's on Tuesday the Seventh Day of March, 1801; With Alterations and Amendments* (Charleston: A. E. Miller, 1818), 1-25. Charleston Library Society; Mitchell, *The History of the Hibernian Society,* 14-15; Donald M. Williams, "Charleston's Irish Connections: Hibernian Society," *Preservation Progress,* Vol. 32 no. 2 (March 1988), 1.

⁴⁵John Blair, "Journal of a Voyage from Larne to Charleston on the Sally of Savanna," June 19, 1796. In the collection of the South Caroliniana Library of the University of South Carolina.

⁴⁶N. Louise Bailey and Walter B. Edgar eds., *Biographical Directory of the South Carolina House of Representatives,* 5 vols. (Columbia: University of South Carolina Press, 1981), 3:105-107; *Biographical Directory of the United States Congress 1774-1989* (United States Government Printing Office, 1989), 704.

⁴⁷Bailey and Edgar, *Biographical Directory of the South Carolina House of Representatives,* 3: 667-668.

⁴⁸Christopher Silver, "A New Look at Old Southern Urbanization: The Irish Worker in Charleston, South Carolina, 1840-1860," in Samuel Hines and George Hopkins, eds., *South Atlantic Urban Studies* Vol. 3 (Charleston, University of South Carolina Press, 1979), 148-149 (hereinafter cited as Silver, *The Irish Worker in Charleston);* W. M. Pine, "History Rides the Winds to Colonial Charleston," *South Carolina Historical Magazine,* Vol. 87 no. 3 (July 1986), 162-165; *South Carolina Gazette,* December 24, 1772; Blair, "Journal of a Voyage From Larne to Charleston on the Sally of Savanna"; Coker, *Charleston's Maritime History,* 172.

⁴⁹Silver, *The Irish Worker in Charleston,* 149; Coker, *Charleston's Maritime History,* 172.

⁵⁰ Pine, *History Rides the Winds,* 163; William Forbes Adams, *Ireland and Irish Emigration to the New World From 1815 to the Famine* (New Haven: Yale University Press, 1932), 425.

⁵¹George Potter, *To the Golden Door: The Story of the Irish in Ireland*

and America (Boston: Little, Brown and Company, 1960), 138-139; Miller, *Emigrants and Exiles,* 195.

⁵²Potter, *To the Golden Door,* 138-139; Considine, *It's the Irish,* 59-60.

⁵³Potter, *To the Golden Door,* 138-140; Miller, *Emigrants and Exiles,* 195.

⁵⁴Benjamin Joseph Klebaner, "Public Poor Relief in Charleston, 1800-1860," *The South Carolina Historical Magazine,* Vol. LV, 1954, 217-218; Adams, *Ireland and Irish Emigration to the New World,* 416; Silver, *The Irish Worker in Charleston,* 145.

⁵⁵*Dublin Evening Post,* March 25, 1819, cited as a footnote in Adams, *Ireland and Irish Emigration to the New World,* 92.

⁵⁶Consadine, *It's the Irish,* 61.

⁵⁷Urich Bonnell Phillips, "The Slave Problem in the Charleston District," *Plantation Town and Country,* (Urbana: University of Illinois Press, 1974), 16; Silver, *The Irish Worker in Charleston,* 150; Potter, *To the Golden* Door, 203; H. M. Henry, *Police Control of the Slave in South Carolina* (Emory Virginia: n. p., 1914), 103-104.

⁵⁸O'Connell, *Catholicity in the Carolinas and Georgia,* 196-197.

⁵⁹Samuel Melanchther Derrick, *Centennial History of the South Carolina Railroad* (Columbia: The State Company, 1930), 53.

⁶⁰Derrick, *Centennial History of the South Carolina Railroad,* 54.

⁶¹Silver, *The Irish Worker in Charleston,* 150; Derrick, *Centennial History of the South Carolina Railroad,* 60.

⁶²Thomas Y. Simons M.D., "A Report on the Epidemic of Yellow Fever as it occurred in Charleston in 1852 with statistics and other observations," *Charleston Medical Journal and Review* Vol. 8 (1854), 371 (here after cited as Simons, "A Report," *CMJR,* 8); Guilday, *The Life and Times of John England,* 2: 160-163.

⁶³Simons, "A Report," *CMJR.,* 8: 364.

⁶⁴Potter, *To the Golden Door,* 203; Consadine, *It's the Irish,* 77; William M. Mathew ed., *Agriculture, Geology, and Society in Antebellum South Carolina: The Private Diary of Edmund Ruffin, 1843* (Athens: University of Georgia Press, 1992), 65.

⁶⁵O'Connell, *Catholicity in the Carolinas and Georgia,* 46-47.

⁶⁶Potter, *To the Golden* Door, 203; Silver, *The Irish Worker in Charleston,* 147-148; Consadine, *It's the Irish,* 77.

⁶⁷Klebner, *Public Poor Relief in Charleston,* 218-219.

⁶⁸Mitchell, *The History of the Hibernian Society,* 21.

⁶⁹Potter, *To the Golden* Door, 203.

⁷⁰Consadine, *It's the Irish,* 77.

⁷¹O'Connell, *Catholicity in the Carolinas and Georgia,* 38-40.

⁷² Guilday, *The Life and Times of John England*, 1: 505-507, 545-550; O'Connell, *Catholicity in the Carolinas and Georgia*, 57; Madden, *Catholics in South Carolina*, 31-33.

⁷³Mitchell, *The History of the Hibernian Society*, 35, 37; *Tribute of Respect to the Memory of Their Late Distinguished Brother Member the Right Rev. Bishop England by the Hibernian Society of Charleston, S. C. Published by the Society* (Charleston: A. E. Miller, 1842), 15, in the collection of the Charleston Library Society; *Constitution and Rules of the Hibernian Society of Charleston, S. C. Incorporated 19th December, 1805. Rules Adopted 1827, Revised 1838, 1868. To which is attached a list of Officers and Members* (Charleston: Courier Job Press, 1868), 29.

⁷⁴P. S. O'Hegarty, *A History of Ireland Under the Union* (New York: Methuen & Co., 1969), 291-292 and 327; Kerby Miller and Paul Wagner, *Out of Ireland: The Story of Irish Emigration to America* (Washington: Elliott & Clark, 1994), 26-27 and 280; Potter, *To the Golden* Door, 140.

⁷⁵ Potter, *To the Golden* Door, 170-171; William D. Griffin, *A Portrait of the Irish in America* (New York: Charles Sons, 1981), 53.

⁷⁶Potter, *To the Golden* Door, 170

⁷⁷Griffin, *A Portrait of the Irish in America*, 53.

⁷⁸Silver, *The Irish Worker in Charleston*, 150-151.

⁷⁹Coker, *Charleston's Maritime History*, 177-178 and 187-190; Silver, *The Irish Worker in Charleston*, 149-150.

⁸⁰Neil C. Pogue, *South Carolina Electric and Gas Company, 1846-1964* (Columbia: The State Printing Company, 1964), 4-5; William Hume, "An Inquiry Into Some of the General and Local Causes to Which the Endemic Origin of Yellow Fever Has Been Attributed by Myself and Others," *Charleston Medical Journal and Review*, Vol. 9 no. 6 (November 1854), 729 (hereinafter cited as Hume, "An Inquiry," *CMJR.*, 9).

⁸¹Hume, "An Inquiry," *CMJR.*, 9: 729.

⁸²Hume, "An Inquiry," *CMJR*, 9: 729-730. Pogue, *South Carolina Electric and Gas Company*, 5.

⁸³Beatrice St. Julien Ravenel, *Architects of Charleston* (Columbia: University of South Carolina Press, 1992), 237-238.

⁸⁴Hume, "An Inquiry," *CMJR.*, 9: 728-729.

⁸⁵Michael P. Johnson and James L. Roark, *Black Masters: A Free Family of Color in the Old South* (New York: W. M. Morton and Company, 1984), 178.

⁸⁶William Hume, "On the Introduction, Propagation and Decline of Yellow Fever in Charleston, During the Summer of 1854," *Charleston Medical Journal and Review*, Vol. X no.1 (January 1855), 22.

[87]*Charleston Courier*, March 12 and 26, 1855; Adams, *Ireland and Irish Emigration to the New World*, 151.

[88]*Charleston Courier*, March 26, 1855.

[89] *Mayor's Report on City Affairs Submitted to the City Council of the City Charleston September 29, 1857*
(Charleston: Walker Evans and Co., 1857), 64.

[90] Jordan, *Police Power*, 129 and footnote 31 on page 137.

[91]"Yellow Fever in Charleston," *Charleston Medical Journal and Review*, Vol 11 (November 1856), 846 (here after cited as "Yellow Fever in Charleston," *CMJR.,* 11*)*.

[92]Ibid.; Frederick Law Olmstead, *Journey in the Seaboard Slave States* (New York:Dix and Edwards, 1856), 151.

[93]Frederick Law Olmstead, *Journey in the Seaboard Slave States* (New York:Dix and Edwards, 1856), 151.

[94]*Charleston Courier*, November 10, 1849.

[95]D. J. Cain, *History of the Epidemic of Yellow Fever in Charleston S.C., in 1854*, (Philadelphia: T. K. and P. G. Collins, 1856), 22-23; Samuel Gaillard Stoney, *This Is Charleston* (Charleston: Carolina Art Association, 1944), 54-55; *Shole's Directory of the City of Charleston 1882* (Sholes & Co. Publishers, 1882), 11.

[96] O'Connell, *Catholicity in the Carolinas and Georgia,* 154; J. J. Chisolm M.D., "A Brief Sketch of the Epidemic of Yellow Fever in 1854 in Charleston," *Charleston Medical Journal and Review*, Vol. X no. 4 (July 1855), 437-438 (here after cited as Chisolm, "Sketch," *CMJR.,10)*; Cain, *History of the Epidemic of Yellow Fever in Charleston S.C. in 1854,* 8

[97]O'Connell, *Catholicity in the Carolinas and Georgia*, 64; M. Foster Farley, *An Account of the History of Stranger's Fever in Charleston, 1699-1876* (Washington: University Press of America, Inc., 1978), first page of Preface.

[98]"Yellow Fever in Charleston," *CMJR,* 11: 846.

[99]Simons, "A Report," *CMJR.*, 8: 364-365 and 370; Farley, *An Account of the History of Stranger's Fever in Charleston*, 89-90.

[100]Simons, "A Report," *CMJR.*, 8: 363-365, 370.

[101]Farley, *An Account of the History of Stranger's Fever in Charleston,* 102-109.

[102]Ibid., 107.

[103]Ibid., 110-123.

[104]Mitchell, *The History of the Hibernian Society,* 74; *News and Courier* March 18, 1883; Silver, *The Irish Worker in Charleston,* 148.

CHAPTER TWO

[105]*South Carolian Gazette*, March 19, 1749.

[106]*South Carolian Gazette and Country Journal*, March 19, 1771.

[107]Josiah Quincy, *Memoirs of the life of Josiah Quincy Junior of the Massachusetts Bay: 1744-1775* (Boston: Little, Brown and Company, 1875), 83.

[108]William D. Griffin, *The Book of Irish Americans* (New York: Times Books, 1990), 10.

[109]*Charleston Mercury and Morning Advertiser*, March 17, 1823.

[110]Ibid.

[111]*Charleston Courier,* March 20, 1837.

[112]Arthur Mitchell, *The History of the Hibernian Society of Charleston, South Carolina, 1799-1981* (Charleston: n.p., 1981), 27-28.

[113]*Charleston Courier,* March 20, 1837; *Charleston Daily Courier,* March 17, 1854, March 18, 1858; *News and Courier,* March 18, 1875.

[114]Petition for the Incorporation of the Irish Mutual Benevolent Society of Charleston, General Assembly Papers, Petitions, 1851, no. 34. In the collection of the South Carolina Department of Archives and History.

[115]*Charleston Daily Courier,* March 17, 1854.

[116]Ibid.

[117]*Charleston Daily Courier,* March 17, 1855, March 17, 1856, March 18, 1857 March 18, 1858, March 18, 1859; *Charleston Mercury,* March 17,1857.

[118]*Charleston Daily Courier,* March 18, 1860.

[119]*Charleston Daily Courier,* March 19, 1861.

[120]*Charleston Daily Courier,* March 17 and 18, 1862, March 17 and 18, 1863, March 18, 1864.

[121]City of Charleston, Y*ear Book, 1883* (Charleston: The News and Courier Book Presses, 1883), 542-543.

[122]*Charleston Daily Courier,* May 5, 1862, E. Milby Burton, *The Seige of Charleston 1861-1865* (Columbia: University of South Carolina Press, 1970), 251-252.

[123]*Charleston Courier,* March 18, 1865.

[124]*Charleston Daily Courier,* March 19, 1866; *Sunday News* (Charleston), March 11, 1917.

[125]*News and Courier,* March 18, 1875, March 18, 1876, March 17, 1877 and March 19, 1878; *Sunday News* (Charleston), March 11, 1917

[126]*News and Courier,* March 6, 1878.

[127]James Armstrong, *Portrayal of Eventful Past as Recounted at Centennial of St. Patrick's Benevolent Society March 17, 1917,* 15. In the collection of the South Carolina Historical Society.

[128]*News and Courier,* March 18, 1901.

[129]*News and Courier,* March 18, 1876.

130 *News and Courier,* March 18, 1884.
131 *News and Courier,* March 17, 1877.
132 Ibid.
133 *News and Courier,* June 19, 1889.
134 *News and Courier,* March 18, 1883, March 18, 1887, March 18, 1892, March 18, 1898, March 19, 1912, March 18, 1916.
135 *News and Courier,* March 17, 1890, March 18, 1895.
136 *News and Courier,* March 17, 1911, March 19, 1912, March 17, 1915, March 17, 1916; *Charleston American,* March 18, 1921.
137 *Charleston Evening Post,* March 16, 1917, March 19, 1918, March 17, 1920, *Charleston News and Courier,* March 18, 1919.
138 *Charleston American,* March 10, 1921.
139 *Charleston American,* March 18, 1921.
140 *News and Courer,* March 17, 1877.
141 *Charleston Daily Courier,* March 18, 1853.
142 *News and Courier,* March 18, 1875.
143 *Charleston Daily Courier,* March 17, 1850, March 17, 1854, March 20, 1855, March 18, 1859.
144 *Charleston Daily Courier,* March 18, 1859.
145 *News and Courier,* March 18, 1885, March 17, 1890.
146 *Charleston Courier,* March 19, 1825, March 20, 1837; *Charleston Daily Courier,* March 18, 1860, March 20, 1868.
147 *Charleston Courier,* March 18, 1825, March 19, 1835, March 20, 1837.
148 *Charleston Courier,* March 17, 1841, *Charleston Daily Courier,* March 18, 1864.
149 *News and Courier,* March 18, 1897.
150 Mitchell, *The History of the Hibernian Society,* 75.
151 *Charleston Daily Courier,* March 20, 1868.
152 *Charleston Daily News,* March 20, 1868.
153 *Charleston Daily News,* March 20, 1868.
154 *News and Courier,* March 18, 1875.
155 *Charleston Daily Courier,* March 18, 1857.
156 Mitchell, *History of the Hibernian Society,* 100-101.
157 *News and Courier,* March 18, 1875.
158 (first three toasts) *Charleston Courier,* March 19, 1825.
159 Charleston *Courier,* March 19, 1835.
160 *Charleston Courier,* March 20, 1837.
161 *Charleston Daily Courier,* March 19, 1866.
162 *News and Courier,* March 18, 1875, March 18, 1888, *Charleston Daily Courier,* March 18, 1853; March 20, 1855, March 18, 1860, March

20, 1868, March 17, 1861, March 17, 1862 , March 17, 1864; *Sunday News* (Charleston)*,* March 11, 1917; *Charleston Mercury,*March 18, 1852.

[163]*Charleston Daily Courier,* March 19, 1861, March 18, 1862.

[164]*Charleston Daily Courier,* March 18, 1862.

[165]*Charleston Daily Courier,* March 17, 1863.

[166]*Charleston Daily Courier,* March 17, 1864; Mitchell, *History of the Hibernian Society,*70.

[167]*Charleston Daily Courier,* March 18, 1864.

[168]Mitchell, *History of the Hibernian Society*, 70-71.

[169] *Charleston Courier*, March 18, 1865; *Sunday News* (Charleston), March 11, 1917.

[170]James Armstrong, *Centennial Address,* 15.

[171]Ibid.

[172]*Charleston Daily Courier,* March 20, 1855

[173]*Charleston Daily* Courier, March 17, 1859

[174]*News and Courier,* March 18, 1875.

[175]Ibid.

[176]*News and Courier,* March 17, 1876

[177]*News and Courier,* March 18, 1885.

[178]*News and Courier,* March 18, 1890.

[179]*News and Courier,* March 18, 1890

[180]*News and Courier,* March 17 and 18, 1892.

[181]*News and Courier,* March 17, 1911; March 19, 1912; March 17, 1915.

[182] *News and Courier,* March 19, 1912.

[183]*News and Courier,* March 17, 1916.

[184]*News and Courier,* March 17, 1922, March 17, 1923; March 17, 1924, March 17 and 18, 1925, March 17, 1926, March 18, 1927, March 17 and 18, 1928, March 18, 1929.

[185]*Charleston Evening Post,* March 17, 1922.

[186]*Charleston Evening Post*, March 17, 1923, March 17, 1924.

[187]*News and Courier,* March 17, 1925, March 17, 1926, March 17, 1927, March 17, 1928, March 17, 1929.

[188]*News and Courier,* March 17, 1922, March 17, 1923, March 17, 1924, March 17 and 18, 1925, March 17, 1926, March 18, 1927, March 17 and 18, 1928, March 18, 1929, March 19, 1935, March 18, 1936.

[189]Mitchell,*History of the Hibernian Society*, 96-98; *The Two Hundredth Annual Banquet Hibernian Society Charleston, South Carolina* (Charleston: The Hibernian Society, 2001), 5-6.

[190]*The Two Hundredth Annual Banquet Hibernian Society Charleston, South Carolina* (Charleston: The Hibernian Society, 2001), 5-6.

[191]Mitchell, *History of the Hibernian Society,* 104.

[192] Gerald F. McMahon, Jr., "A Brief Sketch of the History of the South Carolina Irish Historical Society."
In the possession of Gerald F. McMahon, Jr.
[193] *Post and Courier*, March 16, 1998; March 17, 2000.

CHAPTER THREE
[194] *South Carolina Gazette,* From Monday March 13-20, 1749; Arthur Mitchell, *The History of the Hibernian Society of Charleston, South Carolina 1799-1981* (Charleston: n. p., 1981), 12.

[195] Henning Cohen, *The South Carolina Gazette, 1732-1775* (Columbia: University of South Carolina Press, 1953), 23.

[196] *South Carolina Gazette and Country Journal,* March 23, 1773.

[197] Michael J. O'Brien, "The Irish in Charleston, South Carolina," *Journal of the American Irish Historical Society*, vol. XXV (1926), 143.

[198] Petition for Incorporation of the Friendly Brothers of Ireland, General Assembly Papers, Petitions, 1787, no. 4. In the collection of the South Carolina Department of Archives and History.

[199] Mitchell, *The History of the Hibernian Society*, 13-14.

[200] *Constitution and Rules of the Hibernian Society of Charleston, S.C., Rules Adopted 1827, Revised 1838-68 and Amended 1889, 1894, and 1899* (Charleston: Wm. F. Barragan, 1899), 25 (hereafter cited as *Constitution and Rules of the Hibernian Society Amended 1899*).

[201] John I. Cosgrove, *Sketch of Hibernian Society of Charleston, S. C.* (Charleston: John J. Furlong & Sons, Inc., 1927), 9-11; Mitchell, *The History of the Hibernian Society*, 14.

[202] *Constitution and Rules of the Hibernian Society Unanimously Approved and Adopted, At an Anniversary Meeting, Held at Mr. Burger's on Tuesday the Seventh Day of March, 1801; With Alterations and Amendments* (Charleston: A. E. Miller, 1818), 11 (hereinafter cited as *Constitution and Rules of the Hibernian Society Adopted 1801*). In the collection of the Charleston Library Society.

[203] *Constitution and Rules of the Hibernian Society Unanimously Approved and Adopted, At an Anniversary Meeting, Held on the 17th Day of March, 1827, Revised and Amended on the 5th Day of June 1838* (Charleston: James S. Burgess, 1838), 7 (hereinafter cited as *Constitution and Rules of the Hibernian Society Revised and Amended 1838*). In the collection of the Charleston Library Society. Mitchell, *The History of the Hibernian Society*, 14.

[204] Mitchell, *The History of the Hibernian Society*, 115 Appendix Four.

[205] Thomas Cooper and David J. McCord, eds., *The Statutes at Large*

of South Carolina [1682-1838], 10 vols. (Columbia: A. S. Johnson, 1836-1841), 8: 233-235 (hereinafter cited as Cooper and McCord, *Statutes*).

[206]*Constitution and Rules of the Hibernian Society Amended 1899*, 27; *Constitution and Rules of the Hibernian Society Adopted 1801*, 7; *Constitution and Rules of the Hibernian Society Unanimously Approved and Adopted, At an Anniversary Meeting, Held on the 17th Day of March 1827, Revised and Amended on the 5th Day of June 1838*, 9 (hereinafter cited as *Constitution and Rules of the Hibernian Society Revised and Amended 1838*). In the collection of the Charleston Library Society.

[207]Samuel Melanchthon Derrick, *Centennial History of South Carolina Railroad* (Columbia: The State Company, 1930), 54; Mitchell, *The History of the Hibernian Society*, 15, 19-20, 59.

[208]*Constitution and Rules of the Hibernian Society Adopted 1801*, 10, 17.

[209]Mitchell, *The History of the Hibernian Society*, 22-23, 116-118; John Belton O'Neall, *Biographical Sketches of the Bench and Bar of South Carolina*, 2 vols. (Charleston, S.C.: Courtnay & Co., 1859), 1: 35-38.

[210]Mitchell, *The History of the Hibernian Society*, 21; *Constitution and Rules of the Hibernian Society Revised and Amended 1838*, 14, 15.

[211]Mitchell, *The History of the Hibernian Society*, 28.

[212]Kenneth Severens, *Charleston:Antebellum Architecture and Civic Destiny* (Knoxville: The University of Tennessee Press, 1988), 90-96.

[213]Ibid.

[214]Ibid., 28-38; Augustine T. Smythe, *Centennial Address Delivered before the Hibernian Society of Charleston, S. C. on its One Hundredth Anniversary 18th March 1902* (Charleston: Walker Evans & Cogswell Co., 1902), 42 (hereafter cited as Smythe, *Centennial Address*).

[215]Mitchell, *The History of the Hibernian Society*, 21; Donald M. Williams, "Charleston's Irish Connections," *Preservation Progress*, vol. 32 no. 2 (March 1988), 4; Smythe, *Centennial Address*, 31-33.

[216]*Distress in Ireland Extracts from Sundry Reports and other documents in Relation to the Famine in Ireland* (Charleston: Burgess & James, 1847), 28-33, in the collection of the Charleston Library Society; Mitchell, *The History of the Hibernian Society*, 56-57; Harvey Strum, "South Carolina and Irish Famine Relief," 1846-47, *South Carolina Historical Magazine*, vol. 103 no. 2 (April 2002), 147.

[217]Mitchell, *The History of the Hibernian Society*, 67, 71; *Charleston Mercury*, June 8, 1861; E. Milby Burton, T*he Seige of Charleston, 1861-1865* (Columbia: University of South Carolina Press, 1970), 199; *Charleston Mercury*, May 6, 1862.

[218]Mitchell, *The History of the Hibernian Society*, 70, 71, 74, 77.

[219]Ibid., 86-88.

[220] Ibid., 102.

[221] *Sunday News* (Charleston), March 17, 1901; *News and Courier*, March 19, 1901.

[222] Mitchell, *The History of the Hibernian Society*, 88-90.

[223] Ibid., 75, 93, 100; *Constitution and Branch By-Laws of the Friends of Irish Freedom: Revised by the Irish Race Convention February 22 and 23, 1919* (n. p.: n. p., n. d.).

[224] Mitchell, *The History of the Hibernian Society*, 93.

[225] Ibid, 99.

[226] Ibid., 102-103.

[227] *News and Courier*, March 18, 1954 and May 22, 1975; *Post and Courier*, March 21, 1997.

[228] *The Two Hundredth Annual Banquet Hibernian Society Charleston, South Carolina* (Charleston: The Hibernian Society, 2001), 4.

[229] Petition for Incorporation of the St. Patrick's Benevolent Society, General Assembly Papers, Petitions, 1817, no. 190, in the collection of the South Carolina Department of Archives and History; *Constitution and By-Laws of the St. Patrick's Benevolent Society of Charleston, S.C.* (Charleston: E. Perry & Co., 1887), 1.

[230] Petition for Incorporation of the St. Patrick's Benevolent Society, General Assembly Papers, Petitions, 1817, no. 190. In the collection of the South Carolina Department of Archives and History.

[231] *The Charleston Directory and Register for 1835-6* (Charleston: Daniel J. Dowling, 1835), 157.

[232] Ibid.

[233] *Constitution and By-Laws of the St. Patrick's Benevolent Society of Charleston, S.C.*, 5-6.

[234] Ibid., 5.

[235] Ibid., 23.

[236] Mitchell, *The History of the Hibernian Society*, 53, 55; M. Foster Farley, *An Account of the Histrory of Stranger's Fever in Charleston, 1699-1876* (University Press of America: 1978), 99; Richard C. Madden, *Catholics in South Carolina* (Lanham, MD: University Press of America, 1985), 63-64

[237] *Charleston Mercury,* June 8, 1861.

[238] *Charleston Daily Courier,* March 18, 1868.

[239] *Charleston Daily News,* March 18, 1873.

[240] *News and Courier*, March 18, 1883.

[241] *News and Courier* March 18, 1883; *Constitution and By-Laws of the St. Patrick's Benevolent Society of Charleston, S.C.*, 13.

²⁴²*Constitution and By-Laws of the St. Patrick's Benevolent Society of Charleston, S.C.*, 14.

²⁴³*Charleston Daily Courier*, February 10, 1852 and September 11, 1860; *Sholes' Directory of the City of Charleston 1882* (Charleston: Sholes & Co., 1882), 54; *Sholes' Directory of the City of Charleston 1883* (Charleston: A. E. Sholes, 1883), 56; *The Charleston City Directory 1888* (Charleston: Southern Directory and Publishing Company, 1888), 644. *Charleston SO. CA. City Directory 1895* (Charleston: Lucas & Richardson Co., 1895) 51; *Walsh's Charleston, South Carolina 1908 City Directory* (Charleston: The Walsh Directory Company, Inc. 1908), 92; *Walsh's 1925-1926 Charleston, South Carolina City Directory* (Charleston: Southern Printing and Publishing Company, 1925), 826.

²⁴⁴*Charleston Courier,* March 20, 1837, *Charleston Daily Courier,* March 19, 1866, *News and Courier,* March 18, 1876 and March 17, 1877; Mitchell, *The History of the Hibernian Society,* 35; *Charleston News and Courier,* March 18, 1886 and March 17, 1901.

²⁴⁵James Armstrong, *Portrayal of Eventful Past as Recounted at Centennial of St. Patrick's Benevolent Society March 17, 1917.* In the collection of the South Carolina Historical Society.

²⁴⁶*Charleston American*, March 18, 1921; *Evening Post,* March 17, 1922; March 17, 1923 and March 17, 1924; *Walsh's 1927 Charleston, South Carolina City Directory* (Charleston: Southern Printing and Publishing Company, 1927), 911.

²⁴⁷Cooper and McCord, *Statutes,* 8: 326.

²⁴⁸Mitchell, *The History of the Hibernian Society,* 23.

²⁴⁹Petition for the Incorporation of the Emerald Isle Beveloent Society, General Assembly Papers, Petitions, 1831, no. 110. In the collection of the South Carolina Department of Archives and History.

²⁵⁰Ibid.

²⁵¹Cooper and McCord, *Statutes,* 8: 372-374.

²⁵²Petition for the Incorporation of the Emerald Isle Beveloent Society, General Assembly Papers, Petitions, 1831, no. 110. South Carolina Department of Archives and History.

²⁵³*Charleston Courier,* March 20, 1832.

²⁵⁴*Charleston Courier,* March 18, 1833.

²⁵⁵*Charleston Courier,* March 20, 1832; March 18, 1833 and March 17, 18 and 19, 1834.

²⁵⁶*Charleston* Courier, March 17, 1851 (This notice of the society's St. Patrick's Day activities states that it was the society's second anniversary), March 17, 1852 (This notice of the society's St. Patrick's Day activities states that it was the society's third anniversary).

[257] Petition for the Incorporation of the Irish Mutual Benevolent Society of Charleston, General Assembly Papers, Petitions, 1851, no. 34. In the collection of the South Carolina Department of Archives and History; *The Statutes at Large of South Carolina* (Columbia: Republican Printing Company, 1874), 12: 103.

[258] *Charleston Courier,* March 19, 1850.

[259] *Charleston Courier,* March 18, 1851

[260] *Charleston Courier,* March 18, 1852.

[261] *Charleston Daily Courier,* March 18,1853.

[262] *Charleston* Courier, March 17, 1851; February 5, 1852; March 17, 1852 and March 17, 1855.

[263] *Charleston Daily Courier,* March 21, 1853, June 27, 1853; *Charleston Mercury,* March 21, 1853.

[264] C. Irvine Walker, *Carolina Rifle Club Charleston, S.C. July 30th, 1869* (n. p., n. p., n. d.), 16, 21. Charleston County Library; Richard Zuczek, *State of Rebellion:Reconstruction in South Carolina* (Columbia: University of South Carolina Press, 1996), 138

[265] *News and Courier*, March 17, 1876.

[266] *Charleston Daily Courier*, March 18, 1872. This notice of the club's St. Patrick's Day activities states that it was the first anniversay meeting of the club.

[267] *Charleston Daily News*, May 19, 1872.

[268] Ibid.

[269] *The Statutes at Large of South Carolina* (Columbia: Republican Printing Company, 1872), 15: 310, 311; *Charleston Daily News.* March 18, 1872; *Sholes' Directory of the City of Charleston for 1877-78* (Charleston: A. E. Sholes, 1877), 55.

[270] *Sholes' Directory of the City of Charleston for 1877-78* (Charleston: A. E. Sholes, 1877), 55; *News and Courier*, March 18, 1874.

[271] *News and Courier*, March 18, 1875.

[272] *Charleston Daily Courier*, March 17, 1873. This notice of the club's St. Patrick's Day activities states that it was the first anniversay meeting of the club; *The Statutes at Large of South Carolina* (Columbia: Republican Printing Company, 1872), 15: 320, 321; *Charleston Daily News*, March 18, 1873, *News and Courier,* March 18, 1874.

[273] *News and Courier*, March 15, 1876.

[274] Walker, *Carolina Rifle Club,* 54.

[275] Francis Butler Simkins and Robert Hillard Woody, *South Carolian During Reconstruction* (Chapel Hill: University of North Carolian Press, 1932), 490, 499-501; Walter Edgar, *South Carolina: A History* (Columbia: University of South Carolina Press, 1998), 402-406; Zuczek, 139, 171.

[276]Edgar, *South Carolina: A History,* 402-406; *Sholes' Directory of the City of Charleston for 1877-78* (Charleston: A. E. Sholes, 1877), 53, 55; *News and Courier*, March 18 and 19, 1878.

[277]*Sholes' Directory of the City of Charleston for 1877-1878* (Charleston: A. E. Sholes, 1877), 53,55; *Sholes' Directory of the City of Charleston 1882* (Charleston: Sholes & Company, 1882), 45.

[278]*Directory for 1872-1873* (Charleston: Walker Evans & Cogswell, 1872), 320.

[279]*Charleston Daily Courier,* March 19, 1872.

[280]*Constitution of the Hibernian Park Association Adopted October 1874* (Charleston: Edward Perry, 1875), 3. In the collection of the South Caroliniana Library of the University of South Carolina.

[281]Ibid.

[282]Ibid. 2, 5.

[283]Deed Book B 17 page 118 records of the Register of Mesne Conveyance for Charleston County, South Carolina; *News and Courier*, June 22, 1876.

[284]*The Statutes at Large of South Carolina* (Columbia, S. C., Republican Printing Company, State Printers, 1876), 94.

[285]*News and Courier*, June 22, 1876.

[286]Ibid.

[287]Ibid.

[288]*News and Courier,* June 6, 1878; May 19, 1880; May 14, 1883; May 28, 1883; June 20, 1882; June 27, 1883 and May 19, 1884.

[289]*Directory of the City of Charleston (South Carolina) 1898* (Charleston: Lucas & Richardson, Co., 1898), 63; Deed Book H 25 page 319 records of the Register of Mesne Conveyance for Charleston County, South Carolina: "Plat of Grants Park (Hibernian Park) Charleston, County, S.C." recorded in Plat Book E page 129 records of the Register of Mesne Conveyance for Charleston County, South Carolina; Charleston County Tax Map #464-02-00-00.

[290]*News and Courier*, September 15, 1876.

[291]Ibid.

[292]Alfred B. Williams, *Hampton and His Red Shirts: South Carolina's Deliverance in 1876* (Charleston: Walker, Evans & Cogswell Company, 1935), 229.

[293]Ibid.

[294]*The Charleston Guide and Business Directory for 1885-6* (Charleston: Southern Directory and Publishing Company, 1885), 92.

[295]*News and Courier,* March 18, 1885.

[296] *The Charleston City Directory 1890* (Charleston: Southern Directory and Publishing Company,1890), 731.

[297] John O'Dea, *History of the Ancient Order of Hibernians and the Ladies' Auxillary*, 4 vols. (Philiadelphia: Keystone Printing Co, 1923), 2: 995.

[298] O'Dea, *History of the Ancient Order of Hibernians and the Ladies' Auxillary*, 2: 991-992.

[299] O'Dea, *History of the Ancient Order of Hibernians and the Ladies' Auxillary*, 2: 884-886, 949; *Cathedral of St. John the Baptist Charleston, S.C. Its Consecration and History 1907* (n. p.: n. p., 1907), 45, 47.

[300] *Cathedral of St. John the Baptist Charleston, S.C. Its Consecration and History 1907*, 47; *Charleston, S.C. City Directory for 1901* (Charleston: W. H. Walsh Directory Company, 1901), 72.

[301] *Cathedral of St. John the Baptist Charleston, S.C. Its Consecration and History 1907*, 49; *Walsh's Charleston, South Carolina 1912 City Directory* (Charleston: The Walsh Directory Company, Inc., 1912), 50.

[302] *Charleston City Directory 1895* (Charleston: Lucas & Richardson Co., 1895), 50; *Charleston, S.C. City Directory for 1900* (Charleston: Lucas & Richardson Co., 1900), 58.

[303] *Cathedral of St. John the Baptist Charleston, S.C. Its Consecration and History 1907*, 47, 49.

[304] O'Dea, *History of the Ancient Order of Hibernians and the Ladies' Auxillary*, 2: 1000.

[305] Ibid.

[306] Ibid., 998.

[307] *News and Courier*, March 17, 1890; March 18, 1895; March 17, 1903; March 17,1908; March 17, 1915 and March 17, 1921; *News and Courier*, March 17, 1903; March 17, 1911; March 19, 1912 and March 17, 1915.

[308] *Cathedral of St. John the Baptist Charleston, S.C. Its Consecration and History 1907*, 51.

[309] Ibid.

[310] Ibid.

[311] Ibid.

[312] *News and Courier*, March 17, 1902 and March 17, 1908; *News and Courier*, May 2, 1921.

[313] *Walsh's Charleston, South Carolina 1922 City Directory* (Charleston: The Walsh Directory Company, Inc., 1922), 94; *Walsh's 1925-1926 Charleston, South Carolina City Directory* (Charleston: Southern Printing and Publishing Company, 1925), 822; *Walsh's 1929 Charleston, South*

Carolina City Directory (Charleston: Southern Printing and Publishing Company, 1929), 1034.

[314] *Ancient Order of Hibernians John L. Manning Div.1 Charleston, S.C.* (n. p.: n. p., n. d.), 6. In the possession of John L. Manning Div. 1 Charleston, S.C.

[315] *The Charleston City Directory 1890* (Charleston: Southern Directory and Publishing Co., 1890), 737; *The Charleston City Directory 1891*, (Charleston: Southern Directory and Publishing Co., 1891), 227; *The Charleston City Directory 1892* (Charleston: Southern Direcroty and Publishing Co., 1892), 743.

[316] Gerald F. McMahon, Jr., "A Brief Sketch of the History of the South Carolina Irish Historical Society." In the possession of Gerald F. McMahon, Jr.

[317] Ibid.

[318] Ibid.

[319] Ibid; *Post and Courier*, March 16, 1998 and March 17, 2000.

[320] Gerald F. McMahon, Jr., "A Brief Sketch of the History of the South Carolina Irish Historical Society."

CHAPTER FOUR

[321] *Proceedings at a Special Meeting of The Survivors' Association of Charleston District July 25, 1890*, "The Defense of Charleston Harbor" (Charleston: Walker Evans & Cogswell Company, 1890), 12-16.

[322] Ibid., 12.

[323] *Charleston American*, March 27, 1919; F. M. Salley, *History of Irish Volunteers Company from 1798 to 1836* (Typscript Charleston County Library), 1-2.

[324] Salley, *History of the Irish Volunteers Company*, 2-6.

[325] Ibid., 7-9.

[326] Ibid., 9-11.

[327] Ibid., 12-13.

[328] Ibid., 13-15.

[329] *The Irish Volunteers Memorial Meeting and Military Hall Festival* (Charleston: The News and Courier Book and Job Presses, 1878), 26 (hereinafter cited as *Irish Volunteers Memorial Meeting*); Arthur M. Wilcox and Warren Ripley, *The Civil War at Charleston* (Charleston: The News and Courier and Evening Post, 1966), 10-11; E. Milby Burton, *The Seige of Charleston: 1861-1865* (Columbia: University of South Carolina Press, 1970), 16-19.

[330] *Irish Volunteers Memorial Meeting*, 26.

[331] *Charleston Daily Courier*, September 17, 1861; *Irish Volunteers Memorial Meeting*, 30-33.

[332] *Irish Volunteers Memorial Meeting*, 31.

[333] *Charleston Mercury*, February 21, 1862; Stewart Sifakis, *Compendium of the Confederate Armies: South Carolina and Georgia* (New York: Facts on File, 1995), 50; *Irish Volunteers Memorial Meeting*, 26.

[334] Patrick Brennan, *Secessionville: Assault on Charleston* (Campbell California: Savas Publishing Company, 1996), 70-73 and 76-82.

[335] Ibid., 78-82.

[336] *Charleston Daily Courier*, June 11, 1862.

[337] *Irish Volunteers Memorial Meeting*, 27; Brennan, *Secessionville: Assault on Charleston*, 82.

[338] John O'Dea, *History of the Ancient Order of Hibernians and Ladies' Auxiliary*, 4 vols. (Philadelphia: Keystone, 1923), 2: 960.

[339] Brennan, *Secessionville: Assault on Charleston*, 82.

[340] *Irish Volunteers Memorial Meeting*, 18; *Charleston Daily Courier*, June 12, 1862; Randolph W. Kirkland, Jr., *Broken Fortunes: South Carolina Soldiers, Sailors and Citizens Who Died in the Service of Their Country and State in the War for Southern Independence, 1861-1865* (Charleston: The South Carolina Historical Society, 1995), 37; *News and Courier*, June 19, 1889; *The War of the Rebellion: A Compilation of the Officials Records of the Union and Confederate Armies*, 128 vols. (Washington D.C., U.S. Government Printing Office, 1880-1901), Series 1 Vol. 14: 30 (hereinafter cited as *O. R.*; all citations will be Series I unless otherwise noted).

[341] Burton, *The Seige of Charleston*, 104-106; Wilcox and Ripley, *The Civil War at Charleston*, 33-34.

[342] Brennan, *Secessionville: Assault on Charleston*, 174-177, 181, 185; *Charleston Daily Courier*, June 18, 1862.

[343] *Charleston Daily Courier*, June 18, 1862; *O. R.*, 14: 97; Burton, *The Seige of Charleston*, 108-109; Kirkland, *Broken Fortunes*, 169; *News and Courier*, June 19, 1889.

[344] Burton, *The Seige of Charleston*, 155-159; Stephen R. Wise, *Gate of Hell: Campaign for Charleston Harbor, 1863* (Columbia: University of South Carolina Press, 1994), 246.

[345] Burton, *The Seige of Charleston*, 162-163; *O. R.*, 28: 417-418, 543-544.

[346] James Armstrong, *Portrayal of Eventful Past as Recounted at Centennial of St. Patrick's Benevolent Society March 17, 1917*, 19. In the collection of the South Carolina Historical Society.

[347] Burton, *The Seige of Charleston*, 163-165; Wise, *Gate of Hell*, 97-99; *O. R.*, 28 (Pt. 1): 418, 543-544; Timothy Bradshaw, Jr., *Battery Wagner:*

The Siege, the Men who Fought and the Casualties (Columbia: Palmetto Historical Works, 1993), 46, 149; Kirkland, *Broken Fortunes,* 350.

[348] *O. R.,* 28 (Pt. 1): 418-419; *Charleston Daily Courier,* July 21, 1863; Wise, *Gate of Hell,* 98.

[349] Bradshaw, *Battery Wagner,* 71.

[350] Wise, *Gate of Hell,* 128-129, 131-132, 199-202, 247-249; Bradshaw, *Battery Wagner,* 179.

[351] Burton, *The Seige of Charleston,* 190; Wilcox and Ripley, *The Civil War at Charleston,* 66.

[352] John Johnson, *The Defense of Charleston Harbor Including Fort Sumter and the Adjacent Islands 1863-1865* (1889; Reprinted, Freeport, New York: Books for Libraries Press,1970), 147; Wise, *Gate of Hell,* 205.

[353] *O. R.,* 28 (Pt. 2): 344.

[354] Burton, *The Seige of Charleston,* 194-197; Wise, *Gate of Hell,* 205-209; Wilcox and Ripley, *The Civil War at Charleston,* 66; Johnson, 160-164; *Irish Volunteers Memorial Meeting,* 28.

[355] Sifakis, *Compendium of the Confederate Armies,* 104-105; *Rivers' Account of the Raising of the Troops in South Carolina for State and Confederate Service 1861-1865* (Columbia: The Bryan Printing Co, 1899), 41; *Irish Volunteers Memorial Meeting,* 28. Johnson Hagood, *Memoirs of the War of Secession* (Columbia: The State Company, 1910), 195, 202, 210-216.

[356] Wise, *Gate of Hell,* 209, 214; Hagood, *Memoirs of the War of Secession,* 217.

[357] Hagood, *Memoirs of the War of Secession,* 217-219.

[358] Hagood, *Memoirs of the War of Secession,* 219-225; *Confederate Historian: Roll of the South Carolina Volunteers in the Confederate States Provisional Army,* 5 vols., 3: 273 (hereinafter cited as *Roll of the South Carolina Volunteers*). In the collection of the South Carolina Department of Archives and History.

[359] *Encyclopedia of the Confederacy* (New York: Simon & Schuster, 1993), 496; Hagood, *Memoirs of the War of Secession,* 231-232; *Roll of the South Carolina Volunteers,* 3: 273, 275. South Carolina Department of Archives and History, Columbia, South Carolina; *Irish Volunteers Memorial Meeting,* 29; Clay W. Holmes, *The Elmira Prison Camp: A History of the Military Prison at Elmira N. Y. July 8, 1864 to July 10, 1865* (New York: G. P. Putnam's Sons The Knickerbocker Press, 1912), 457.

[360] Hagood, *Memoirs of the War of Secession,* 253-257; *Roll of the South Carolina Volunteers,* 3: 273, 275. In the collection of the South Carolina Department of Archives and History; *Irish Volunteers Memorial Meeting,* 29.

[361] *Irish Volunteer Memorial Meeting,* 29; *Roll of the South Carolina*

Volunteers, 3: 273, 275. In the collection of the South Carolian Department of Archives and History.

[362] Hagood, *Memoirs of the War of Secession*, 315-317; *Irish Volunteers Memorial Meeting*, 29; Compendium of the Confederate Armies, 104.

[363] *The Charleston American*, March 27, 1919; *Charleston Directory for 1872-1873* (Charleston: Walker Evans and Cogswell, 1872), 309; *Sholes' Directory of the City of Charleston for 1877-78* (Charleston: A. E. Sholes, 1877), 53; *News and Courier*, March 18, 1875; March 18, 1876.

[364] *Sholes' Directory of the City of Charleston for 1877-78* (Charleston: A. E. Sholes, 1877), 53; *Irish Volunteers Memorial Meeting*, 23-24; *Charleston American*, March 27, 1919.

[365] *Sholes' Directory of the City of Charleston for 1877-78* (Charleston: A. E. Sholes, 1877), 53.

[366] *News and Courier*, June 29, 1878.

[367] Ibid.

[368] *Irish Volunteers Memorial Meeting* 23-24; *Charleston Daily Courier*, October 21, 1853; March 15, 1858; *Sholes' Directory of the City of Charleston 1882* (Charleston: Sholes & Co., 1882), 45; *News and Courier*, June 19, 1889.

[369] *News and Courier*, March 29, 1888; April 2, 3, 6, 7, 1888; June 19, 1889; Jonathan H. Poston, *The Buildings of Charleston: A guide to the City's Architecture* (Columbia, S.C.: University of South Carolina Press, 1997), 642-643.

[370] *News and Courier*, June 19, 1889.

[371] *Charleston American*, March 27, 1919; *News and Courier*, March 20, 1917.

[372] *News and Courier*, June 19, 1916; March 20, 1917; *Sunday News* (Charleston), March 26, 1916; *Charleston* American, March 27, 1919; Mitchell, *The History of the Hibernian Society*, 54.

[373] *News and Courier*, March 20, 1917; *Charleston American*, March 27, 1919.

[374] Ibid.

[375] *Charleston American*, March 27, 1919; Mitchell, 54; Irish Volunteers of Charleston, *Minutes 1915-1929*, in the collection of the South Caroliniana Library of the University of South Carolina.

[376] *Charleston Daily Courier*, March 21, 1853; June 27, 1853; March 17, 1854; March 18, 1859; *Charleston Mercury*, March 21, 1853.

[377] Statutes at Large of South Carolina (Columbia, South Carolina: Republican Printing Company, State Printers, 1874), 12: 269; *Roll of the South Carolina Volunteers*, 5: 94. South Carolian Department of Archives

and History, Columbia, South Carolina; *Irish Volunteers Memorial Meeting*, 12.

[378] *Charleston Daily Courier,* March 17, 1854; *The Charleston City and General Business Directory for 1855* (Charleston: David M. Gazlay, 1855), 17; *Charleston Daily Courier*, March 18, 1856; March 18, 1858; *The Charleston Directory 1859* (Charleston: Mears and Turnbull, 1859), 261.

[379] *Cyclopedia of Eminent and Representative Men of the Carolinas of the Nineteenth Century* South Carolina, 2 vols. (Spartanburg, S.C.: The Reprint Company, 1972), 1: 162; *Irish Volunteers Memorial Meeting*, 12.

[380] *Irish Volunteers Memorial Meeting,* 13; Burton, 11-13; Wilcox and Ripley, *The Civil War at
Charleston*, 4.

[381] Ibid.

[382] Richard C. Madden, *Catholics in South Carolina: A Record* (Lanham, MD: University Press of America, Inc., 1985), 77, *Irish Volunteers Memorial Meeting,* 13.

[383] *Irish Volunteers Memorial Meeting,* 13-14 ; Robert N. Rosen, *Confederate Charleston: An Illustrated History of the City and the People During the Civil War* (Columbia, South Carolina: University of South Carolina Press, 1994), 130.

[384] *Charleston Mercury,* May 7, 1861

[385] *Charleston Mercury,* May 10, 1861

[386] *Charleston Daily Courier,* June 7, 1861; *Charleston Mercury,* June 8, 1861.

[387] *Charleston Daily Courier*, September 9, 1861; *Charleston Mercury,* February 21, 1862.

[388] *Charleston Mercury,* February 11, 20 and 24, 1862; April 5, 1862; *Charleston Daily Courier,*
February 13, 1862; April 1, 5, 1862.

[389] *News and Courier*, November 19, 1874; March 18, 1877; *Charleston Daily Courier,* March 17, 1854 (states that this is the company's first anniversary), June 16, 1853; *Charleston Mercury,* May 3, 1861; Dumas Malone ed., *Dictionary of American Biography*, (New York: Charles Scribner's Sons, 1962), 7: 98-99.

[390] *The Charleston City and General Business Directory for 1855* (Charleston: David M. Gazlay, 1855), 17; *The Charleston Directory 1859* (Charleston: Mears and Turnbull, 1859), 263; *Charleston Daily Courier,* June 16, 1853; *Charleston Mercury,* May 3, 1861; John Amasa May and John Reynolds Faunt, *South Carolina Secedes* (Columbia, South Carolina: University of South Carolina Press, 1960), 130-131.

[391] John Amasa May and John Reynolds Faunt, *South Carolina Secedes*

130-131; Mary Conner Moffett, *Letters of General James Conner C. S. A.* (Columbia, S.C.: The R. L. Bryan Co., 1950), 23-25.

[392] *Irish Volunteers Memorial Meeting*, 13-14; *Charleston Mercury*, May 4, 1861.

[393] *Charleston Daily Courier*, September 9, 19, 1861.

[394] *Charleston Mercury*, February 21, 1862.

[395] *News and Courier*, March 18, 1874; November 19,1874; March 18, 1877.

[396] *News and Courier*, March 18, 1877.

[397] Alfred B. Williams, *Hampton and His Red Shirts: South Carolina's Deliverance in 1876* (Charleston: Walker, Evans & Cogswell Company, 1935), 152-153.

[398] *Sholes' Directory of the City of Charleston for 1877-78* (Charleston: A. E. Sholes Publishing, 1877), 55; *Sholes' Directory of the City of Charleston 1882* (Charleston: Sholes & Co., 1882), 44; Statutes at Large of South Carolina (Columbia, South Carolina: James Woodrow, State Printer, 1882), 17: 679-680.

[399] *News and Courier,* June 22, 1876; June 29, 1878; March 18, 1886; *The Lucas and Richardson Company's Directory of the City of Charleston, South Carolina 1898* (Charleston: Lucas & Richardson Co., 1898), 61.

[400] *Charleston Daily Courier*, March 18, 1854; March 20, 1855; *The Charleston City and General Business Directory for 1855* (Charleston: David M. Gazlay, 1855), 17.

[401] *Year Book-1883 City of Charleston, So. CA.* (Charleston: The News and Courier Book Presses, 1883), 542-547 (Hereinafter cited as *City of Charleston Year Book-1883*).

[402] *Charleston Daily Courier*, March 18, 1858; March 18, 1859.

[403] *Charleston Daily Courier*, January 3, 1861; April 8, 1862.

[404] *Irish Volunteers Memorial Meeting*, 14; *Charleston Mercury,* June 8, 1861.

[405] *Charleston Daily Courier*, July 12, 1861; *Rivers' Account of the Raising of Troops in South Carolina*, 17; *Irish Volunteers Memorial Meeting,* 14.

[406] *Charleston Daily Courier*, July 12, 1861; Ron Field, *South Carolina Volunteers in the Civil War 1st South Carolnia Volunteers (Gregg's)* (Lower Swell, Gloucestershire: Design Folio, 1991). 43.

[407] *Irish Volunteers Memorial Meeting,* 14-15.

[408] Ibid., 16, 35.

[409] Ibid., 35.

[410] Ron Field, *South Carolina Volunteers in the Civil War 1st South Carolina Volunteers*, 44.

[411][Alexander O'Donnell], "Address to the Irishmen of Charleston December 1861," South Carolina Volunteers, First Regiment, South Caroliniana Library, University of South Carolina.

[412]J. F. J. Caldwell, *The History of a Brigade of South Carolinians: First Known as "Gregg's"and Subsequently as "McGowan's Brigade"* (Philadelphia: King & Bird, 1866. Dayton Ohio: Morningside Press, 1984), 32, 34-36.

[413]*Charleston Daily Courier*, July 9, 1862.

[414]William Woods Hassler, *A. P. Hill: Lee's Forgotten General* (Chapel Hill: University of North Carolina Press, 1962), 70; Irish Volunteer Minutes, 20; Sifakis, *Compendium of the Confederate Armies*, 54.

[415]*O. R.*, 12 (Pt. 2): 684-690.

[416]Hassler, *A. P. Hill: Lee's Forgotten General*, 90- 91; Caldwell, *The History of a Brigade of South Carolinians*, 64.

[417]*O. R.*, 12 (Pt. 2): 671.

[418]Edward McCrady, Jr., "Gregg's Brigade in the Second Battle of Manassas," *Southern Historical Society Papers*, Volume XIII (1885), 34.

[419]Hassler, *A. P. Hill: Lee's Forgotten General*, 92.

[420]*Irish Volunteers Memorial Meeting*, 16.

[421]*News and Courier*, January 5, 1883.

[422]*Irish Volunteers Memorial Meeting*, 20; A. S. Salley, Jr., *South Carolina Troops in Confederate Service*, 3 vols. (Columbia: The R. L. Bryan Company, 1913), 1: 370, 372, 380, 381, 386, 388, 389, and 393; *Roll of the South Carolina Volunteers*, 2: 12; *Cyclopedia of Eminent and Representative Men of the Carolinas of the Nineteenth Century South Carolina*, 2 vols. (Spartanburg, South Carolina: The Reprinting Company, 1972), 1: 162.

[423]*O. R.*, 19 (Pt.1): 952-955, 981, 987-988; Hassler, 100-104; Salley, *Troops in Confederate Service*, 1: 370, 373, 379, 384, 385, 387, 394; *Roll of the South Carolina Volunteers*, 2: 12.

[424]Caldwell, *The History of a Brigade of South Carolinians*, 93; Salley, *Troops in Confederate Service*, 1: 371, 372, 381, 383, 384, 388, 390, 393 and 396; *Irish Volunteers Memorial Meeting*, 20.

[425]*Cyclopedia of Eminent and Representative Men of the Carolinas of the Nineteenth Century*, 1: 163-166; *Evening Post*, November 2, 1903.

[426]Caldwell, *The History of a Brigade of South Carolinians*, 101; Sifakis, *Compendium of the Confederate Armies*, 54; Peter J. Parish, *The American Civil War* (New York: Holmes & Meier, 1975), 278; Salley, *Troops in Confederate Service*, 1: 371, 381, 391 and 392.

[427]Caldwell, *The History of a Brigade of South Carolinians*, 137-140; *Irish Volunteers Memorial Meeting*, 16; *Roll of the South Carolina Volunteers*, 2: 12, in the collection of the South Carolian Department of Archives

and History, Columbia, South Carolina; Salley, *Troops in Confederate Service,* 1: 373 and 374.

[428]*Roll of the South Carolina Volunteers,* 2: 12-13, in the collection of the South Carolina Department of Archives and History, Columbia, South Carolina; Salley, *Troops in Confederate Service,* 1: 373, 375, 386, 391, 394, 395 and 396; Caldwell, 188-196; *Irish Volunteers Memorial Meeting.* 20.

[429]Ibid.

[430]*Charleston Evening Post,* August 16, 18, 1930; Mitchell, 85.

[431]*Charleston Evening Post,* August 16, 1930.

[432]Salley, *Troops in Confederate Service,* 1: 370-397; *News and Courier,* June 19, 1889; R. A. Brock ed. "Paroles of the Army of Northern Virginia, R. E. Lee, Gen., C.S.A., Commanding Surrender at Appomatox C. H., VA., April 9, 1865 to Lieutenant-General U. S. Grant Commanding Armies of The U.S.," *Southern Historical Society Papers,* Vol. XV (1887, reprinted 1990), 371.

[433]*Charleston Daily Courier*, August 26, 1861; Colin Thomas and Avril Thomas, *Historical Dictionary of Ireland* (Lanham, Maryland: The Scarecrow Press Inc., 1997), 170.

[434]*Charleston Mercury,* February 17, 21 and 24, 1862; April 5, 1862; *Charleston Daily Courier*, August 26, 1861; April 1, 5, 1862.

[435]*Charleston Daily Courier,* September 27, 1861; *City of Charleston Year Book-1883,* 542-544; . *Charleston Mercury,* February 17, 1862; *Statutes at Large of South Carolina* (Columbia, South Carolina: Reprinted by Republican Printing Company, State Printers, 1875), 13: 61-63.

[436]*Charleston Mercury,* February 17 and 21, 1862; April 5, 1862; *Charleston Daily Courier*, April 1 and 5, 1862.

[437]*Charleston Daily Courier*, September 26, 1861.

[438]Wilcox and Ripley, *The Civil War at Charleston,* 24-26; Walter Edgar, *South Carolina: A History* (Columbia: University of South Carolian Press, 1998), 360 361.

[439]*Charleston Daily Courier*, January 13, 1862.

[440]*Statutes at Large of South Carolina* (Columbia, South Carolina: Republican Printing Company, State Printers, 1875), 13: 9-13; *Charleston Mercury,* February 10 and 20, 1862.

[441]*Charleston Daily Courier*, February 7, 1862.

[442]*Charleston Mercury,* February 11, 1862.

[443]*Charleston Mercury,* February 21 and 24, 1862.

[444]*Charleston Mercury,* February 24, 1862.

[445]*Charleston Mercury,* February 24, 1862.

[446]*Charleston Daily Courier*, February 25, 1862.

[447]*Charleston Mercury,* March 11, 1862.

⁴⁴⁸*Charleston Mercury,* April 15, 1862; Sifakis, *Compendium of the Confederate Armies,* 50.

⁴⁴⁹*Charleston Daily Courier,* March 25, 1862; April 1 and 5, 1862; *Charleston Mercury,* March 31, 1862; April 5, 1862.

⁴⁵⁰*Charleston Daily Courier,* April 6, 1862.

⁴⁵¹*Rivers' Account of the Raising of Troops in South Carolina for State and Confederate Service 1861-1865* (Columbia: The Bryan Printing Co, State Printers, 1899), 86; *City of Charleston YearBook-1883,* 544-547.

⁴⁵²*News and Courier,* March 17 and 18, 1875.

⁴⁵³*News and Courier,* March 18, 1875.

⁴⁵⁴*News and Courier,* March 17, 1876; June 28, 1876; March 19, 1877.

CHAPTER FIVE

⁴⁵⁵ *News and Courier,* March 18, 1901

⁴⁵⁶ Sir Leslie Stephen and Sir Sidney Lee eds., *Dictionary of National Biography*, (London: Oxford University Press, 1921-1922), 13: 194-196; D. J. Hickey and J. E. Doherty, *A Dictionary of Irish History Since 1800* (Totowa, New Jersey: Gill and Macmillan, 1980), 242, 361-362.

⁴⁵⁷ *Dictionary of National Biography,* 13: 194-196, 14: 780; Hickey and Doherty, *A Dictionary of Irish History,* 361-362.

⁴⁵⁸ *Charleston Daily Courier,* March 15 and 17, 1853.

⁴⁵⁹ *Charleston Daily Courier,* March 21, 1853.

⁴⁶⁰ *Charleston Daily Courier,* March 18, 1853, April 8, 1853; *Charleston Mercury,* March 21, 1853.

⁴⁶¹ Arthur Mitchell, *The History of the Hibernian Society of Charleston, South Carolina, 1799-1981* (Charleston: n. p., 1981), 67 and 68: Robert N. Rosen, *Confederate Charleston: An Illustrated History of the City and the People During the Civil War* (Columbia, South Carolina: University of South Carolina Press, 1994), 130.

⁴⁶² *Dictionary of National Biography,* 14: 777-781; Hickey and Doherty, *A Dictionary of Irish History,* 416-417.

⁴⁶³ *Charleston Daily Courier,* March 17 and 18, 1859; *Charleston Mercury,* March 18, 1859.

⁴⁶⁴ *Charleston Daily Courier,* March 19, 1866, William D'Arcy, *The Fenian Movement in the United States 1858-1886* (Washington: The Catholic University of America Press, 1947), 12-16.

⁴⁶⁵ *Charleston Daily Courier,* March 19 and 23, 1866.

⁴⁶⁶ Mitchell, *The History of the Hibernian Society,* 75.

⁴⁶⁷ Robert Kee, *Ireland: A History* (Boston: Little, Brown and Company, 1980), 111-112.

⁴⁶⁸ Ibid., 112; D'Arcy, *The Fenian Movement in theUnited States*, 99-118, 151.

⁴⁶⁹ D'Arcy, *The Fenian Movement in the United States*, 159-161.

⁴⁷⁰ Kee, *Ireland: A History*, 112-113.

⁴⁷¹ Kee, *Ireland: A History*, 112-117; Hickey and Doherty, *A Dictionary of Irish History*, 276 and 358.

⁴⁷² *Charleston Daily News*, February 6, 1868.

⁴⁷³ Mitchell, *The History of the Hibernian Society*, 75.

⁴⁷⁴ Charles Callan Tansill, *America and the Fight for Irish Freedom 1866-1922* (New York: The Devin-Adair Co., 1957), 37-38; D'Arcy, *The Fenian Movement in the United States*, 348.

⁴⁷⁵ Hickey and Doherty, *A Dictionary of Irish History*, 231, 251.

⁴⁷⁶ *Dictionary of National Biography*, 14: 323.

⁴⁷⁷ T. A. Jackson, *Ireland Her Own: An Outline History of the Irish Struggle for Freedom and Independence* (New York: Internations Publishers, 1947), 310-315; S. J. Connelly, *The Companion to Irish History* (Oxford: Oxford University Press, 1998), 431; *Dictionary of National Biography*, 15: 322-324.

⁴⁷⁸ Kee, *Ireland: A History*, 120.

⁴⁷⁹ Tansill, *America and the Fight for Irish Freedom*, 51-55; Hickey and Doherty, *A Dictionary of Irish History*, 394-395.

⁴⁸⁰ Norman Duncan Palmer, *The Land League Crisis* (New Haven: Yale University Press, 1940), 142; B. Barry O'Brien, *The Life of Charles Stewart Parnell 1846-1891*, 2 vols. (New York Harper and Brothers,1898), 1: 195.

⁴⁸¹ Palmer, *The Land League Crisis*, 142.

⁴⁸² Ibid., 143-145.

⁴⁸³ Ibid., 147; Tansill, *America and the Fight for Irish Freedom*, 56-57; O'Brien, *The Life of Charles Stewart Parnell*, 1: 197; *News and Courier*, January 20, 1880; Hickey and Doherty, *A Dictionary of Irish History*, 460.

⁴⁸⁴ Mary Doline O'Connor, *The Life and Letters of M. P. O'Connor* (New York: Dempsey & Carroll, 1893), 193.

⁴⁸⁵ O'Connor, *Life and Letters of M. P. O'Connor*, 193-194.

⁴⁸⁶ Thomas N. Brown, *Irish-American Nationalism 1870-1890* (West Port Connecticut: Greenwood Press, 1966), 104; *News and Courier*, May 2, 1883; *Shole's Directory of the City of Charleston 1883* (Charleston: A. E. Sholes, 1883), 56.

⁴⁸⁷ Palmer, *The Land League Crisis*, 148, 291-295; Michael Davitt, *The Fall of Feudalism in Ireland* (London & New York: Harper & Brothers, 1904), 333-335.

488 Davitt, *The Fall of Feudalism in Ireland*, 335-338.

489 Palmer, *The Land League Crisis*, 298-300; Tansil, *America and the Fight for Irish Freedom*, 69;

D. George Boyce, *Ireland 1828-1923 From Ascendency to Democracy* (Oxford: Blackwell Publisher, 1992), 50; B. Barry O'Brien, *The Life of Charles Stewart Parnell 1846-1891*, 2 vols. (New York: Harper and Brothers, 1898), 1: 350.

490 O'Brien, *The Life of Charles Stewart Parnell*, 1: 351, 365-369, Hickey and Doherty, *A Dictionary of*
Irish History, 389, 461.

491 Hickey and Doherty, *A Dictionary of Irish History*, 389.

492 *News and Courier*, May 2, 1883; Brown, *Irish-American Nationalism*, 155; Tansil, *America and the Fight for Irish Freedom*, 77.

493 *News and Courier*, June 8, 1883.

494 Hickey and Doherty, *A Dictionary of Irish History*, 462; Emily Hahn, *Fractured Emerald: Ireland* (New York: Weathervane Books, n.d.), 283: *The Charleston City Directory 1887* (Charleston: Southern Directory and Publishing Company, 1887), 694.

495 *News and Courier*, March 6, 1888; May 1, 1888.

496 *News and Courier*, March 6, 1888.

497 Ibid.

498 Ibid.

499 Ibid.

500 Ibid.

501 *News and Courier*, May 2, 1888; E. Culpepper Clark, *Francis Warrington Dawson and the Politics of Restoration: South Carolina, 1874-1889* (Alabama: University of Alabama Press, 1980), 10 and 198.

502 *News and Courier*, May 2, 1888

503 Ibid.

504 Ibid.

505 Alan Dures, *Modern Ireland* (London: Wayland Publishers, 1973), 52-53.

506 Brown, *Irish-American Nationalism*, 177; Kirby A. Miller, *Emigrants and Exiles* (New York: Oxford University Press, 1985), 446; *Charleston City Directory 1895* (Charleston: Lucas & Richardson Co., 1895), 50; *Directory of the City of Charleston 1899* (Charleston: Lucas & Richardson Co., 1895), 88.

507 Dures, *Modern Ireland*, 59; Kirby Miller, *Emigrants and Exiles*, 447-448; Constantine Fitzgibbon, *Out of the Lion's Paw: Ireland Wins Her Freedom* (New York: American Heritage Press, 1969), 31.

508 Fitzgibbon, *Out of the Lion's Paw*, 31-42; Dures, *Modern Ireland*,

57-61; F. X. Martin, ed., *Leaders and Men of the Easter Rising Dublin 1916* (Ithaca, New York: Cornell University Press 1967), 139-141.

[509] Martin, ed., *Leaders and Men of the Easter Rising Dublin 1916*, 144-145; P. S. O'Hegarty, *History of Ireland Under the Union* (London: Methuen & Co., 1952), 687-688; Dures, *Modern Ireland*, 61.

[510] Tansil, *America and the Fight for Irish Freedom*, 188-189.

[511] Ibid., 189.

[512] *News and Courier*, November 1, 1920; *Charleston American*, March 18, 1921.

[513] O'Hegarty, *History of Ireland Under the Union*, 697, 701; Tansil, *America and the Fight for Irish Freedom*, 196.

[514] Tansil, *America and the Fight for Irish Freedom*, 196.

[515] Martin, ed., *Leaders and Men of the Easter Rising Dublin 1916*, 190-198.

[516] Martin, ed., *Leaders and Men of the Easter Rising Dublin 1916*, 181-185; Allen J. Ward, *Ireland and Anglo-American Relations 1899-1920* (Canada: University of Toronto Press, 1969), 106; Tansil, *America and the Fight for Irish Freedom*, 198; Fitzgibbon, 58-59.

[517] Ward, *Ireland and Anglo-American Relations*, 106-107.

[518] Robert Kee, *The Green Flag: The Turbulent History of the Irish National Movement* (New York: Delacorte Press, 1972), 548-549; Dures, *Modern Ireland*, 62; Ward, 107; Tansil, *America and The Fight for Irish Freedom*, 199.

[519] Tansil, *America and the Fight for Irish Freedom*, 202; Fitzgibbon, *Out of the Lion's Paw*, 89-90; Michael Foy and Brian Barton, *The Easter Rising* (Gloucestershire: Sutton Publishing, 1999), 225-226.

[520] The Earl of Longford and Thomas P. O'Neill, *Eamon De Valera* (Boston: Houghton Mifflin Company, 1971), 1-2, 38-39, 50.

[521] Tansil, *America and the Fight for Irish Freedom*, 200-201; Robert Kee, *The Green Flag*, 581; Fitzgibbon, *Out of the Lion's Paw*, 83-84; W. E. Vaughan, *A New History of Ireland*, 8 vols. (Oxford: Clarendon Press, 1996), 6: 218-220; Joseph Lee, *The Modernization of Irish Society 1848-1918* (Dublin: Gill and Macmillan, 1973), 155-156; F. X. Martin, ed., *Leaders and Men of the Easter Rising Dublin 1916*, 131; Ward, *Ireland and Anglo-American Relations*, 141-142; Lawrence J. McCaffrey, ed., *Irish Nationalism and the American Contribution* (New York: Arno Press, 1976), 80.

[522] *News and Courier*, June 26, 1940; Mitchell, *History of the Hibernian Society*, 93-94; *Constitution and Branch By-Laws of the Friends of Irish Freedom; Revised by the Irish Race Convention February 22 and 23, 1919* (n. p., n. d.), 6; Tansil, *America and the Fight for Irish Freedom*, 367; *Charleston American*, February 23, 1919.

523 Ward, *Ireland and Anglo-American Relations,* 172; Tansil, *America and the Fight for Freedom,* 296-297.

524 *Charleston American,* February 17, 1919.

525 *News and Courier,* February 17, 1919.

526 *Charleston American,* February 23, 1919.

527 Ibid.; Tansil, *America and the Fight for Irish Freedom,* 299-303.

528 Ward, *Ireland and Anglo-American Relations,* 214.

529 Patrick McCartan, *With Devalera in America* (New York: Brentano, 1932), 141-145; Tansil, *America and the Fight for Irish Freedom,* 347-353; Ward, *Ireland and Anglo-American Relations,* 216-218; Longford and O'Neill, *Eamon De Valera,* 95.

530 Ward, *Ireland and Anglo-American Relations,* 218; Tansil, *America and the Fight for Irish Freedom,* 350-353; McCartan, *With De Valera in America,* 142-145.

531 Longford and O'Neill, *Eamon De Valera,* 95 and 105-108; Tim Pat Coogan, *Eamon De Valera: The Man Who Was Ireland* (New York: Harper Collins Publishers, 1993), 156; Ward. 217-219.

532 Tansil, *America and the Fight for Irish Freedom,* 365-368; Longford and O'Neill, *Eamon De Valera,* 108-109; Coogan, *Eamon De Valera,* 173-175.

533 John P. Grace to Andrew J. Ryan, June 28, 1920, quoted in Tansil, *America and the Fight for Irish Freedom,* 367-368.

534 *News and Courier,* April 10, 1920.

535 *News and Courier,* April 6, 1920.

536 *News and Courier,* April 11, 1920; *Charleston American,* April 11, 1920.

537 *Charleston American,* April 11, 1920.

538 Ibid.

539 Ibid.

540 Ibid.

541 *News and Courier,* April 11, 1920; *Charleston American* April 11, 1920.

542 *Charleston American,* April 12, 1920.

543 John Coles, *Movie Theaters of Charleston: Hollywood Meets the Holy City* (Mt. Pleasant, S.C.:
Graphic Data Services, 1994), 46.

544 Tansil, *America and the Fight for Irish Freedom,* 386-391.

545 Ibid., 392-394; Ward, *Ireland and Anglo-American Relations,* 232; *News and Courier,* November 1, 1920, March 7, 1921.

546 William H. Kautt, *The Anglo-Irish War, 1916-1921: A People's War* (Westport, Connecticut: Praeger Publishers, 1999), 70-79 and 87-96.

[547] Ibid., 78; Coogan, *Eamon De Valera*, 184; Ward, *Ireland and Anglo-American Relations*, 229-231.

[548] *News and Courier*, November 1, 1920; *Charleston Evening Post*, November 1, 1920; *Charleston American*, November 1, 1920.

[549] Ward, *Ireland and Anglo-American Relations*, 232; Tansil, *America and the Fight for Irish Freedom*, 414-417.

[550] *News and Courier*, February 27 and 28, 1921.

[551] *News and Courier*, February 28, 1921; Tansil, *America and the Fight for Irish Freedom*, 409-414; Ward, *Ireland and Anglo-American Relations*, 239-241.

[552] *News and Courier*, March 5, 6 and 7, 1921.

[553] *News and Courier*, March 7 and 8, 1921.

[554] *News and Courier*, March 7, 1921; *Charleston Evening Post*, March 7, 1921.

[555] Ibid.

[556] *News and Courier*, March 8, 1921.

[557] *News and Courier*, March 18, 1921.

[558] Ward, *Ireland and Anglo-American Relations*, 241-242; *Charleston American*, May 1, 1921.

[559] Hickey and Doherty, *A Dictionary of Irish History*, 565-566; Boyce, *Ireland 1828-1923 From Ascendancy to Democracy*, 100-103.

Made in the USA
Columbia, SC
15 June 2021